# Building Hypermedia Applications

# Building Hypermedia Applications

**A Software Development Guide**

**Gary Thomas Howell**

**McGraw-Hill, Inc.**

New York   St. Louis   San Francisco   Auckland   Bogotá
Caracas   Lisbon   London   Madrid   Mexico   Milan
Montreal   New Delhi   Paris   San Juan   São Paulo
Singapore   Sydney   Tokyo   Toronto

Library of Congress Cataloging-in-Publication Data

Howell, Gary Thomas.
    Building Hypermedia applications : a software development guide /
    Gary Thomas Howell.
        p.      cm.
    Includes index.
    ISBN 0-07-030601-X
    1. Hypermedia systems.    2. Computer software—Development.
    I. Title.
    QA76.76.H92H68    1992
    005.75—dc20                                              92-11191
                                                             CIP

    2 3 4 5 6 7 8 9 0   DOC/DOC   9 8 7 6 5 4 3 2

ISBN 0-07-030601-X

*The sponsoring editor for this book was Jeanne Glasser.*

*Printed and bound by R. R. Donnelley & Sons Company.*

# Contents

# Section II   Hypermedia Project Development

# Preface

Hypermedia is a technology that has finally come of age. With the unprecedented power of the desktop personal computer, individuals now have the ability to create their own Hypermedia applications. This book has a threefold purpose: to explain what Hypermedia is and what it can be used for; to explain software development, first in general and then specifically for Hypermedia applications; and to examine hardware and software that is commercially available for developing your application.

## Section One—Introduction to Hypermedia

Section One is devoted to introducing you to Hypermedia. Hypermedia is a relatively new technology that is actually a combination of two more established technologies—Hypertext and Multimedia. The first chapter concentrates on the history of the two individual technologies and how they merge into one. Particular emphasis is placed on the terminology involved. For those readers who are already familiar with hypermedia, please bear with me. While the first chapter explains the what of Hypermedia, the second and last chapter of Section One gives the why. Chapter Two concentrates on the identification of the strengths and weaknesses of hypermedia. Current and potential future uses of hypermedia are also examined. Reading Section One will give you answers to the following questions.

What is Hypermedia?

What is the terminology involved?

What are the strengths and weaknesses of Hypermedia?

What types of applications are suited to Hypermedia solutions?

## Section Two—Hypermedia Project Development

Section Two concentrates on Hypermedia project development. References are made to decisions that must be made with respect to hardware, but Section Two concentrates on software development. Chapter Three gives a detailed overview of five popular software development techniques and develops a sixth. Chapters Four through Seven are more Hypermedia specific. In Chapter Four, guidelines for obtaining system and software requirements and specifications are given. A sample Hypermedia project using the concepts defined in the chapter is also begun in Chapter Four. This sample project is followed to completion in Chapters Five, Six, and Seven. Chapter Five introduces Hypermedia system and software design and implementation. Particular emphasis is placed on designing for maintainability. Integration and maintenance of Hypermedia systems are covered in Chapter Six. The sample project is fully implemented and strategies for system and software testing and maintenance are described.

## Section Three—Software and Hardware Options

Section Three emphasizes commercially available hardware and software. Chapter Seven covers the advantages and disadvantages of three general categories of programming languages. Chapter Eight presents hardware and software options available on the IBM PC and compatible computers. Chapter Nine examines hardware and software options on the Macintosh personal computer.

# Acknowledgments

To my wonderful wife, Alesia, for putting up with me all these years.

To my children, Sharon, Eric, and Ryan for accepting the answer "Daddy's busy."

To the staff at McGraw-Hill for their patience with a new author.

To Tony and Tod, who took the brunt of my departure from the Air Force, Good Luck.

**AND**, special thanks for everything to JWM, my good friend and colleague. Best of luck in your present and future efforts.

*Gary Thomas Howell*

# Building
# Hypermedia
# Applications

# Introduction to Hypermedia

# What is Hypermedia?

The word Hypermedia, as illustrated in Figure 1.1, is a fusion of Hypertext and Multimedia. It follows that Hypermedia technology is a fusion of Hypertext technology and the concept of Multimedia.

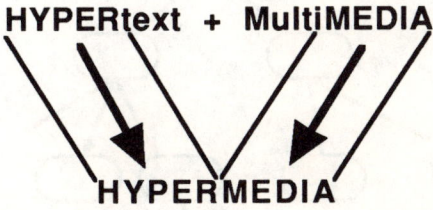

Figure 1.1 Hypermedia–the word.

This chapter will define these two separate entities and the terminology surrounding them and will explain how they come together to form Hypermedia.

## HYPERTEXT

The term Hypertext was first coined by Theodor Holme Nelson, recognized ideologist of Hypertext and author of "Xanadu" (a Hypertext engine), in reference to a radically new way of storing and
viewing information.  Before Hypertext, the most common way to
gather information from text was sequentially (i.e., a book is read
from front to back).  However, when attempting to retrieve information quickly, the text is not read from cover to cover.  Generally, you
proceed to the index, look up the subject of interest, and go directly to
the location of the pertinent information.  If you don't find the exact
information you are looking for in that location, then go back to the
index to find another reference.  This goes on until you either find
the information or get tired of looking.

With Hypertext, the text is fashioned in multiple layers.  In reference to the previous example, the pseudo-index would be the top layer
and the locations of the information would be at the next level.  The
text could be ordered in a pyramid-like structure (see Figure 1.2), or
in something a little less structured (see Figure 1.3).  The point being, the hierarchy of information is designed to fit the application,
not some predefined layout.

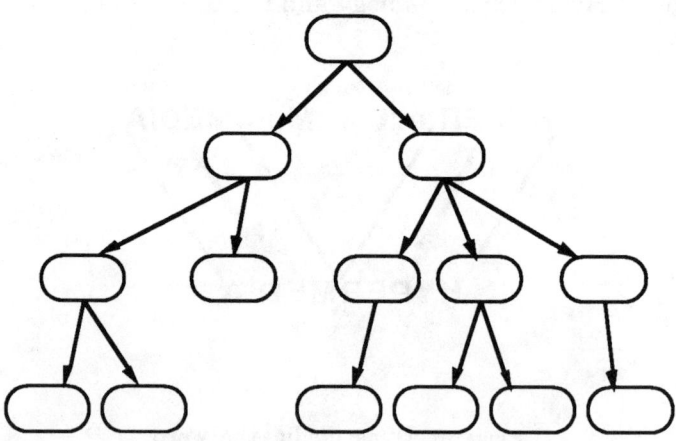

**Figure 1.2** Standard pyramid hierarchy of data.

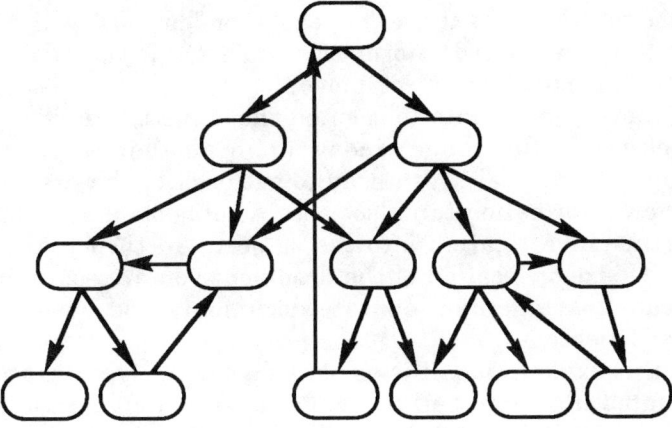

Figure 1.3 Data layout can be less structured in Hypertext.

Generally speaking, Hypertext applications are written to run in a windowing environment (i.e., there can be multiple windows or text viewing ports open at any given time). Applications are mouse driven; there is no command line interface. Actually, Hypertext is simply composed of points, nodes, and links (see Figure 1.4).

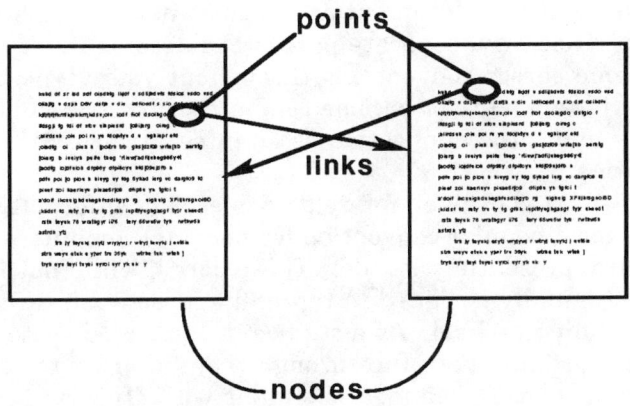

Figure 1.4 Points, nodes, and links.

Located within the text are "hot spots" or "buttons" which provide the links to other related information (points). If you wish to know more about a particular subject, move the mouse over the subject and click. If there is more information on the subject, it is displayed as a point either in the same window or in another window that is popped up. There is always a way to get back to the previous level and the new information can also contain hot spots and/or buttons to allow further investigation into the subject. In theory, there is no limit on the size or location of the document you are searching. Hypertext can link together separate documents and even link over networks if neccessary.

From this explanation, it is obvious that with Hypertext you have an automated index built in to the document. Related pieces of information (points) or related chunks of text (nodes) are connected together by pointers to other pieces of information (links).

## Points, Nodes, and Links

Points, sometimes called link anchors, are usually the most fundamental piece of information in a document. They consist of either a word or a phrase that can be expanded upon. In order for the viewer of a Hypertext document to visually distinguish between regular text and a point, the cursor (mouse, pointer, etc.) will typically change shape when it passes over a point. It is not essential that all Hypertext cursors change to the same shape when they pass over a point. It is important, however, that within a single Hypertext document consistency is maintained. For example, you wouldn't want the cursor to change to a pointed finger when passing over a point in one part of a document and then switch to another convention, like a circle, in a separate part of the document. If you maintain the same cursor conventions throughout your Hypertext document, the viewers will not become confused or frustrated and will be more likely to use the application as an integral part of their day-to-day activities.

A node is a container for related pieces of information. Currently, the most popular convention for personal computers is that of a note card representing a node. These cards, while not limited in size, were originally designed to represent those 3 x 5 cards some of us used to study in school. As a study aid, you would write down one concept per card and then flip through them in order to commit the concepts to memory. The idea is similar with Hypertext. There is generally one concept to a card or node, but there can be many points within the node which lead to other nodes of related information. You, as the viewer, can simply flip through the cards sequentially, but you are not limited to merely flipping through the cards.

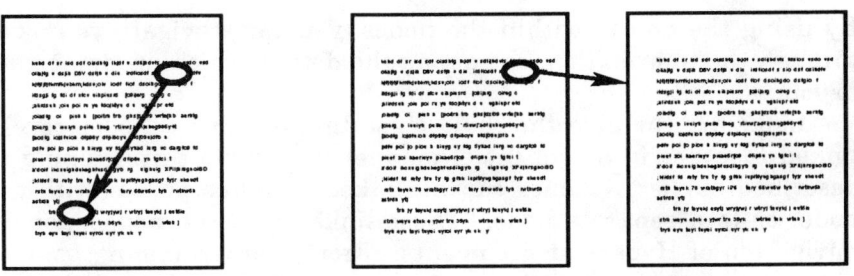

**point-to-point**                    **point-to-node**

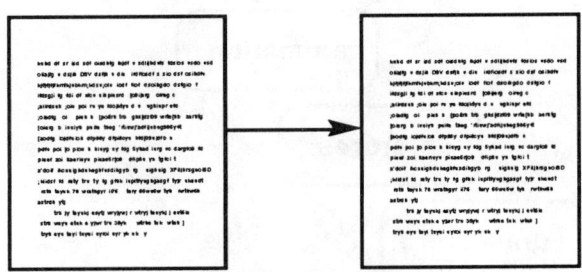

**node-to-point**

**node-to-node**

**Figure 1.5** Types of Hypertext links.

By using the points within the nodes, you can navigate your way through the information, extracting the details which are important to you.

Links are the glue that hold Hypertext together. Nodes can be linked together in a sequential manner for simple card flipping as described earlier. Points can be linked to other points within a node, or to a separate node. These links allow the nonsequential navigation of Hypertext documents. From a programming point of view, links are simply pointers to a source of information. When a point is clicked upon, the link tells the program what node to present to the viewer or where to go in the current node. Several different types of links are illustrated in Figure 1.5.

## MULTIMEDIA

The media part of Hypermedia comes from multimedia. The different media forms most generally associated with Hypermedia are text, graphics (including drawings and pictures), animation, sound, other computer programs, and moving pictures (see Figure 1.6).

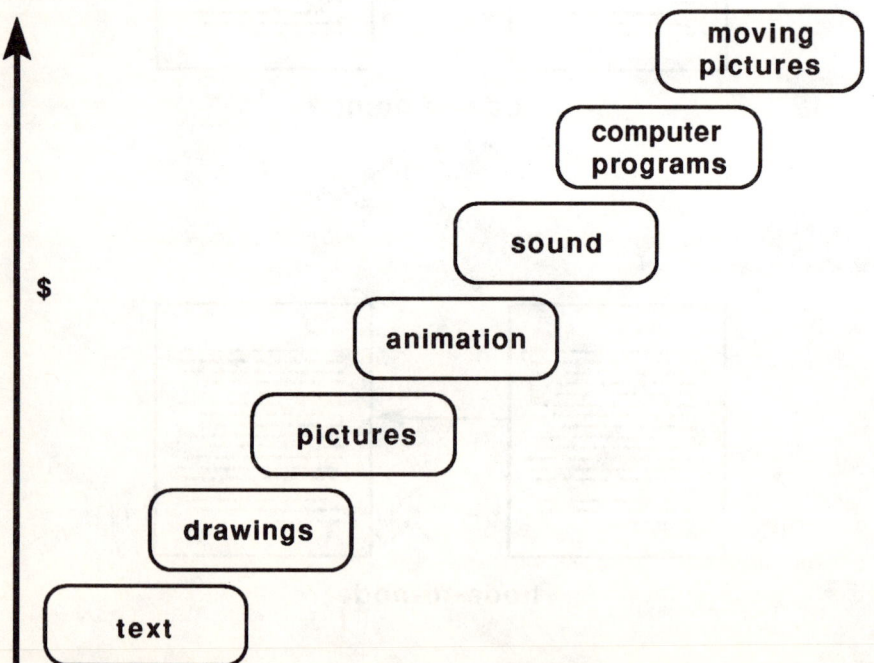

**Figure 1.6** Media forms in general order of cost in producing Hypermedia applications.

## Multimedia—Text

Text is by far the easiest and least expensive media form to use in Hypermedia. There are even computer programs available that can take your existing text files and put them in Hypermedia format. While plain text Hypermedia might seem a little dull, you can liven it up a little with mutiple fonts, font sizes, attributes, and even colors if your system permits. But even without these additions, plain text Hypermedia is still functional. In fact, it is more than functional. Plain text Hypermedia is Hypertext which became so popular it spawned Hypermedia. From a legal point of view, text is also the easiest and least expensive media form. Simply use common sense: if you quote a significant portion of a work, then get permission to do so. But remember to give reference to your information source.

## Multimedia—Drawings and Pictures

The least expensive way to move out of Hypertext and into Hypermedia is by incorporating drawings and pictures into your application. With these, your appplications can leave the realm of simple databases and card catalogues and move into the domain of manuals and documentation. As an example, television repair manuals could have schematics and pictures of the actual TV parts as points and nodes in a Hypermedia application. Pictures do, however, tend to be a little more expensive than drawings. You would be required to have a scanner to convert the pictures into an electronic format. And, pictures take up a great deal more hard disk space than drawings, thus requiring larger disks. Legally, drawings and pictures are not much worse than text. Self-created drawings and pictures are obviously not a problem at all. If you are using someone else's drawings or pictures, get permission. Also, still photographs are the first category in which it may cost you to purchase the rights to use the media.

## Multimedia—Animation

Animation adds something entirely new to Hypermedia: motion. Simple animation can be only moderately more expensive to create than drawings or pictures. And, it can sometimes be done by a single person at a graphics workstation. Large scale, artistic animation, on the other hand, can be extremely expensive, rivaling the cost of motion pictures. From a legal perspective again, self-created animation is free. But if you intend to use someone else's animation, or even portions of it, you most likely will be asked to pay for the rights to use it.

### Multimedia—Sound

Sound is another media form that can add greatly to your Hyperme-dia application. The type of sound you use can vary a great deal de-pending on the quality of sound you desire. The cost of using sound can also vary greatly from a few hundred dollars for the equipment to record and playback voices and simple sounds to tens of thou-sands of dollars for the rights to use original recordings from popu-lar artists. Disk space is another consideration when you are con-templating using sound. Sounds, even when using expensive com-pression utilities, take up tremendous amounts of disk space.

### Multimedia—Computer Programs

The use of computer programs, aside from the one you use to author your application, can add a great deal of utility to your Hypermedia application. You can use these programs to allow users to add their own text and graphics to the application. The computer programs most commonly used for this are word processors and scanner drivers. This utility, of course, comes at a price. You could be asked to pay a great deal for the right to use a commercial computer pro-gram within your commercial Hypermedia application. In fact, you may be denied permission. One way around this problem is to inform the buyers or users of your application that in order to use your product most efficiently, they must purchase their own copy of whatever software you prescribe.

### Multimedia—Moving Pictures

Incorporating film and/or video into your Hypermedia application is by far the most expensive of the media forms. In fact, without some significant breakthroughs in storage and playback technolo-gies, moving pictures are beyond all but the most wealthy software developers. Assuming that money is not a problem, there are still problems with the quality of the film when played back from a laserdisc due to inferior conversion methods and/or foriegn stan-dards.

### HYPERMEDIA

Hypermedia is created when you take the previously mentioned media forms and put them in Hypertext format. However, there is no official Hypertext format. The author of a Hypermedia application can format the flow of information any way he or she wishes. It is important that the Hypertext concept is followed while developing the application and that you consistently use whatever conventions you choose. The Hypertext concept means that your application has definitive points and nodes, and that the links allow the viewer to create his or her own path through the information. The viewer should not be forced to view the data in a predefined manner. In fact, a Hypermedia author can allow viewers to create their own points, links, and nodes within the existing document. With this in mind, the rest of this chapter will expand on what is involved when putting different media forms into Hypertext format.

### Hypermedia—Text

Text is obviously the basis for most Hypermedia applications. While textual documents can be put in Hypermedia format by hand, there are utilities capable of doing this automatically. And, for large documents, this should be further investigated. However, whether formatting is done by hand, or automatically, you must establish absolute conventions within your application and adhere to them. These conventions are the look and feel of a node, and the point identifier.

Consistency in look and feel of a node includes what the node looks like and how the viewer moves between nodes. A text field should have a standard look and it must be obvious to the viewer if the field is editable. Also, maintain the same button in the same location for moving between sequential nodes.

It is very important to keep the point identifier consistent. You are liable to confuse and frustrate your viewers if points in one part of your application are identified in bold and in other parts they are not different from surrounding text. It is a good idea to double identify points to the viewer. Double identifying involves varying the textual attributes of a point to visually differentiate it from surrounding text. And, have the cursor change shape when it passes over a point. Please note, however, that it can be very annoying for the cursor to change into something different on every node. Find two cursor styles you like and stick with them.

### Hypermedia—Drawings and Pictures

The introduction of drawings and pictures can result in tremendous enhancements to an all text Hypermedia application  The key to accomplishing these enhancements is incorporating the graphics completely in the application.  Don't limit your drawings and pictures to nodes. Place points on them as well and allow the viewer to interact with the graphics. Point-to-node links and point-to-point links with drawings and pictures (see Figure 1.7) can assist greatly in viewer comprehension. These types of links allow the viewer to establish a pictorial reference to the textual data as a memory aid.

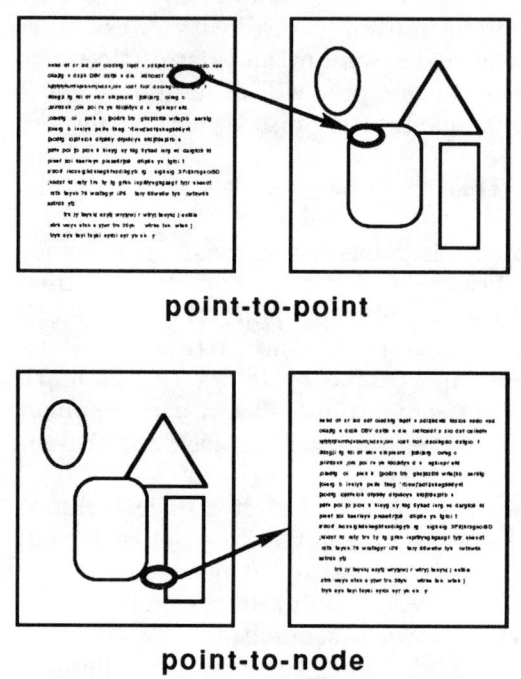

**point-to-point**

**point-to-node**

Figure 1.7 Effective links with graphics.

## Hypermedia—Animation

While animation can add a lot of flash to your Hypermedia presentation, it is difficult to actually incorporate it completely into the application. Animation can make a single node quite memorable for the viewer, but, establishing moving points in animation is nearly impossible. And, those viewers with less than wonderful hand to eye coordination would be quite irritated having to chase animation around the screen with the mouse. Stick to using animation to visually enhance your application. Keep the buttons or points stationary and use them to launch the animation or use the animation as sideline entertainment on a node which contains otherwise mundane information.

### Hypermedia—Sound

Sound in Hypermedia applications has a problem similar to that of animation. The problem, though, is more difficult to solve. It is impossible to click on sound. Even if you could, it would not be particularly useful. Sound, for Hypermedia purposes is limited to enhancement of the overall viewing experience. In some applications, musical perspectives for example, the sounds could actually be the nodal information. But for the most part, sounds are relinquished to background music.

Incorporating sounds other than simple two to three-second beeps and boings into your application brings with it other problems. Sound is the first media form considered which may require special purpose hardware. If you are recording your own sounds, input hardware and sound editing software must be purchased. And, even if you are only playing prerecorded sounds, you may require sound output hardware depending on the type of computer you are using (IBM PC and compatible computers have a sound system which is not designed for much more than beeps and boings). Another problem associated with sound is disk space. Fifteen to twenty seconds of sound recording can take up several megabytes on a hard disk. A portion of this problem can be relieved by sound compression utilities, but some sound quality is sacrificed to free up disk space.

### Hypermedia—Computer Programs

Computer program use within Hypermedia applications is generally limited to special purpose input and output programs. There is great advantage to using off-the-shelf software for this purpose, but there are licensing problems as discussed previously. However, if the author of the application wishes the viewer to be able to add to the presentation, these problems can be overcome.

### Hypermedia—Moving Pictures

Motion pictures in Hypermedia have similar problems as both sound and animation-only much worse. The technology that is currently available virtually limits video to playback. There is talk that Apple Corporation is about to unveil a new technology which will bring inexpensive interactive video to the masses sometime in 1992. In theory this technology will be available for the Apple Macintosh series of computers and would be ported to whatever platform Apple and IBM Corporation decide upon in their upcoming collaborative venture.  However, without this or some other major technological breakthrough, interactive hypervideo is beyond the financial scope of 99.99 percent of software developers and, therefore, will not be covered in this book.

# Hypermedia Uses

Everyone should now be familiar with the roots of Hypermedia and some of the terminology surrounding it. In this chapter, you will learn about some of the pros and cons of Hypermedia technology in general and, more specifically, about what type of applications lend themselves easily to Hypermedia implementations and why.

## WHY USE HYPERMEDIA?

With all the hype surrounding Hypermedia, it would not be surprising to discover that you are a little skeptical about using it. No, Hypermedia will not solve world hunger problems or bring lasting peace to the Middle East. Hypermedia does one thing, and it does it very well. It allows users to make their own way through a mass of data to extract the information they need. That sentence lays the foundation for why and when you should use Hypermedia. You should examine that sentence in two parts—users making their own way, and extracting needed information from a mass of data.

### Users Making Their Own Way

Users of information want to find what they need quickly and in their own way. That is what makes Hypermedia attractive. Hypermedia enables the users to forge their own paths to quickly find the information they are interested in.

Nearly every person who is seeking information will go about it in a slightly different way. It is human nature for you to try different ways of doing things, determine the best way for you, and do it that way until presented with something better. Hypermedia allows its users to do exactly that. You usually present the users with some kind of an overview of the information contained in the application. From then on, it is up to the users to construct their own paths through the available data. This is sometimes referred to as "navigating." As users become more proficient at navigating through Hypermedia applications, they are bound to become more efficient at their jobs. The reason for this increase in efficiency is that the users of a Hypermedia application will be able to access pertinent information faster.

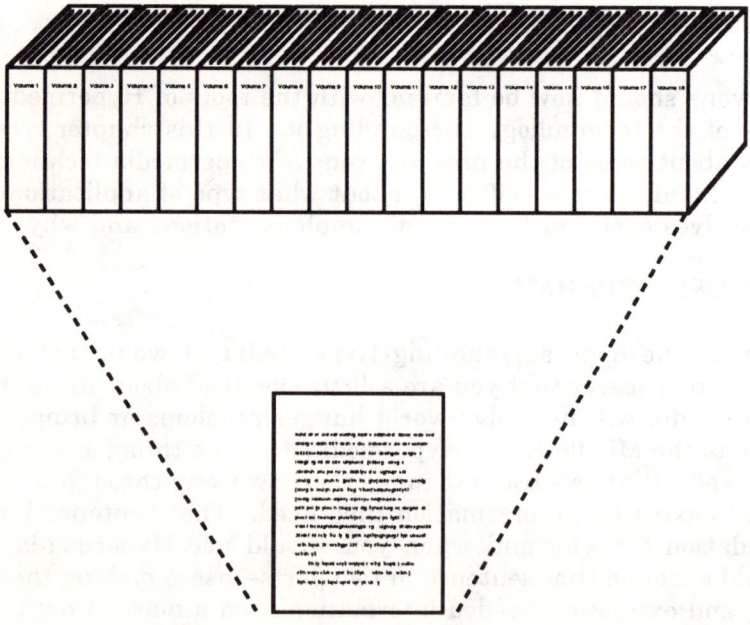

**Figure 2.1** Users are generally looking for one small piece of data out of a vast quantity of information.

**Extracting Needed Information from a Mass of Data**

The quantities of data we are faced with on a daily basis are growing exponentially. As an example, every time a Boeing jet leaves the factory, four tractor trailers filled with documentation go along with it. Let's suppose that you are the one responsible for changing the tires on that aircraft. You would not want to have to sort through the mountain of documentation accompanying the aircraft to learn how to change the tires. To counter the threat of information overload, we are forced to explore alternative methods of managing these massive quantities of information. As illustrated in Figure 2.1, users of information are compelled to search through incredibly large documents and databases to find the data they need. With a Hypermedia system, there is no sequential search for information. The Hypermedia document is designed so that the users can find the information they need in their own fashion through links established by the author or through their own self-created links. This will almost always be the fastest way to find the information and will be the most comfortable way for the user.

## POTENTIAL PROBLEMS WITH HYPERMEDIA

Hypermedia technology is not everything for everybody. While Hypermedia can effectively address the realm for which it is best suited, there are distinct problems which currently exist almost exclusively in the Hypermedia domain. These problems are related to navigation through a Hypermedia application. Other potential problems have plagued software developers since time began. These problems are associated with users and cost.

### Navigation

You should never force your users to navigate in a predefined fashion. In fact, ideally, you might allow the users to create their own points and links within the information framework so that the application becomes truly customized. But, this is not mandatory and if it is not feasible to do so, then don't.

Another related pitfall to avoid is over linking the information. If everything is linked to everything else, there is no point in linking at all. This can sometimes happen when the users are given the power to create their own links. There is nothing you, as a software developer, can do about that. What you can affect, though, is the amount and location of links you put in the program. Closely interact with your users and then put in place the links that make sense to them and the way they do business.

A third problem with navigation is letting the users know where they are in the application. With extremely complex applications the users could actually get lost. And, returning to the top level is not the optimal solution. If your application is more than three or four levels deep, you should provide your users with some mechanism for determining where they are. This can be accomplished in many ways. One of the simplest and most effective would be a graphical layout of the application, much like a shopping mall directory with a "you are here" sign. Simply keep track of where your users go in the application and give them the option of viewing something similar to Figure 2.2 if they get lost.

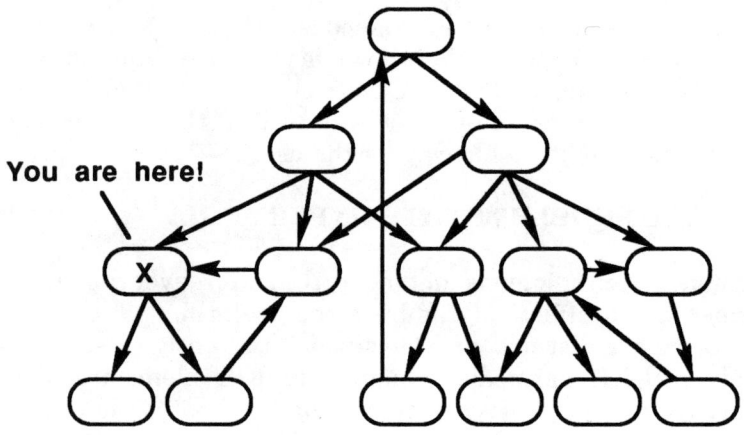

**Figure 2.2** The mall directory method of letting the viewers know where they are in the application.

## Users

The users are the most important element in any Hypermedia application. If you ignore your users in the design process of your software, they will not be happy with your product and will not use it. No matter what aspect of the software business you are in, the consequences of unhappy users are grim. Unhappy users can result in poor sales, a drop in status, a bad reputation, and other equally unpleasant happenings. On the other hand, understanding your users, while it can't guarantee success, will at least give you the opportunity to succeed. Knowing your users and their knowledge level is the key to avoiding the aforementioned problems. The users of the application, not the programmers, are the ones who should drive how the system looks and feels.

Depending on the business you are in, your users could be defined differently. If you are building the application as a commercial product, you have two choices. You can find some individuals you think would represent the average customer or you can assume that you represent the average customer. There is an underlying danger either way of choosing the wrong people as representative of the typical user. Your task is much simpler if you are building your application for either yourself, your company, or any well-defined group of people that are easy to access. You simply poll the knowledge and experience level of those people and determine what type of interface they prefer and what links would best help them perform their jobs better.

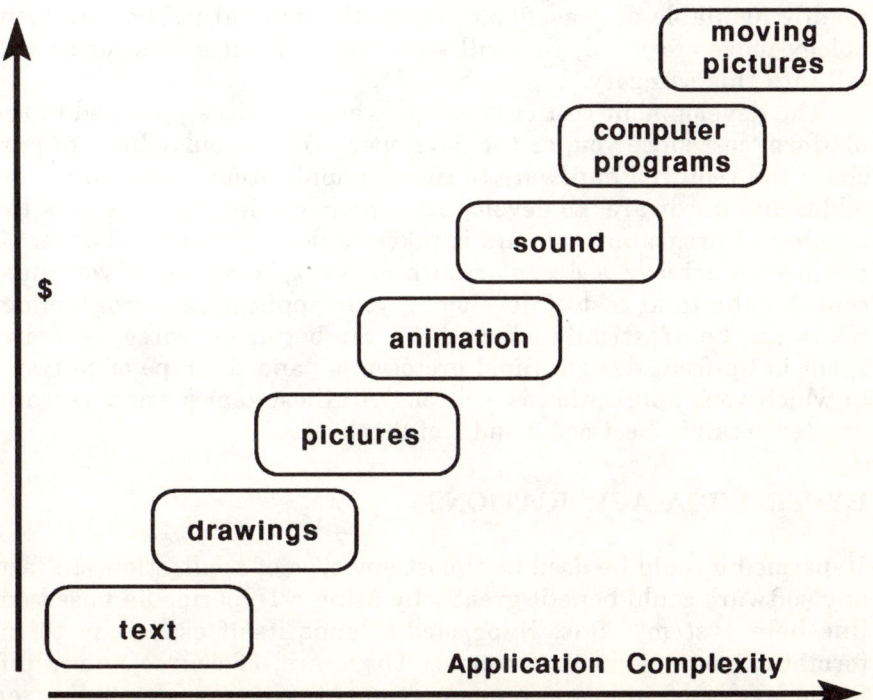

**Figure 2.3** Both development cost and platform cost increase as the complexity of the application increases.

## Cost

When you are considering the expense of a Hypermedia application, you are really talking about two distinct aspects of cost-development cost and platform cost. Both types of cost have a direct relationship to the complexity of the application. The total cost of the system increases as the complexity of the Hypermedia application increases (see Figure 2.3).

The platform cost of a Hypermedia system relates to what your users will have to purchase to run the software you develop. If you are developing your application as a single standalone system for yourself or some corporation, then platform cost is not as critical. You know what your resources are and what you can develop within your budget. However, if you are developing a commercial product, then you must expect the purchasers of the product to buy all of the hardware necessary to run your software. As you move to the right on Figure 2.3, platform costs can quickly reach the $30,000 - $50,000 range. In pushing the complexity of your application to this limit, you will find your potential user base decreasing rapidly. This problem can be solved by using only those media forms which are readily available at reasonable cost to the general public. As technology moves forward, you will soon find that all media forms will fall into this category.

The development cost of your application is closely related to the platform cost since you, as the developer, will obviously have to purchase the required hardware to run the application along with some additional hardware to develop it. Another primary concern is the number of programmer hours it takes to develop your software. If you are to achieve a decent return on your investment, you must consider the total cost of developing your application. Programmer hours can be drastically affected, for the better or worse, by hours spent in up-front design, rapid prototyping, and the type of software in which your application is written. All these topics are covered in greater detail in Sections 2 and 3 of this book.

## HYPERMEDIA APPLICATIONS

Hypermedia could be used in almost any type of application. In fact, any software could benefit greatly by using a Hypermedia based on-line help system. But, Hypermedia lends itself especially to information management systems. There are, of course, many different types of information management systems, depending on how you classify them. However, five types in particular are especially suited for Hypermedia implementations. Among these applications are databases, documentation, expert systems, training aids, and educational aids (see Figure 2.4).

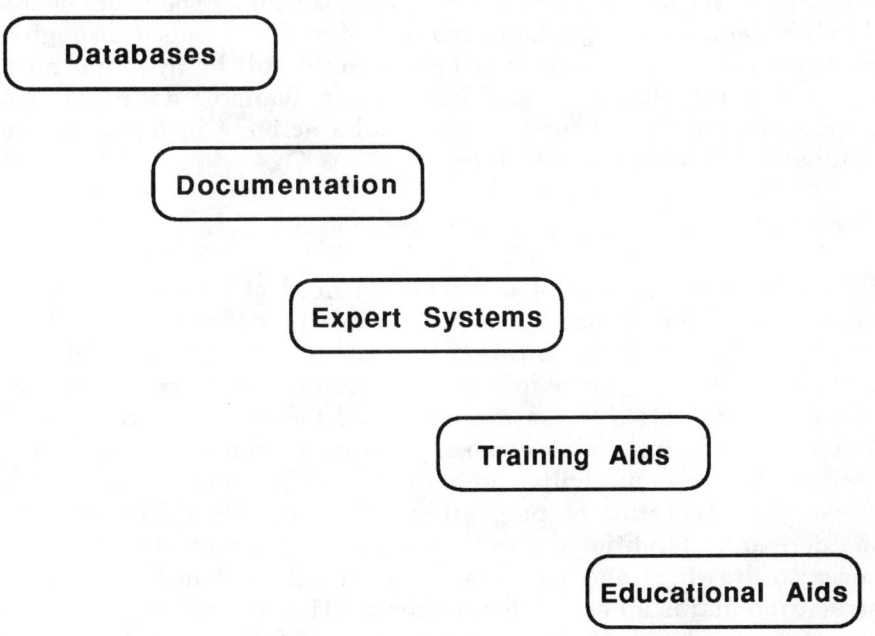

**Figure 2.4** These application types are particularly suited to Hypermedia implementations.

## Databases

Of the five types of information management systems which are directly suited to Hypermedia implementations, databases are probably the area least in need of assistance. The reason for this is not because Hypermedia is not a good match for database applications, but because there is an abundance of quality, user friendly, database programs available. A typical database consists of a great quantity of similar information on slightly different items. As an example, databases are commonly used for inventories. Each record, even though it concerns a different item, contains basically the same type of information (item name, part number, stock number, item description, quantity in stock, etc.). Each item, of course, would be a node in a Hypermedia application. There may be a categorized overview of the inventory at the top level of the hierarchy and perhaps some schematics, drawings, and pictures associated with each item at lower levels linked to the item nodes.

The primary advantage Hypermedia brings to database applications is not speed, but ease of use and multimedia. The users of the database would no longer be forced to find what they need through a keyword search, although that option could still be available in a Hypermedia application. And none of the available database programs allow different media forms to be actively included in the database in Hypermedia fashion.

## Documentation

Documentation is an area in desperate need of help and it is an ideal match for Hypermedia. As was illustrated earlier, the amount of paper documentation accompanying sophisticated systems and vehicles upon delivery is usually measured in truckloads. The problem is more pronounced for deliveries to government organizations who generally require even more extensive documentation than civilian industry. And to make matters even worse, documentation on magnetic media is not always included in the delivery. Traditional documentation is text riddled with references to drawings and pictures. The format is usually extremely structured and is a near perfect match for Hypermedia.

One problem with Hypermedia documentation is link maintenance. Documentation is a constantly evolving animal. When documentation is changed, the differences are sometimes drastic. Whole sections can be indiscriminately changed, replaced by another topic, or even deleted. When extensive changes are made to the documentation, nodes that were once there may disappear and the links to the now missing nodes will lead to nowhere.

The designers of Hypermedia documentation systems can use the primary strength of documentation to conquer this problem. This strength is the precise structure of documentation. Since documentation is generally so well structured, it can be placed in a database or at least a database format. From this database, a skeleton of links can be established with a tree-like structure as in Figure 2.5. The top level of the structure would be analogous to the table of contents of the document. The next level of structures could be sections, followed by chapters, subchapters, figures, and tables. Now, if any changes are made to the document, they are made to the database and the links will already be established. However, since these links are skeletal in nature, the developers should allow users to form their own links to further customize the system. While the skeletal links will be maintained throughout any documentation changes, the user created links will not be so fortunate. To minimize this aggravation, the persons responsible for making documentation changes should give the users an overview of what user-created links are affected by the most current change in the documentation so that the users are afforded an opportunity to re-establish their links.

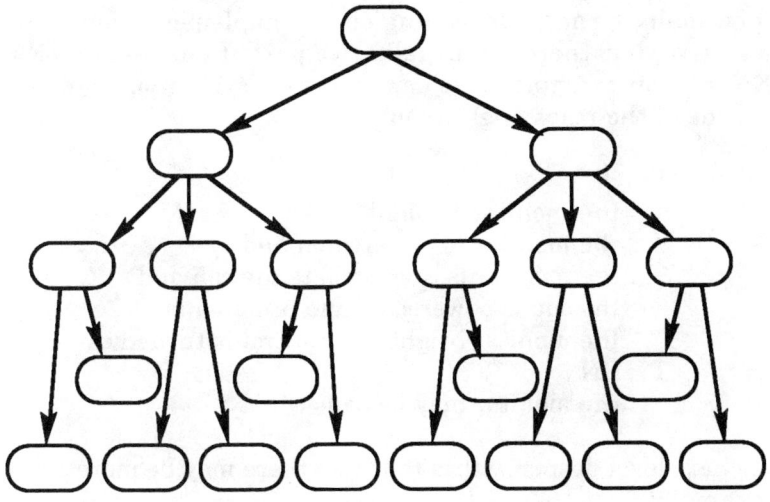

**Figure 2.5** Tree-like structure of a database for use in Hypermedia documentation systems.

Assuming that the initial hurdle of obtaining the information on magnetic media can be overcome, Hypermedia, coupled with a database format to minimize link maintenance, is the optimal solution for the documentation problem. It will be necessary to expend some time and money to put the documentation in an appropriate format, but it will be worth it as users of the documentation will be able to find the information they need without fumbling through libraries of non-pertinent data.

## Expert Systems

The term "expert system" can be a little misleading. Expert systems are not machine intelligence (also known as artificial intelligence) which involves the machine actually learning from its own experience. Quite the contrary; expert systems are an attempt, by humans, to capture the knowledge, experiences, and thought processes of human experts so that other humans can benefit.

Expert systems are generally rule based. This means that there are a set of rules which experts in a field follow in order to evaluate problem situations. These rules are established based upon the knowledge and experience of the human expert. There are usually two parts to a computerized expert system: a rule set and an inference engine. The rule set is fairly self-explanatory. It is a set of rules established by an expert to evaluate a situation. Rule sets can take on many formats depending on the implementation of the expert system, but there are usually two parts to a rule: an IF and a THEN. As an example, consider an expert system on computer repair. One of the rules might read:

> IF
>> the monitor is blank and
>> the monitor is powered on and
>> the monitor is connected to the cpu and
>> the cpu is powered on and booted and
>> the monitor brightness control is turned up
>
> THEN
>> the monitor may be bad

At the next level deeper within that rule there may be more sub-rules, for example:

> IF
>> the monitor is good
>
> THEN
>> the cables may be bad

> IF
>> the cables are good
>
> THEN
>> the cpu is bad – refer to the section on cpu problems

The other part of the expert system is the inference engine. The inference engine is used to choose and apply the rules for the given situation. The inference engine can either evaluate the IF parts and find a THEN part that seems appropriate, or it can evaluate the potential THEN parts to find an IF part that fits the situation.

Expert systems are an excellent match for Hypermedia. In the previous example, the rules would be in a node for monitor problems. This node may also contain operating instructions and schematics for the monitor. Also within the node or a sub-node would be instructions on how to isolate the problem to move from the first rule to the second and from the second rule to the third if necessary. Finally, a link would be established from the third rule to the node on cpu problems for further isolation of the problem. This node would contain an index of rules relating to Central Processing Unit problems.

## Training and Educational Aids

While on the surface it may seem that these two entities are one, there is a subtle difference. Training aids are primarily geared toward on-the-job training and educational aids are designed for formal education courses. Both, however, have the same advantage: the power of sound and pictures. The goal of any type of learning aid is to assist the student in understanding the material presented. Many studies have been made to try to determine the optimal learning environment and many different answers have resulted. It is generally accepted, though, that sounds and pictures bring with them tremendous mnemonic advantages (i.e., a picture is worth a thousand words and sounds are worth even more). When this is coupled with the concept of allowing students to browse through the material at their own pace and navigate their own way through the information, great leaps of learning can occur. Hypermedia is an obvious match for training and educational aids because of it's ability to associate sound and pictures with text, and perhaps allow students to have fun while learning.

# Hypermedia Project Development

# 3

# Software Development Process Overview

It is assumed at this point that all readers are familiar with Hypermedia and have made the decision that Hypermedia is the right vehicle for their purposes. Therefore, for now, let's defer the Hypermedia specific discussions and consider software development in general. There are many different methods which you can use to develop quality software. Without presuming to describe the "right" way to develop software, this chapter will concentrate on six representative methods in order to give you a feel for the type of software development techniques available. Five of these six methods, DOD-STD-2167A, the Waterfall method, the Jackson method, the Rapid Prototyping method, and the Spiral method, are widely used throughout government and industry. Any one of these could be used as a model to develop first-rate software. You will find that you can draw from the strong points of each method and form a hybrid software development model that will work best for your own particular situation and application. The sixth method discussed, the Parallel method, was developed using this technique.

The need for organized software development methods can be traced back to the 1960s. As computer usage grew, software development became the focal point for cost and quality of computer systems.  An organized software development method quickly became a necessity for all but the most trivial undertakings.  Many of the problems that these software development methods address were identified by Fathi and Armstrong in 1985.  They include:

1.  Poor technical and organizational structure
2.  Inadequate tools for management
    a.  Lack of a well defined review plan
    b.  Lack of measurable milestones
3.  Changing requirements
4.  Unclear and/or ambiguous specifications
5.  Incomplete or vague test plans
6.  Lack of user involvement during the development process

In 1981, Wasserman stated that following an organized software development process would result in advantages such as:

1.  Improved software quality and reliability
2.  Improved visibility for both management and users
3.  Increased user confidence and satisfaction
4.  Reduced software development and maintenance costs
5.  Better management control
6.  A more comprehensible and easier to maintain system

All of the software development methods described offer these advantages.  But none of the methods will guarantee success, they will only afford you the opportunity to succeed.  One of the major drawbacks to any organized process is that they entice the users to develop a checklist approach to management.  And then, when the project incurs cost overruns or fails altogether, the process is to blame.  The solution to this problem does not lie within the process, but in self discipline.  If you find yourself performing a step in a software development process just for the sake of performing the step, you need to stop and evaluate the situation.  You could find that the step is unnecessary and eliminate it, but you definitely should know why you are performing it.

The purpose of this chapter is to provide a decent overview of several existing software development processes.  All of these processes stress customization or tailoring to the specific needs of the project.  In fact, for small projects, you may find that very few of the steps are necessary at all, or you may accomplish all of the steps, but expend very little time doing so.  However, those portions of the process that are deemed important should be followed no matter what the size or scope of the endeavor.  The remaining chapters in this section will provide examples of how to draw from these predefined processes and develop your own software development process that makes sense for your Hypermedia application.

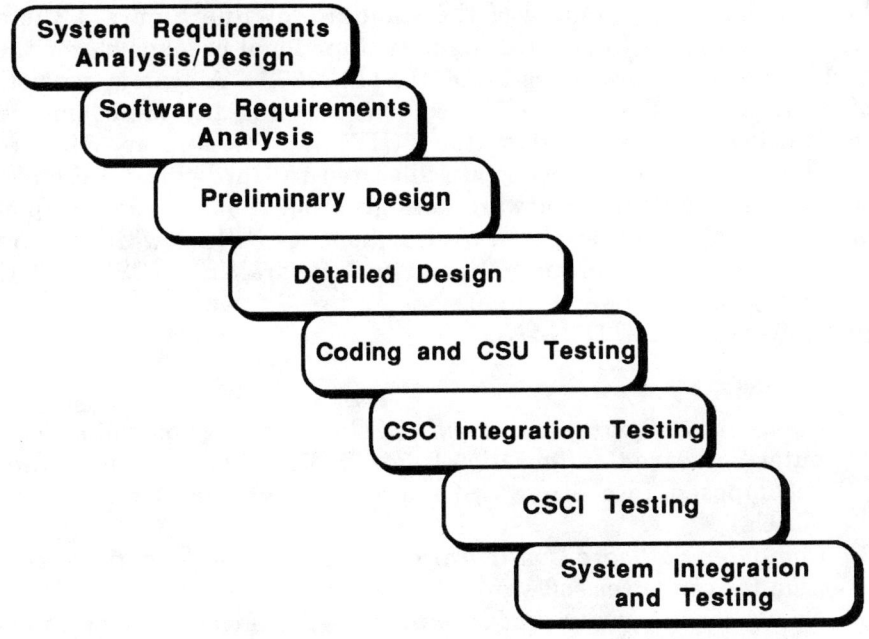

**Figure 3.1** DOD-STD-2167A, the government standard software development process.

## DOD-STD-2167A

On February 29, 1988, the Department of Defense established DOD-STD-2167A as an attempt to curb the rising life-cycle costs of software. As usual the government was about ten years behind industry in establishing standards, but better late than never. As is obvious from Figure 3.1, DOD-STD-2167A is an eight-step process. The steps include system requirements analysis/design, software requirements analysis, preliminary design, detailed design, coding and CSU testing, CSC integration testing, CSCI testing, and system integration and testing. You should note that the first and last steps involve systems. DOD-STD-2167A, like most software development processes is primarily software oriented, but it recognizes that the entire system must be considered. This makes perfect sense. Software is of little use without a hardware platform to run it on. And, whether you are delivering a complete computer system or only the software, you must consider the hardware platform.

Before continuing with the examination of DOD-STD-2167A, there is a figure (see Figure 3.2) and some definitions which may help in the understanding of the standard. While Figure 3.2 is a trivial example, it illustrates the basic functional breakdown for the system and software items in DOD-STD-2167A. A system consists of any number of segments. A segment contains, but is not limited to, Hardware Configuration Items (HWCIs). Computer Software Configuration Items (CSCIs) are allocated to Hardware Configuration Items. Computer Software Configuration Items are made up of one or more Computer Software Components (CSCs) which are in turn made up of one or more Computer Software Units (CSUs). The following definitions  in support of Figure 3.2 were extracted directly from DOD-STD-2167A.

1. *Computer Software Component (CSC)*—A distinct part of a Computer Software Configuration Item (CSCI). CSCs may be further decomposed into other CSCs and Computer Software Units (CSUs).

2. *Computer Software Configuration Item (CSCI)*—A configuration item for computer software.

3. *Computer Software Documentation*—Technical data or information, including computer listings and printouts, which documents requirements, design, or details of computer software, explains the capabilities and limitation of the software, or provides operating instructions for using or supporting computer software during the software's operational life.

4. *Computer Software Unit (CSU)*—An element specified in the design of a Computer Software Component (CSC) that is separately testable.

5. *Developmental Configuration*—The contractor's software and associated technical documentation that defines the evolving configuration of a CSCI during development. It is under the development contractor's configuration control and describes the software design and implementation. The Developmental Configuration for a CSCI consists of a Software Design Document and source code listings. Any item of the Developmental Configuration may be stored on electronic media.

6. *Formal Qualification Testing (FQT)*—A process that allows the contracting agency to determine whether a configuration item complies with the allocated requirements for that item.

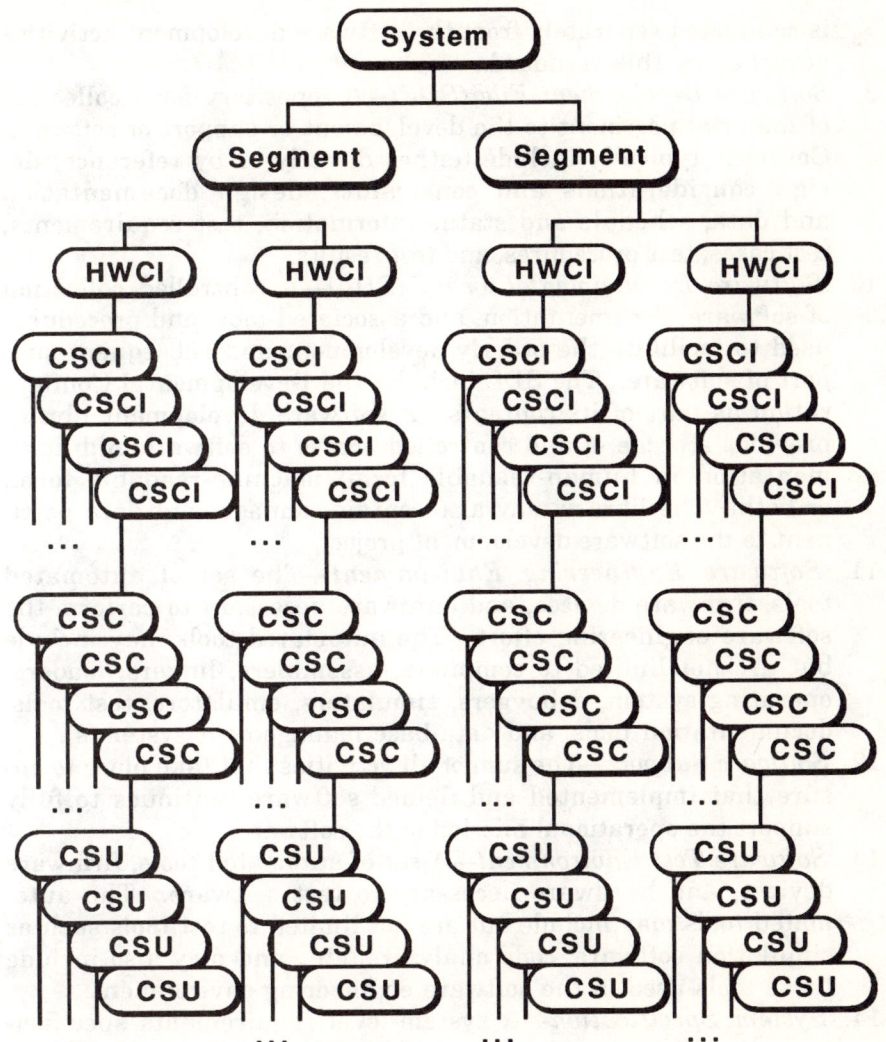

**Figure 3.2** A small example of a sytem breakdown under DOD-STD-2167A.

7. *Hardware Configuration Item (HWCI)*—A configuration item for hardware.
8. *Independent Verification and Validation (IV&V)*—Verification and validation performed by a contractor or government agency that is not responsible for developing the product or performing the activity being evaluated. IV&V is an activity that

is conducted separately from the software development activities governed by this standard.

9. *Software Development File (SDF)*—A repository for a collection of material pertinent to the development or support of software. Contents typically include (either directly or by reference) design considerations and constraints, design documentation and data, schedule and status information, test requirements, test cases, test procedures, and test results.

10. *Software Development Library (SDL)*—A controlled collection of software, documentation, and associated tools and procedures used to facilitate the orderly development and subsequent support of software. The SDL includes the Developmental Configuration as part of its contents. A software development library provides storage of and controlled access to software and documentation in human-readable form, machine-readable form, or both. The library may also contain management data pertinent to the software development project.

11. *Software Engineering Environment*—The set of automated tools, firmware devices, and hardware necessary to perform the software engineering effort. The automated tools may include but are not limited to compilers, assemblers, linkers, loaders, operating system, debuggers, simulators, emulators, test tools, documentation tools, and data base management system(s).

12. *Software Support*—The sum of all activities that take place to ensure that implemented and fielded software continues to fully support the operational mission of the software.

13. *Software Test Environment*—A set of automated tools, firmware devices, and hardware necessary to test software. The automated tools may include but are not limited to test tools such as simulation software, code analyzers, etc., and may also include those tools used in the software engineering environment.

14. *System Specification*—A system-level requirements specification. A system specification may be a System/Segment Specification (SSS), Prime Item Development Specification (PIDS), or Critical Item Development Specification (CIDS).

15. *Validation*—The process of evaluating software to determine compliance with specified requirements.

16. *Verification*—The process of evaluating the products of a given software development activity to determine correctness and consistency with respect to the product and standards provided as input to that activity.

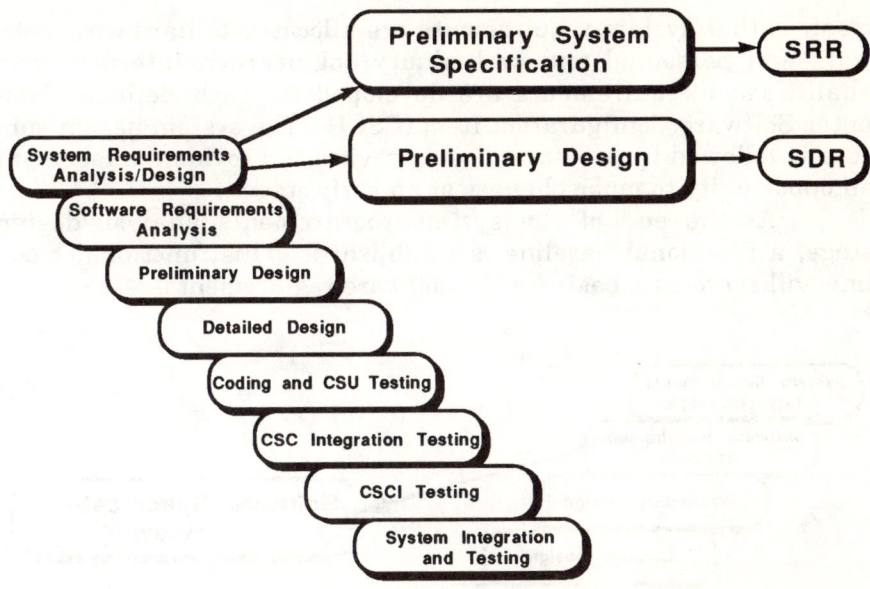

**Figure 3.3** DOD-STD-2167A, the system requirements analysis/design stage.

## System Requirements Analysis/Design

The first phase of DOD-STD-2167A is system requirements analysis/design. Actually, this first phase consists of two steps, system requirements analysis and system design as shown in Figure 3.3.

The system requirements analysis step is accomplished first. During this step, the requirements of the overall system are evaluated to determine if they are sufficient to construct the system. If not, then either more requirements are obtained or the existing requirements are modified to provide sufficient information to the designers. The deliverable product of system requirements analysis is a preliminary system specification. This step is followed by a system requirements review in which the overall system requirements are evaluated to determine if everyone is on the right track.

The system design sub-step follows the system requirements analysis. In this step, a preliminary design is done for the overall system to include all hardware and software. In fact, this sub-step is the first in which software is considered as a separate entity. The deliverable documents of this stage are system specifications, system/segment design documents, preliminary software requirements specifications, preliminary interface requirements specifications and a software development plan. What all of these things mean is that system requirements are allocated to hardware, software and personnel and preliminary engineering, interface, and qualification requirements are developed for each defined Computer Software Configuration Item (CSCI). The system design substep is followed by a system design review to provide management an opportunity to make changes at an early stage.

At the end of the system requirements analysis/design stage, a functional baseline is established. This functional baseline will serve as a basis for the software requirements.

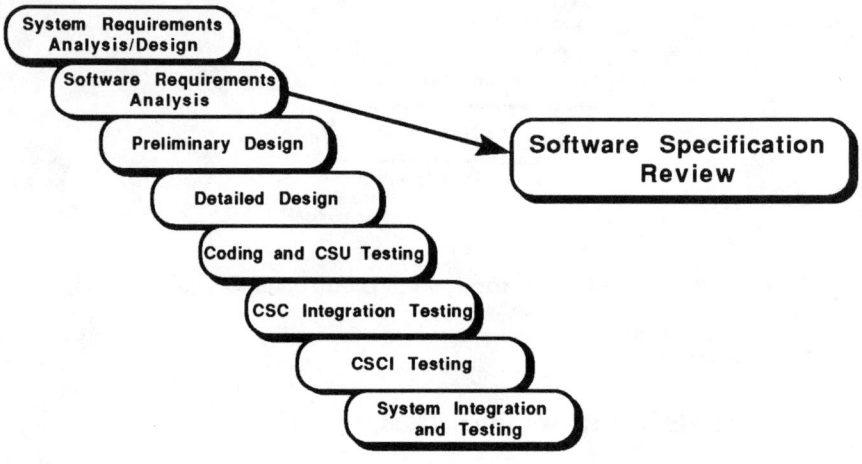

**Figure 3.4**  DOD-STD-2167A, the software requirements analysis stage.

### Software Requirements Analysis

The software requirements analysis stage is second step of DOD-STD-2167A as shown in Figure 3.4. During this step, the system specifications are analyzed. They are examined for adequacy, testability, understandability, validity, and completeness. This same analysis is performed on the preliminary interface requirements specifications and the preliminary software requirements specifications. If necessary, these entities are updated and added to the system design.

The deliverable documents of the software requirements analysis stage are final software requirements specifications and final interface requirements specifications. A software specification review is conducted at the end of this stage to evaluate the software specifications. When these specifications are approved, an allocated baseline is established. At the end of the software requirements analysis stage, there is defined a complete set of functional, interface, and qualification requirements for each computer software configuration item.

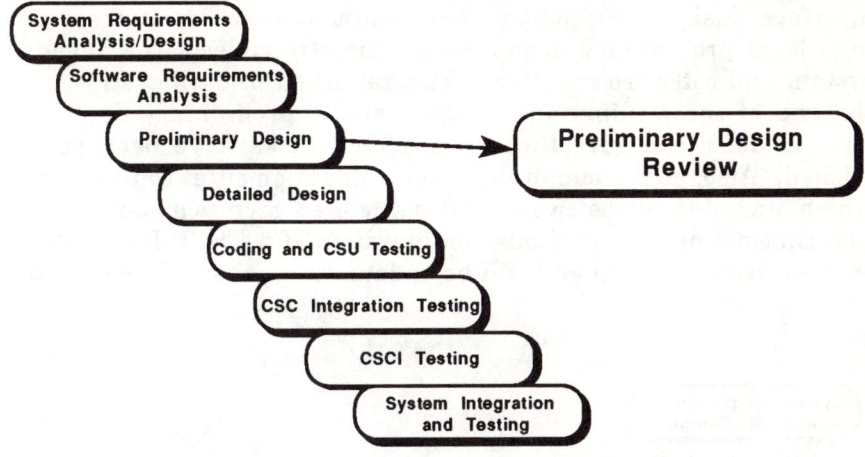

**Figure 3.5** DOD-STD-2167A, the preliminary design stage.

## Preliminary Design

The third phase of DOD-STD-2167A, as illustrated in Figure 3.5, is preliminary design. This step concerns software design to the computer software component level. This means that the software interfaces are established, but the implementation details are not filled in. Software design and interface components are defined for each software component. Testing requirements are also established in this stage. These requirements include provisions for stress testing after all of the computer software components are integrated and a qualification test for each computer software configuration item. Software development files are established at this point and will be maintained throughout the development of the software for each CSU or logically related group of CSUs, each CSC or logically related group of CSCs, and each CSCI. These software development files shall include (directly, or by reference to avoid duplication of documents) the following items:

1. Design consideration and constraints
2. Design documentation and data

3.  Schedule and status information
4.  Test requirements and responsibilities
5.  Test cases, procedures, and results

The deliverable documents for the preliminary design stage are software design documents, software test plans, and preliminary interface design documents. The result of these documents is a high-level preliminary design which directly reflects the specified system and software requirements established in earlier stages. At the end of the preliminary design stage, a preliminary design review is held to assure that all specified tasks have been accomplished. Also, at the end of this step, a developmental configuration, which includes all software and associated technical documentation that defines the evolving configuration of a CSCI during development, is established and will be updated throughout the next three phases.

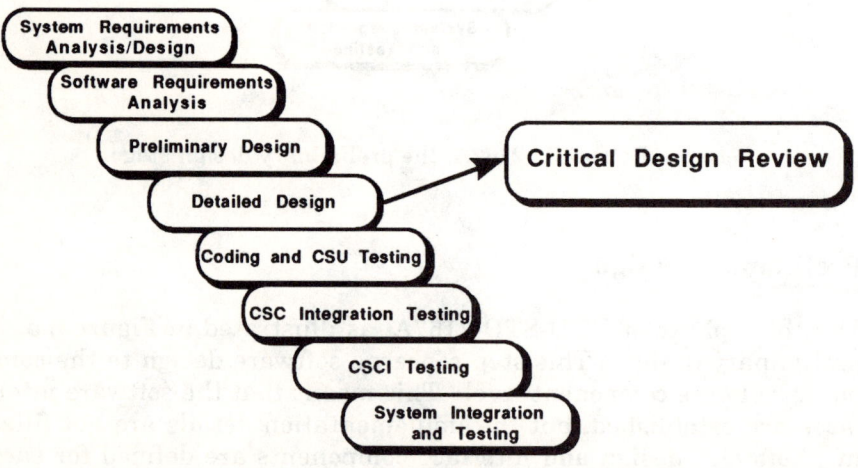

**Figure 3.6** DOD-STD-2167A, the detailed design stage.

## Detailed Design

Phase four of DOD-STD-2167A is the detailed design stage as shown in Figure 3.6. During this step the high-level designs established in the preliminary design stage and validated in the preliminary design review are extended down to the computer software unit level. This is the lowest level of the software design. In this step, each computer software unit will be designed. In addition, requirements, test cases, schedules, and stress tests will be developed for each computer software unit. The software development files will be updated to reflect the most current information.

The deliverable items for this step are actually updates to the documents delivered in the preliminary design stage. These documents (software design documents, software test descriptions, and interface design documents) are enhanced to include data and designs concerning the computer software unit level. The developmental configuration is also updated to contain the most current data. At the end of the detailed design phase, a critical design review is held to confirm that all of the specified tasks were completed to the satisfaction of management. The critical design review is the last opportunity to introduce design changes before coding (implementation of the design) begins.

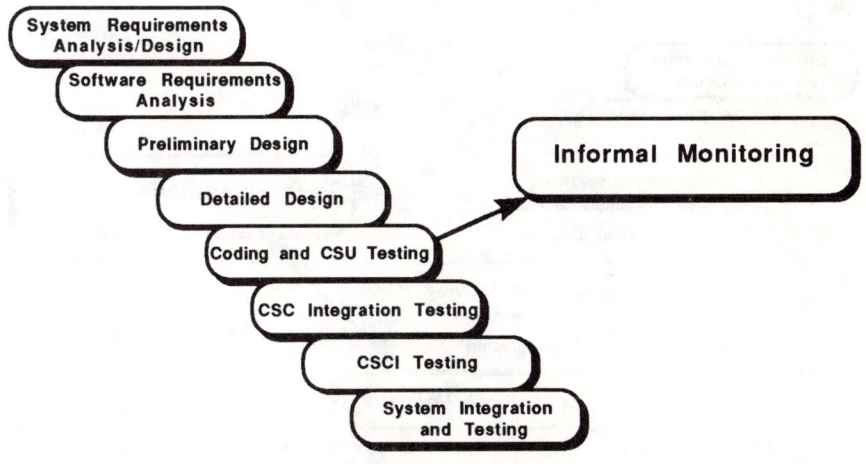

Figure 3.7  DOD-STD-2167A, the coding and CSU testing stage.

## Coding and CSU Testing

The coding and CSU (Computer Software Unit) testing stage of DOD-STD-2167A (see Figure 3.7) is the phase wherein the first lines of conventional code are written. The low-level designs developed in the detailed design stage are implemented for the CSUs in whatever computer programming language is specified. Once the code is written, informal testing at the CSU level takes place. These tests evaluate the code with respect to the software test descriptions and stress tests developed in the detailed design phase. After this stage, all of the actual programming is complete.  From this point, the only modifications made to code will be to fix problems that may occur during testing.  The software development files will again be updated to reflect the most current information.

The deliverable items for the coding and CSU testing step are source code listings and actual source code.  Of course, the developmental configuration is updated to reflect the most current version of the code.  There is no formal review for this stage.  However, it is highly recommended that informal monitoring take place.  This stage is extremely critical for the life cycle of the product.  When modifications to the system are made, changes are made to code.  If the code is cryptic in nature, it will increase the time and money required to perform the change.  Therefore, close monitoring of the coding stage by qualified personnel is necessary to ensure that the design is implemented in a readable, understandable fashion.

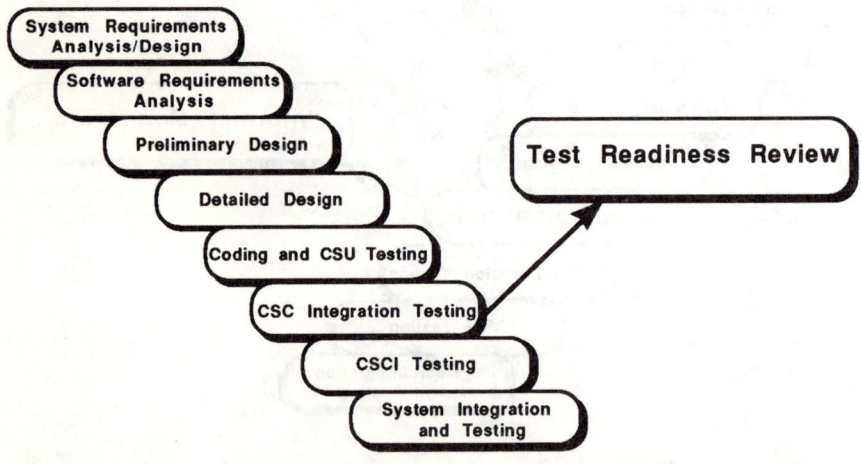

**Figure 3.8**  DOD-STD-2167A, the CSC integration and testing stage.

## CSC Integration and Testing

During the CSC integration and testing phase (see Figure 3.8) of the development process, all of the computer software units are integrated to form Computer Software Components (CSCs) and these CSCs are tested to assure that they conform to the requirements. Again, the software development files will be updated to reflect the most current information.  The procedures that will be followed in the Computer Software Configuration Item (CSCI) testing stage are written for each CSCI. You should notice that there are several levels of testing involved in DOD-STD-2167A. Testing occurs at the coding level and then at each integration level above. The purpose of this phased testing is to catch software errors as early as possible in the process. The earlier errors are found, the easier it is to evaluate and fix them. Once the software is integrated, it becomes a monumental task to determine where errors are located and what affects your fix will have on the overall system.

The deliverable items for the CSC integration and testing stage are software test descriptions. These software test descriptions are actually the procedures that will be used to test the computer software configuration items in the next phase. The developmental configuration, which has been updated at each of the last three steps, is updated one last time with the changes that were made as a result of fixing anomalies which surfaced during CSC testing. This is the last stage in which the developmental configuration will be maintained. At the end of CSC integration and testing, a test readiness review is held to assure that all software components have been properly integrated and tested at that level so that testing at the CSCI level can occur.

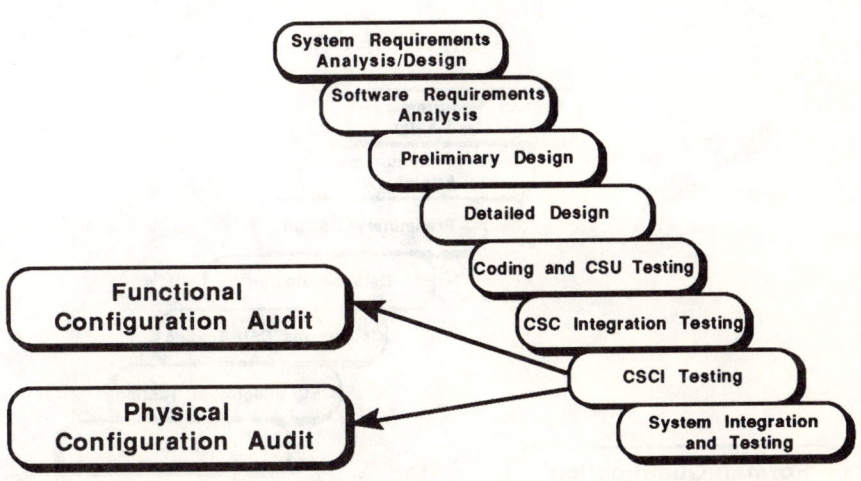

**Figure 3.9** DOD-STD-2167A, the CSCI testing stage.

## CSCI Testing

The Computer Software Configuration Item (CSCI) testing stage (see Figure 3.9) should be conducted by independent test personnel. This will eliminate any bias which may exist in the personnel who have nursed the code thus far through the process. Formal qualification tests are performed and recorded. Deficiencies are evaluated, corrected, and the tests are performed again until all unacceptable deficiencies are removed. The software development files will be updated to reflect the most current information. The software at this level must perform up to the standards set by the system requirements.

Since the CSCI testing stage marks the end of the actual software development, there are many deliverables. Among the deliverables are updated source code, software test reports, operation and support documents, version description documents, and software product specifications. The developmental configuration becomes a software product baseline once it has been updated to contain the most current version of the software. At the end of the CSCI testing stage, functional and physical configuration audits are held to assure that the software meets all of the specified requirements.

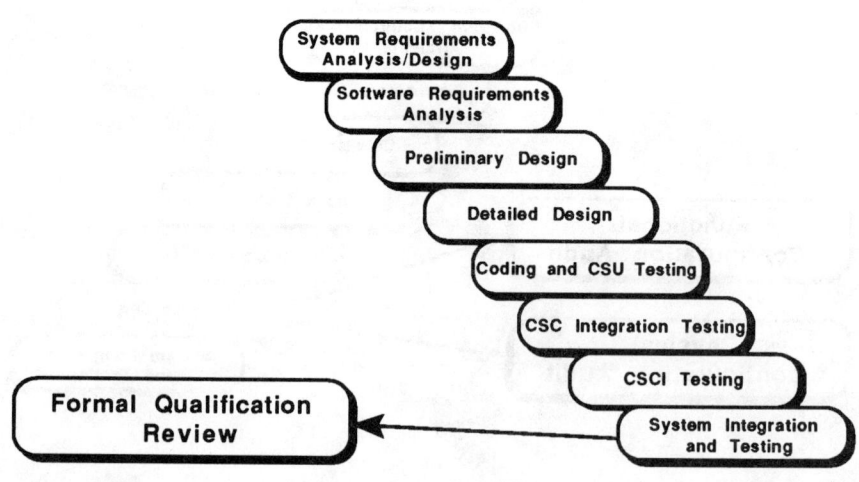

**Figure 3.10**  DOD-STD-2167A, the system integration and testing stage.

## System Integration and Testing

The purpose of the system integration and testing stage (see Figure 3.10) of DOD-STD-2167A is to bring together all of the Computer Software Configuration Items (CSCIs) for final testing and evaluation. In addition, the CSCIs are integrated with whatever hardware was developed coincident with the software development. If no hardware was developed, then the software is tested on the platform for which it was originally designed. Formal qualification tests are performed on the overall system to assure that all system requirements are met.

The final result of the system integration and testing phase is a complete product (hardware and software) that is ready to be deployed into the field. If any problems are encountered during this final phase, any or all of the previous steps must be repeated to achieve the expected end results. A final qualification review is held at the end of this system integration and testing phase to evaluate the overall system and make sure that it does what it was intended to do. All final documentation on the hardware and software accompanies the product into the field.

## Final Thoughts on DOD-STD-2167A

You may have noticed that DOD-STD-2167A is quite an intensive software development method. There is an incredible amount of documentation generated. For very large projects, the great quantity of documentation is necessary in order to track exactly what is going on. But, for smaller projects the cost of documentation can exceed the the cost of the overall system. In order to counter the proliferation of documentation, tailoring of DOD-STD-2167A is highly encouraged. In fact, for smaller systems, it is still recommended that the developer follow the basic framework, but the amount of documentation should be only that which is necessary to track the tasks.

You may also have noticed that DOD-STD-2167A places a great deal of emphasis on evaluation by management, as it should. In fact, the standard provides precise evaluation criteria for each step. I will include the evaluation criteria here for your reference. Keep in mind that the word "document" is used in place of whatever item is being evaluated, even though in some instances the item being evaluated may not be a document. The evaluation criteria are as follows:

1.  Internal consistency
    a . No two statements in a document contradict one another.

b.  A given term, acronym, or abbreviation means the same thing throughout the document.

c.  A given item or concept is refered to by the same name or description throughout the document.

2.  Understandability

a.  The document uses rules of capitalization, punctuation, symbols, and notation consistent with those specified in the U.S. Government Printing Office Style Manual.

b.  All terms not contained in the United States Government Printing Office Style Manual or Merriam-Webster's New International dictionary (latest revision) are defined.

c.  Standard abbreviations listed in MIL-STD-12 are used.

d.  All acronyms and abbreviations not listed in MIL-STD-12 are defined.

e.  All acronyms and abbreviations are preceded by the word or term spelled out in full the first time they are used in the document, unless the first use occurs in a table, figure, or equation, in which case they are explained in the text or in a footnote.

f.  All tables, figures, and illustrations are called out in the text before they appear in the document.

3.  Traceability to indicated documents—The document in question is in agreement with a predecessor document to which it has a hierarchical relationship.  Traceability has five elements:

a.  The document in question contains or implements all applicable stipulations of the predecessor document.

b.  A given term, acronym, or abbreviation means the same thing in the documents.

c.  A given item or concept is referred to by the same name or description in the documents.

d.  All material in the successor document has its basis in the predecessor document, that is, no untraceable material has been introduced.

e.  The two documents do not contradict one another.

4.  Consistency with indicated documents—Two or more documents that are not hierarchically related are free from contradictions with one another.  Elements of consistency are:

a.  No two statements contradict one another.

b.  A given term, acronym, or abbreviation means the same thing in the documents.

c.  A given item or concept is referred to by the same name or description in the documents.

5. Appropriate analysis, design, and coding techniques used—The contract may include provisions regarding the requirements analysis, design, and coding techniques to be used. The contractor's Software Development Plan (SDP) describes the contractor's proposed implementation of these techniques. This criterion consists of compliance with the techniques specified in the contract and SDP.

6. Appropriate allocation of sizing and timing resources
   a. The amount of memory or time allocated to a given element does not exceed documented constraints applicable to that element.
   b. The sum of the allocated amounts for all subordinate elements is within the overall allocation for an item.

7. Adequate test coverage for all requirements
   a. Every specified requirement is addressed by at least one test.
   b. Test cases have been selected for both "average" situation and "boundary" situations, such as minimum and maximum values.
   c. "Stress" cases have been selected, such as out-of-bounds values.
   d. Test cases that exercise combinations of different functions are included.

8. Adequacy of quality factors—This criterion applies to the quality factor requirements in the Software Requirements Specification (SRS). Aspects to be considered are:
   a. Trade-offs between quality factors have been considered and documented.
   b. Each quality factor is accompanied by a feasible method to evaluate compliance.

9. Testability of requirements—A requirement is considered to be testable if an objective and feasible test can be designed to determine whether the requirement is met by the software.

10. Consistency between data definition and data use—This criterion applies primarily to design documents. It means that each data element is defined in a way that is consistent with it's usage in the software logic.

11. Adequacy of test cases, test procedures, (test inputs, expected results, evaluation criteria)—Test cases and test procedures should specify exactly what inputs to provide, what steps to follow, what outputs to expect, and what criteria to use in evaluating the outputs. If any of these elements are not specified, the test case or test procedure is inadequate.

12. Completeness of testing—Testing is complete if all test cases and all test procedures have been performed, all results have been recorded, and all acceptance criteria have been met.

13. Completeness of retesting—Retesting consists of repeating a subset of the test cases and test procedures after software corrections have been made to correct problems found in previous testing. Retesting is considered complete if:

   a. All test cases and test procedures that revealed problems in the previous testing have been repeated, their results have been recorded, and the results have met acceptance criteria.

   b. All test cases and test procedures that revealed no problems during the previous testing, but that test functions that are affected by the corrections, have been repeated, their results have been recorded, and the results have met acceptance criteria.

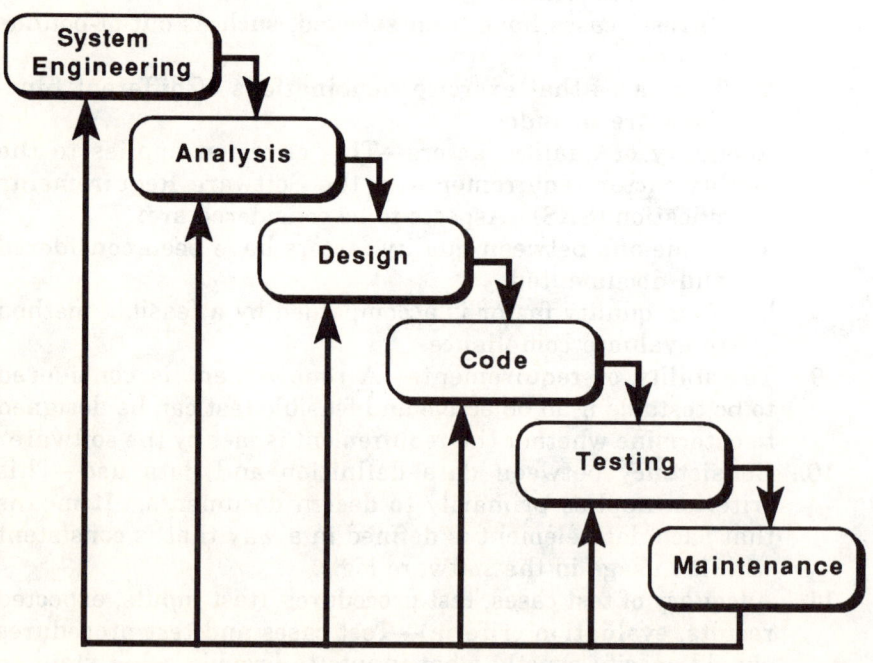

**Figure 3.11** The Waterfall method is modeled after the conventional engineering cycle.

## THE WATERFALL METHOD

The Waterfall method of software development, as illustrated in Figure 3.11, is named after the cascading appearance it presents in graphical form.  Like DOD-STD-2167A, the Waterfall method resulted from industry attempts to curb the rising life-cycle costs of commercial software.  This method offers a systematic, sequential approach to software development that is modeled after the classical engineering cycle.  Notice from Figure 3.11 that during the maintenance phase, the developer may choose or be forced to return to any of the five preceding phases in order to effectively implement changes, fix errors encoutered by users, or accomodate new operating systems or other associated software.  After backing up to the appropriate level, the sequential process is again followed to completion.  This cyclic process will continue throughout the life cycle of the product.  There are six primary phases in the Waterfall Method.  The six phases are system engineering, analysis, design, code, testing, and maintenance.

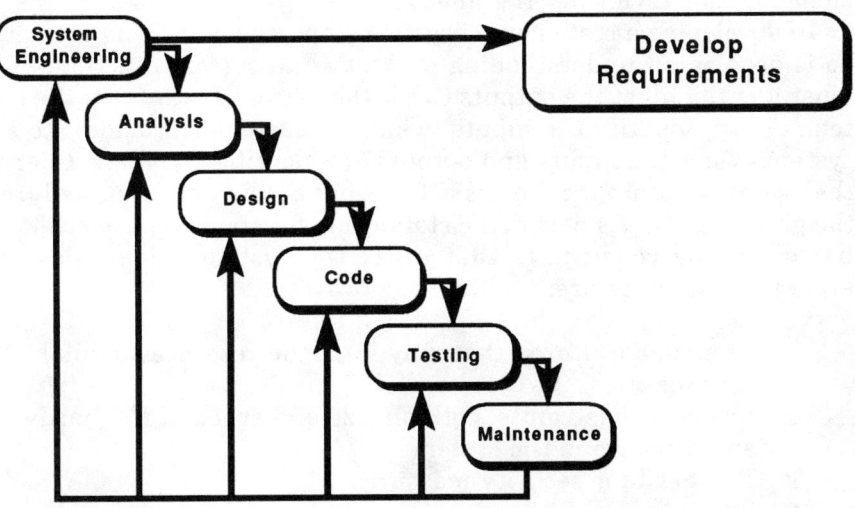

**Figure 3.12** System engineering amounts to designing and refining system requirements.

### System Engineering

System engineering, the first phase of the waterfall method, is actually a multiple-step process.  System engineering is often the most neglected portion of a software development effort. The many steps and iterations involved can be particularly frustrating for a new developer. However, if properly performed, the system engineering phase will save many more hours than it takes to accomplish. Over the life-cycle of the product, the hardware and software will evolve to meet requirements not previously considered. If the system engineering phase is given the time it deserves, these changes can occur without expending a great deal of time and money. If the system engineering phase is ignored or only accomplished to check off a block, then later changes to the system will likely take considerably more time and be much more expensive. In actuality, system engineering involves the predevelopment consideration of the future of the system and how changes will be made to it. The result of the system engineering phase is a set of requirements (see Figure 3.12). These requirements define exactly what the customer expects out of the product. Some of the steps involved in system engineering are developing a statement of system scope, isolating top-level processes and entities, allocating processes and entities to physical system elements, developing a statement of scope for each allocated system element, and reviewing the allocation.

In developing a statement of system scope, the first thing you must do is develop an understanding of the overall system function. You must identify all of the outputs (what the customer wants) of the system. Then, identify the inputs (what the customer provides) to the system. Once the inputs and outputs are identified, you must derive the overall system functions based on what outputs are expected from the given inputs. As part of the statement of system scope, you should list all of the constraints that affect the system. Some possible system constraints are:

1.  Economic concerns that may limit the resources available to the project
2.  Physical constraints, both on size and speed of the hardware and software in the system
3.  The need for security measures
4.  Special reliability needs
5.  Expandability, so the system can grow with the future needs of the customer
6.  Extensibility, or ease of modification

To isolate top-level processes and entities, you should first examine your statement of scope and select the entities. Essentially, the entities are the nouns, the objects that do something. Then you select the processes. The processes are the things that the entities are doing, the actions. Now you have a list of entities and what they do based on the statement of system scope.

The next step is allocating processes and entities to physical system elements. With allocation, you begin to think about system implementation, how to actually solve the system problem. Of course, there are many different ways to solve any problem and software is no exception. You should develop several potential allocations and then evaluate them. Some of the criteria you could use to evaluate the potential allocations are:

1. What is the cost and schedule risk?
2. Does the payoff justify the risk? Is it profitable?
3. Does the technology exist and is it mature?
4. Is the necessary hardware available?
5. Are adequately trained personnel available?
6. Is the allocation legally sound?

Based on your answers to these questions and some weighting for intangibles (yes, there is something to say for gut feelings), you should select the allocation that provides the optimal solution for your particular project.

Developing a statement of scope for each allocated system element is a way of defining interfaces between the individual entities of the system which are now allocated to specific hardware, software, documents, procedures, etc. The results of this step are a complete set of interfaces between the allocated entities and processes.

Ideally, at this point you should review your proposed allocation with the customers or potential customers to determine if you have actually solved the problem. Some of the things you should be concerned with in the review are:

1. Have major functions been thoroughly defined?
2. Are interfaces between system elements defined?
3. Have adequate performance bounds been established?
4. Have design constraints been defined?
5. Did you select the best alternative?
6. Is the selected alternative feasible?
7. Have you considered system validation and verification?

Don't be surprised if the answers to some of the above questions are not acceptable. Systems engineering nearly always involves iterations. In fact, you will notice that the first time through is always the hardest. It is definitely easier to modify an existing solution than to develop one from scratch.

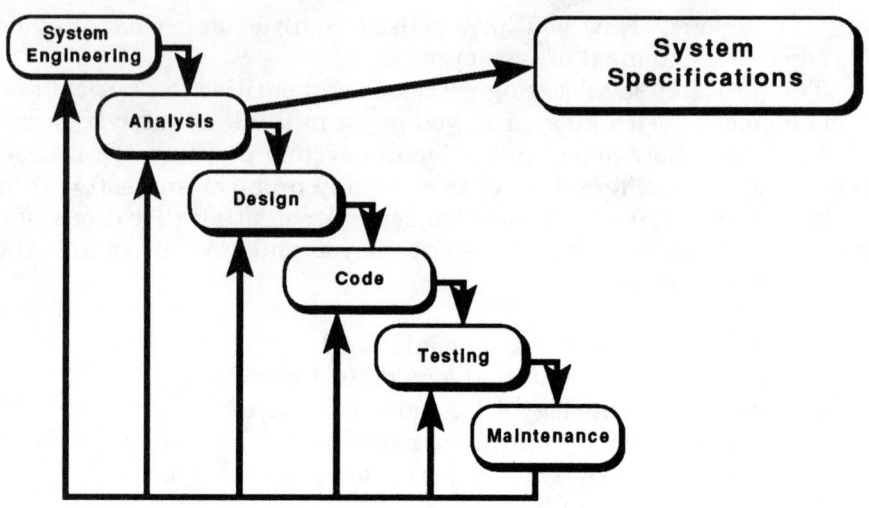

**Figure 3.13**  In the Waterfall method, analysis results in a set of system specifications.

## Analysis

The second phase of the Waterfall method is analysis. During the analysis phase, the requirements that were developed in the system engineering phase are further refined and evolve into system specifications (see Figure 3.13). Notice, at this point, that we are now concerned primarily with the system software. As with system engineering, analysis is not a one-step process. Among these steps are developing the software scope, identifying objects and operations, applying fundamental analysis principles, developing a software flow model, developing a data dictionary, writing narratives for data and control flow, considering software validation, forming a software specification, and reviewing the specification.

The first step in analysis is developing the software scope. Take a careful look at the requirements developed in the system engineering phase. If there are any ambiguities, clarify them now into objects and operations. Then identify all objects and operations in your requirements. This is done in similar fashion as when you identified entities and processes for the entire system. You should classify as an object anything that sends or receives information or stores data. Classify as an operation anything that transforms input data into output data.

There are three fundamental analysis principles. The first is to evaluate all components of the information domain: data flow, data content, and data structure. The second principle is to partition objects and operations to obtain a hierarchical view of the problem. This principle divides the problem into understandable sections. The third principle is to create a model of the software system. This model should emphasize what the software will accomplish, not how the software will be implemented.

To develop a complete software flow model, first use data flow diagrams to show how data moves through the software. Then, create control flow diagrams to show how control influences the software.

A data dictionary represents a complete definition of each data item in your software system. All data items, even if they are composites of other data items, should be clearly defined.

The next step in analysis is writing narratives for data and control flow. These narratives should be in a pseudo-code format. In other words, use English narrative, but put it in a programming format. These narratives will be the foundation for the software design.

In considering software validation, you should focus on how the software will be tested and what general types of tests should be considered. You should not be designing any test cases at this point.

When all of the previous steps are put together, they form a software specification. One possible sample format for a software specification is as follows:

1.0　　Introduction
　　1.1　　Overall system reference
　　1.2　　Business objectives
　　1.3　　Software project constraints
2.0　　Software Description
　　2.1　　Objects and operations
　　2.2　　Flow model
　　2.3　　Data dictionary
　　2.4　　System interface description
3.0　　Narratives
　　3.n　　Flow n description
　　　　3.n.1　Processing narrative
　　　　3.n.2　Restrictions/limitations
　　　　3.n.3　Performance requirements
　　　　3.n.4　Design constraints
　　　　3.n.5　Supporting diagrams
4.0　　Validation Criteria
　　4.1　　Testing strategy
　　4.2　　Classes of tests
　　4.3　　Expected responses
　　4.4　　Special considerations

5.0    Document Reference
6.0    Tables, Charts, Graphs, etc.

The final step in the analysis process is reviewing the specification. Ideally, the customer or potential customer will be involved with the review. The overall goal of the review should be to examine the software specification to determine if all of the system requirements have been satisfied by the software portion of the system. A sub-goal of the review is to assure that the software specification is sound and unambiguous. The software specification will be the basis for the software design and, therefore, must be completely clear. If any ambiguities are found, portions of the analysis phase must be repeated to clarify them.

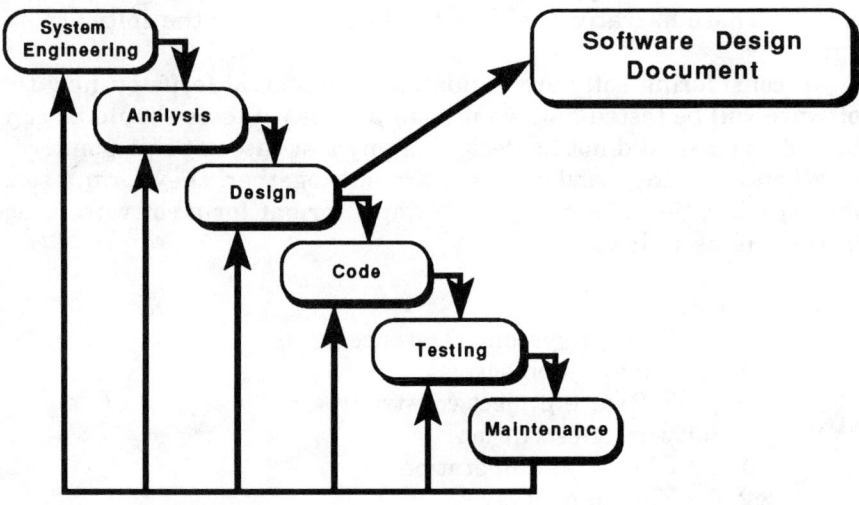

**Figure 3.14** The Waterfall method. The design phase results in a software design document.

## Design

As shown in Figure 3.14, the end result of the design phase of the Waterfall method is a software design document. There are several steps in developing the software design. Among these are refining the software specification, applying fundamental design concepts, extending work started in the analysis phase, developing the program structure, developing a procedural design for each module, developing a preliminary test strategy, creating a design document, and reviewing the design document.

Refining the software specification may not actually be necessary if the specification contains enough detail to begin the design. If it does not, then you must further refine and clarify the software specification so that all the necessary information is present in sufficient detail.

The nine fundamental design concepts are critical to achieving a supportable software design. These concepts are:

1. Develop representations for data, program structure, and procedural detail.
2. Understand the structural elements that make up a software architecture.
3. Understand data structures and their impact on design.
4. Know the difference between architectural and procedural software representations.
5. Understand refinement in the derivation of a design.
6. Understand the importance of software modularity.
7. Utilize information hiding.
8. Design program elements that exhibit effective modularity and functional independence.
9. Use abstraction to refine the design.

During the analysis phase, a data dictionary was developed. Now, you can extend the work you started in the analysis phase by developing data structures which represent the data you identified as necessary in your data dictionary. Review your data dictionary and select those objects that are likely candidates to be represented as data structures. Then define the data structures.

The next step is to develop your program structure. This process involves breaking the overall software design into as many smaller parts (modules) as necessary for easy understanding of the code. Then, develop a software architecture for the overall software system by graphically creating a high-level software design with the software modules you created. From this high-level design, you should be able to completely identify the individual software modules and how they fit into the overall system.

Now that you have the modules defined and a high-level design, you can concentrate on a detailed design. The detailed design or procedural design involves a low-level design. The procedures within each of the modules are designed and graphically laid out much in the same way that the high-level design did for the overall system. A program design language or pseudocode should be used to represent data structures and procedural logic. A program design language is not a formal programming language. It is an English-like description of the software functionality that is formatted much like a traditional program. Program design language is easily translated into actual code.

At this point the design is essentially finished. However, there is testing to consider. Now that you have developed the data structures and the program structure, you should develop a test strategy to adequately test based on the latest design information.

After the test strategy is developed, you are ready to create a software design document. This document will be used as a foundation for the coding phase. A possible sample format for a software design document consists of:

1.0   Scope
    1.1   System objectives
    1.2   Hardware, software, and human interfaces
    1.3   Major software functions
    1.4   Major design constraints
2.0   Reference Documents
    2.1   Software documentation
    2.2   System documentation
    2.3   Technical reference
3.0   Design Description
    3.1   Data description
        3.1.1   Data flow
        3.1.2   Data structure
    3.2   Program structure
    3.3   Interfaces
4.0   Modules
    *for each module:*
    4.1   Processing narrative
    4.2   Interface description
    4.3   Modules used
    4.4   Data organization
5.0   File Structure and Global Data
    5.1   External file structure
        5.1.1   Logical structure
        5.1.2   Logical record description
        5.1.3   Access method
    5.2   Global data
    5.3   File and data cross reference
6.0   Requirements Cross Reference
7.0   Test Provisions
    7.1   Test guidelines
    7.2   Integration strategy

7.3     Special considerations
8.0     Notes

The final step in the design process of the Waterfall method is reviewing the software design document to assure clarity and completeness. Ideally the customer or potential customer will be actively involved with the review. This will give your potential customers the opportunity to assert their opinions about how the software appears to them. The overall goal of the review should be to examine the software design document to determine if all of the system requirements have been satisfied by the software portion of the system. While maximum interaction with customers is ideal at this stage, the organizers of the design review should not allow completely new requirements to be introduced at this stage. Any new requirements for software performance should be delayed until the maintenance phase. A sub-goal of the review is to assure that the software design document is sound and unambiguous. The software design document will be the basis for the actual coding and, therefore, must be completely clear. If any ambiguities are found, portions of the design phase must be repeated to clarify them. Another evaluation point is the testing provisions. The testing guidelines and integration strategy must be thoroughly thought out. These two items will be used as a basis for the actual test cases which will be developed in the coding phase.

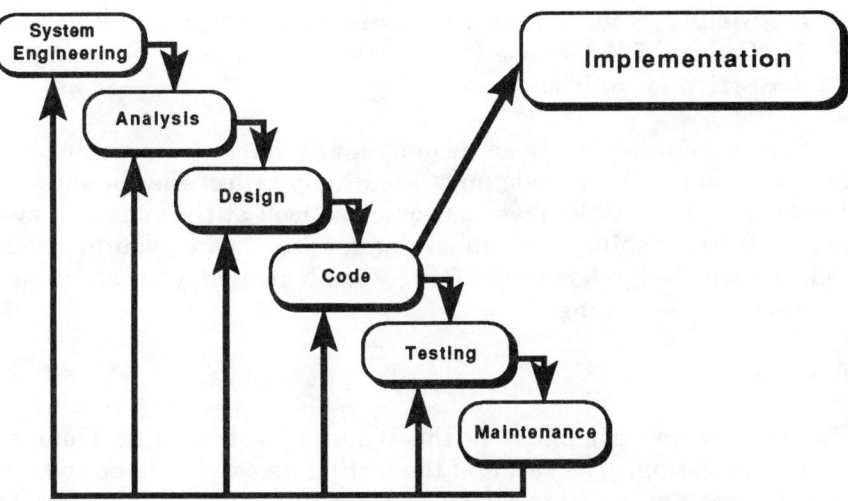

**Figure 3.15** In the Waterfall method, the code phase finally produces actual software.

## Code

The next phase is the coding phase. In the coding phase, the design you have been working on for so long is finally implemented (see Figure 3.15). As with all the other phases of the Waterfall method, the coding phase has several guidelines to follow. Among these guidelines are using the design document as a guide, using good coding style, and reviewing the code.

The design document should contain all the information you need to implement the design in a programming language. In fact, if you are good at writing pseudocode, a great deal of the programming will already be done. The program structure you developed should help you determine the order in which to code the modules. One good strategy for coding is the branch strategy. In the branch strategy you code one branch of the code from top to bottom and then move on to the next branch. Use the procedural design and pseudocode you developed in the design phase as a guideline to coding.

If your code is to be readable, understandable, and maintainable, you should use good coding style. There are eight guidelines to developing good code. The guidelines are:

1.   Always aim for simplicity and clarity.
2.   Use meaningful variable names.
3.   Use consistent formatting conventions.
4.   Use short headers to describe each module.
5.   Establish commenting conventions.
6.   Simplify your statement construction and program layout.
7.   Code all I/O for ease of data transfer and error checking.
8.   Strive for efficient code.

At this point, review the code and assure that it is traceable to the design document. The code must accurately reflect the the intent of the design. If possible have someone else look at the code and evaluate it for readability and understandability. Once you are satisfied that the design has been properly implemented, you can go on to the next phase—testing.

## Testing

The next to the last phase in the Waterfall software development method is testing. The result of the testing phase should be software that is free (or reasonably free) of errors and performs in the manner described by the requirements (see Figure 3.16). There are a myriad of different ways to test software and you must choose one or a combination of several that fits your project.  For the Waterfall method, the recommended steps in the testing phase are:

1.  Develop a test plan.
2.  Apply fundamental testing principles.
3.  Use white box techniques.
4.  Use loop testing.
5.  Use black box techniques.
6.  Review the testing strategy.
7.  Fix errors.

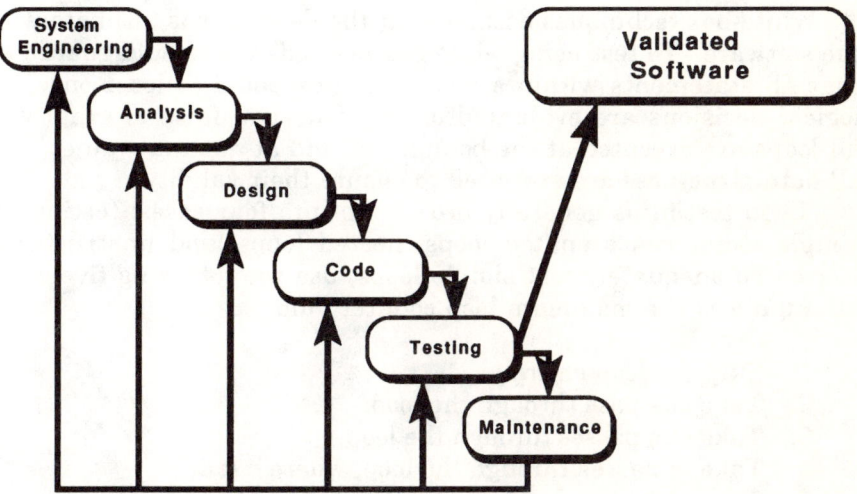

**Figure 3.16** In the Waterfall method, the testing phase results in validated software.

There are two types of testing you should consider when developing a test plan.  One type is designed to test the software to assure that the design was correctly implemented (i.e., there are no logic errors, infinite loops, faulty interfaces, etc.).  To accomplish this, you should define an approach for testing each module in the program structure independently for any errors and then test the interfaces between the modules for errors.  Then, integrate the modules into one piece of software and test the whole.  The other type of testing concerns whether the software does what the customer wanted it to do.  The key to doing this type of testing is to use the requirements as a guide.  Test to make sure that each requirement is completely satisfied.

The next concept is to use fundamental testing principles in designing your test cases. The four fundamental testing principles are:

1. Design your test cases with the object of uncovering errors in the software.
2. Design tests systematically. Don't rely solely on intuition, but don't rule it out either.
3. The testing strategy starts at the module level.
4. Record all test results and save all test cases for use during the maintenance phase.

White-box techniques assume that the developer is intimate with the software. To test using white-box methods you should guarantee that all statements within a module are executed at least once, all logical decisions are evaluated on the true and false alternatives, all loops are executed at the boundaries and at nominal values, and all data structures are exercised to ensure their validity.

Loop testing is generally broken up into four cases: testing for simple loops, concatenated loops, nested loops, and unstructured loops. To adequately test simple loops, use the following five steps (assume $n$ is the maximum loop counter value):

1. Skip the loop entirely.
2. Take one pass through the loop.
3. Take two passes through the loop.
4. Take $m$ passes through the loop, where $n < n$.
5. Take $n-1$, $n$, and $n+1$ passes through the loop.

For nested loops, use the following four steps:

1. Start at the innermost loop and set all other loops to minimum values.
2. Perform the simple loop tests for the innermost loop.
3. Work outward, performing the simple loop test on the next loop while keeping outer loops at minimum values and inner loops at nominal values.
4. Continue until all loops are tested.

For concatenated loops there are two options. If the loops are independent of one another, use simple loop testing on each loop. If the loops are dependant upon one another, use the nested loop approach. Finally, for unstructured loops, you should redesign the loop using structured programming constructs.

Black-box testing techniques assume that the tester knows nothing about how the software functions internally, but everything about what the software is supposed to do. Black-box testing is designed to assure that the software satisfies the overall requirements of the software.

The next step in the testing process is reviewing the testing strategy. When reviewing your strategy, the following questions should be answered:

1. Have test steps been identified and sequenced?
2. Are the tests traceable to the requirements?
3. Are major software functions demonstrated?
4. Is a test schedule defined?
5. Have available test resources and tools been identified?
6. Has a record keeping method been established?
7. Has work to develop test drivers been scheduled?
8. Have white- and black-box tests been specified?
9. Have all logic paths been tested?
10. Are all test cases listed with expected results?
11. Is error handling tested?
12. Are boundary values tested?
13. Are timing and performance tested?

Once the testing has been performed, you must fix whatever errors were encountered. Make sure that you carefully evaluate any changes you make to the software to fix errors. You could easily introduce more errors with your fix. Identify where you believe the change should occur, and then determine what other parts of the software will be affected by your proposed change. Once you are absolutely sure that your change will not have any adverse effects on other parts of the software, make the change and then retest the test that failed and any other tests that may have been affected by the change. The overall requirements testing should be performed after any change to the software. Once all the errors have been fixed, you are ready to field the software.

## Maintenance

Maintenance is the final phase of the Waterfall method of software development. The purpose of the maintenance phase is to make changes to the software after it has been fielded. There are many possible reasons to make changes to the software. Among these reasons are enhancements to the system, correcting errors found through use, and accommodating new operating systems, computers, and peripherals. Whatever the reason, it is apparent that change must occur.  Because of this, there should be a formal process for making software changes.  This formal process is an iteration of all or part of the Waterfall method.

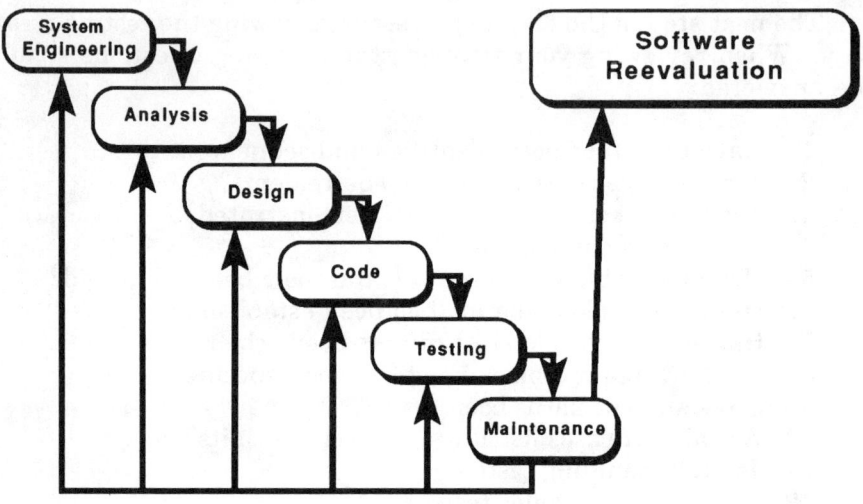

**Figure 3.17**  In the Waterfall method, the maintenance phase results in a software re-evaluation.

In the Waterfall method, the result of the maintenance phase is a reevaluation and then a reengineering of the software (see Figure 3.17).  First, you must evaluate the proposed software change to determine whether the request is reasonable, practical, and technologically feasible.  If you are still determined to make the change, you must determine the scope of the change so that you will know at what level to reenter the Waterfall development process.  If the proposed change requires it, you may need to go back to the software engineering phase and treat the change as a new requirement of the system.  Or, if the change is relatively small, you may only need to make slight modifications to the code and then test the affected portions of the code and reperform the overall requirements testing to assure that no other requirement was affected by your change.  Or, the change could be somewhere in between those two extremes.  In any case, it is imperative that no matter how small the change you make, you make changes to the documentation as well.  If you don't, when the next change comes along that is larger in scope, the code will not agree with the documentation and the changes will take much longer to make.  After you decide at what level to enter the process, follow the process through to the end just as though the software was new. This will assure that all requirements on the software, even the new ones, are met and that old requirements are not pred-judiced by the new ones.

### Final Thoughts on the Waterfall Method

While DOD-STD-2167A placed an emphasis on keeping manage-ment informed, the Waterfall method virtually ignores manage-ment. In defense of the Waterfall method, it is implied that a soft-ware development team has the sole responsibility for developing and fielding the software and that this team would be performing its own reviews and making all the decisions. This is a little idealis-tic. There are very few software development teams in industry with that kind of autonomy. But, for very small companies or indi-vidual developers, the Waterfall method performs all the necessary software development steps without the overhead of management re-views and all of the paperwork required by DOD-STD-2167A. And the Waterfall method could be slightly modified to keep upper level management well informed of the status of the software without compromising much of the simplicity of the method. Overall, the Waterfall method is outstanding in its simplicity as a software de-velopment process and especially recommended to small develop-ers.

### THE JACKSON METHOD

The overall Jackson design method is shown in Figure 3.18. The Jackson method, named after its originator, Michael Jackson, au-thor of *Principles of Program Design*, is a result of the structured programming revolution which took place in the early 1970s. Up until that time, programs were written in a cryptic fashion which was sometimes only understood by the writer of the code. This quickly became unacceptable and great emphasis was placed upon finding consistent, easy-to-understand ways of designing and de-veloping programs. The Jackson method is based on representing data and program structures in the same set of design constructs which makes the program design very easy to understand. This method makes maximum use of pseudocode. Once the design con-structs are complete, the entire program is described in pseudocode. This pseudocode is then translated directly into a high-level, medium-level, or low-level programming language. The Jackson method has six phases: requirement specification, structure prob-lem logic, structure program logic, allocate program operations, code and compile, and program.

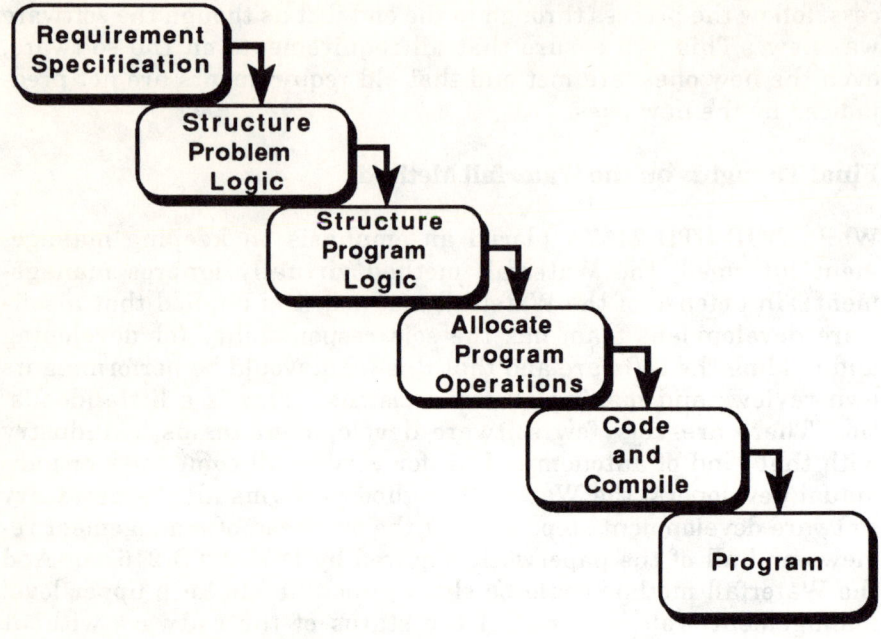

**Figure 3.18** The basic form of the Jackson method.

## Requirement Specification

According to the requirement specification phase of the Jackson method (see Figure 3.19), the first step in the software development process is to evaluate the input and output requirements of the system, determine what the program is supposed to do, and identify the appropriate data components.  The input/output requirements and the system functionality are fairly self-explanatory.  But it is important to define these items in sufficient detail.  In the Jackson method there are three specific types of data components: input, output, and internal.  Input and output data types should be defined at this point.  Once the system input and output are defined, the internal data should be examined.  The internal data types are broken down into five sub-types: files, records, parameters, characters, and fields.  Of course, there are other things to consider, such as programming language, hardware and software configuration, timing constraints, and sizing constraints.  But the primary goal is to define the data and decide what is to be done with it.  The Jackson method defines precise ways of describing the input and output, and internal data structures so that they can be easily ported into a logic diagram.  There are three basic design constructs endorsed by the Jackson design methodology (see Figure 3.20):  sequence, selection, and iteration.

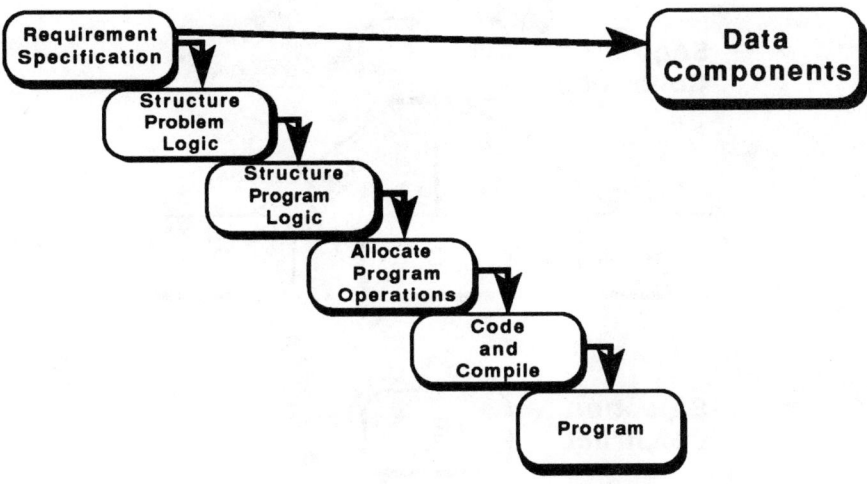

**Figure 3.19**  In the Jackson method, the requirement specification phase results in descriptions of all data components.

The sequence construct implies that "A" is made up of "B," "C," and "D" in that order.  The selection construct differs from the sequence construct by the small "o" in the top right hand corner of the second level constructs.  It implies that "E" is made up of either "F," or "G," or "H" exclusively.  The iteration construct implies that "I" is made up of zero or more "Js."  This construct will have only one second level construct which is annotated with an asterisk.

### Structure Problem Logic

The purpose of the second phase of the Jackson method is to structure the problem logic (see Figure 3.21).  Now that the data components are completely defined, you can draw out graphically what is to be done with the data from a problem viewpoint (i.e., transform the input data into output data).  The same constructs which were used to identify the data components are used to develop the problem logic. The problem logic should completely identify how input data are manipulated to form output data.  There are two distinct steps in the structure problem logic phase: defining relationships between data components, and identifying correspondences between data structures.

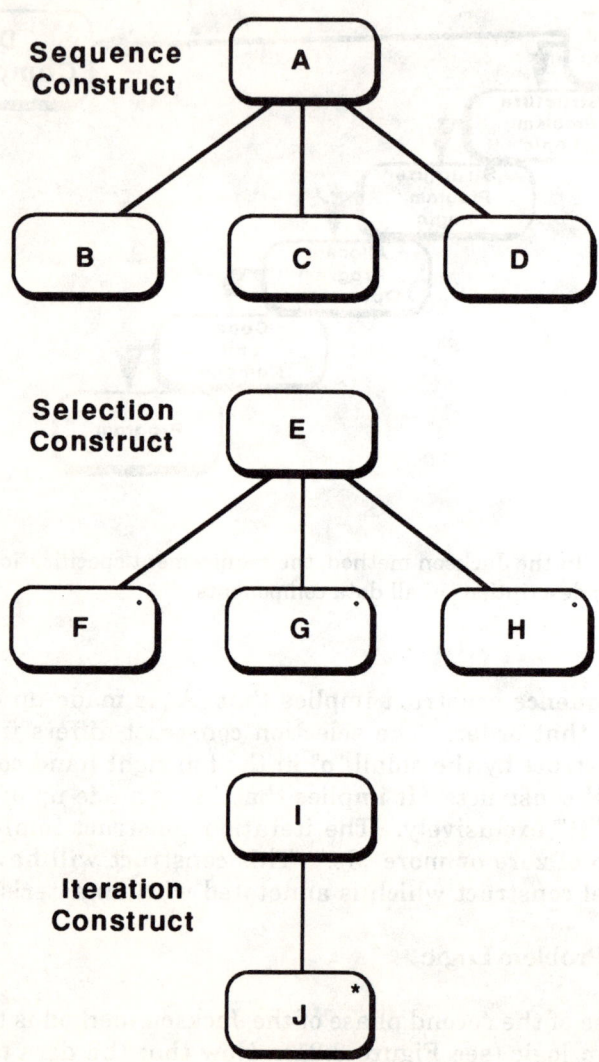

**Figure 3.20** The three basic design constructs.

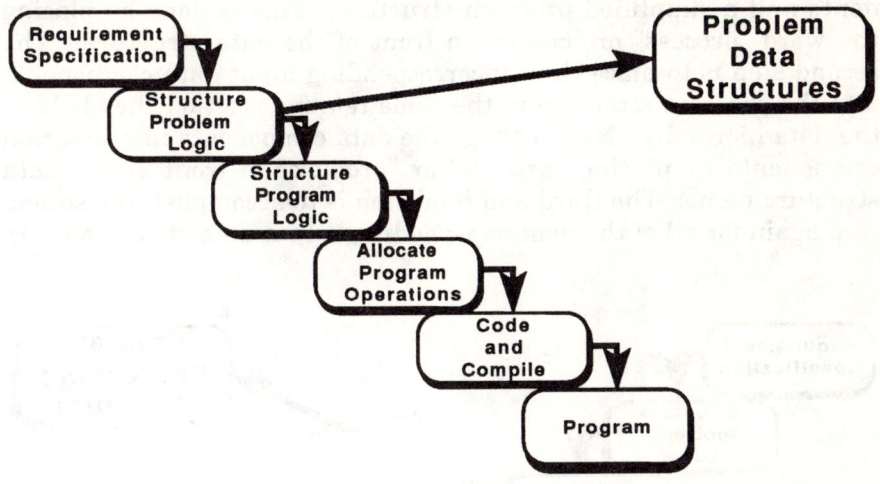

**Figure 3.21** In the Jackson method, the structure problem logic phase results in data structures for the problem domain.

Having already identified the data components, the next step is to develop relationships between those data components. Maximum user interaction is recommended during this phase to assure that input and output data structures and their relationships are complete and correct. This done, the following three rules should be used to identify correspondences between data structures for the purpose of classification and consolidation:

1. The same number of each of the different data components must be present.
2. Corresponding components must occur in the same order
3. Each set of components must be able to be processed together.

Jackson suggests that the most effective way to apply these rules is to start with the data structure with the least number of components, start at the top, and move down the problem logic diagram.

### Structure Program Logic

The purpose of the structure problem logic phase of the Jackson software development method is to translate the problem logic into a program processing structure (see Figure 3.22). There are three distinct steps in this phase. In the first step, processes are defined for corresponding data components, thus creating program components and a simplified program structure. This is done by placing the word "process" or "create" in front of the data structure. The second step is to place the noncorresponding input data components into the program structure in the same relative position they held in the data hierarchy. Next, change the data components into program components by placing "process" or "produce" in front of the data structure name. The third and final step is to accomplish the second step again for all of the noncorresponding output data structures.

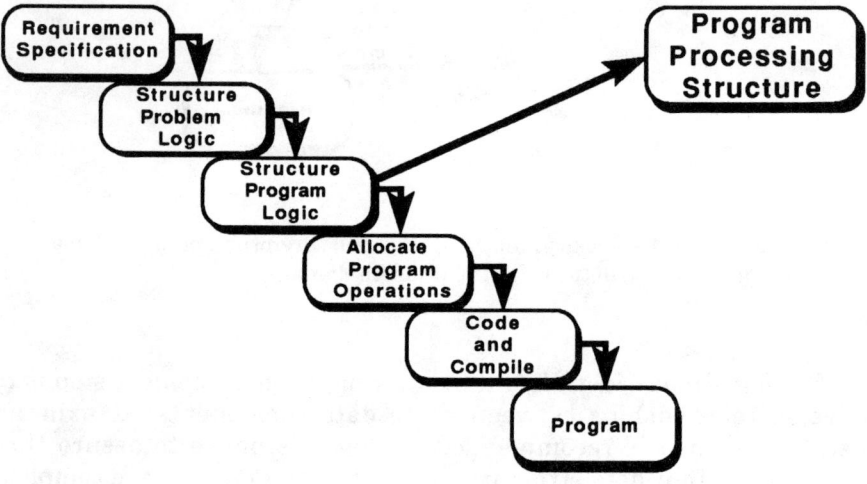

**Figure 3.22**  In the Jackson method, the structure program logic phase results in a processing structure for the program domain.

At the end of the structure problem logic phase you are left with a complete definition of all of the data structures and an easy to read diagram outlining the logic of the entire program. There should be a one-to-one correspondence between the problem structure diagram and the program structure diagram.

### Allocate Program Operations

The result of the allocate program operations phase as illustrated in Figure 3.23 is a readable logic diagram for the entire program. To accomplish this goal, you must know what the user wants the program to do and the target language for the program. These two items will identify what specific operations are to be carried out and in what level of detail the operations must be defined. Then, Jackson recommends the use of a checklist to ensure that all required operation are accounted for. The checklist consists of six major program functions as follows:

1. Termination operations—stop processing once the required tasks are completed
2. Open and close operations—for files, databases, etc.
3. Output operations—direct program results to the user
4. Calculations—create output from the available data
5. Input operations—read input from assorted sources for use in processing
6. Manage internal variables—for initialization of variables and counters

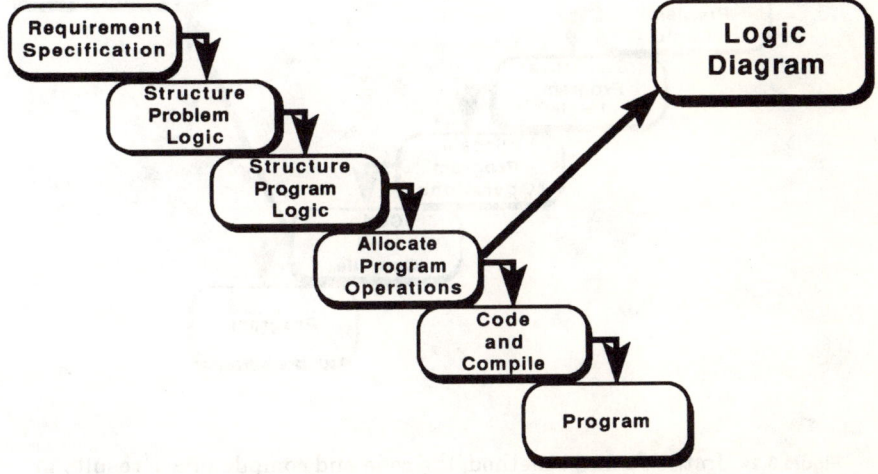

**Figure 3.23**  In the Jackson method, the allocate program operations phase results in a logic diagram.

Once all of your program logic structures have been identified and classified as one of the above types of operations, you can draw a complete logic diagram of the program in preparation for coding.

**Code and Compile**

The results of the code and compile phase of the Jackson method is executable code (see Figure 3.24). In preparation for the code and compile phase, you should take the program logic diagram developed in the allocate program operations phase and develop a structured narrative.  A structured narrative or pseudocode is an English-like description of all the details of the program.  The structure of the descriptions is similar to that of any structured programming language and should be directly translatable into any programming language.  If you find at this level that there is insufficient definition of a process, you may have to return to one of the previous phases to obtain further information.  There must be sufficient definition to completely implement the operation at the level prescribed by the implementation programming language.

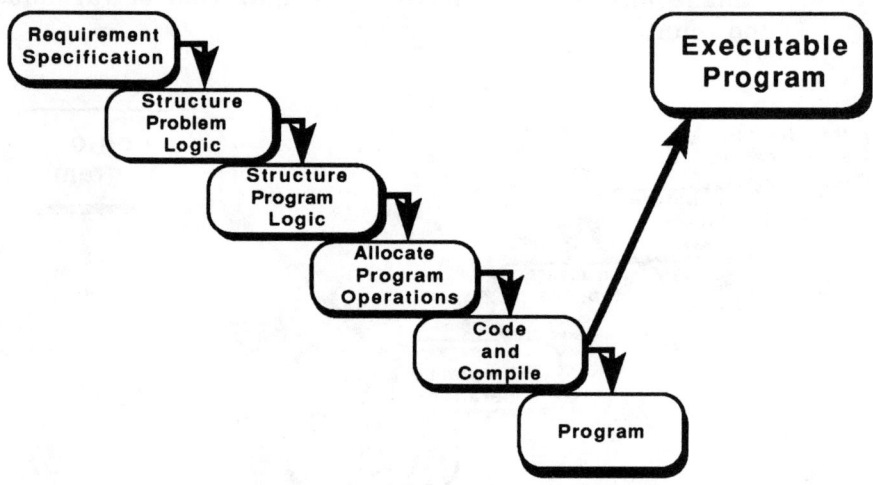

**Figure 3.24**  In the Jackson method, the code and compile phase results in an executable program.

## Program

The final phase of the Jackson software development method is the program phase which results in validated software (see Figure 3.25).  The program phase is essentially a testing, validation, and fielding phase.  The Jackson method contends that because of the structured design methodology, you need only test the three major design constructs (sequences, selections, and iterations) to ensure that there are no software errors and that the system meets all specified requirements.  To test a sequence you must assure that each action within the sequence is checked at least once.  To test a selection, exercise each possible selection at least once. And, for iterations, check the upper and lower boundaries, a median value, and an out of bounds value. Once the testing is completed and all found errors are corrected, the program is ready to be fielded.

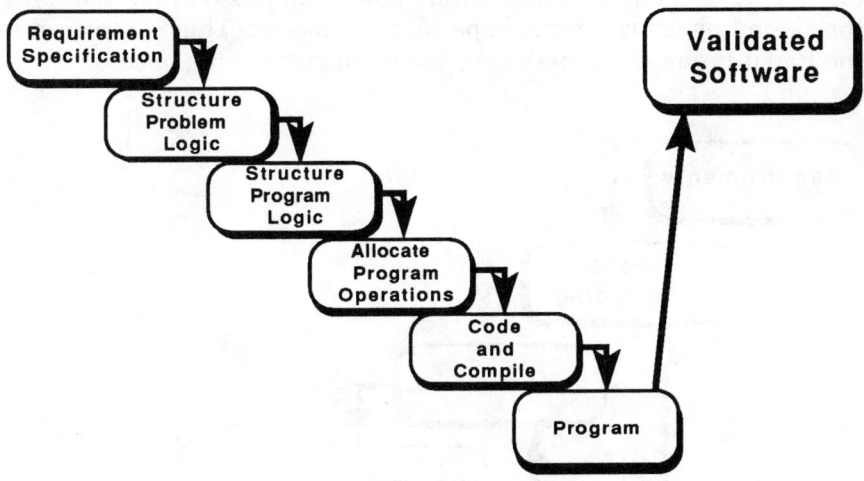

**Figure 3.25** In the Jackson method, after testing, the program phase results in validated software.

## Final Thoughts on the Jackson Method

The Jackson design method is an excellent tool for designing programs of any complexity level. It provides a high level of understanding for both the user and the programmer, traceability to requirements, and direct relationships between data and program constructs. Self-admittedly, however, the Jackson design method is not a complete life-cycle tool. It is an outstanding software design and implementation tool, but does not adequately address system requirements and specifications, software requirements, complete testing, and implementation and production aspects of the life-cycle. Because of these shortcomings, the Jackson method is best used as a supplement to a more complete life-cycle software development method.

## THE RAPID PROTOTYPING METHOD

The Rapid Prototyping method is very similar to the Waterfall method as illustrated in Figure 3.26. In fact, it is a derivative of the Waterfall method. The major difference between the two software development methods is the second phase. In the Waterfall method, the second phase is a formal specification phase. This is replaced in the Rapid Prototyping method by the rapid prototyping phase.

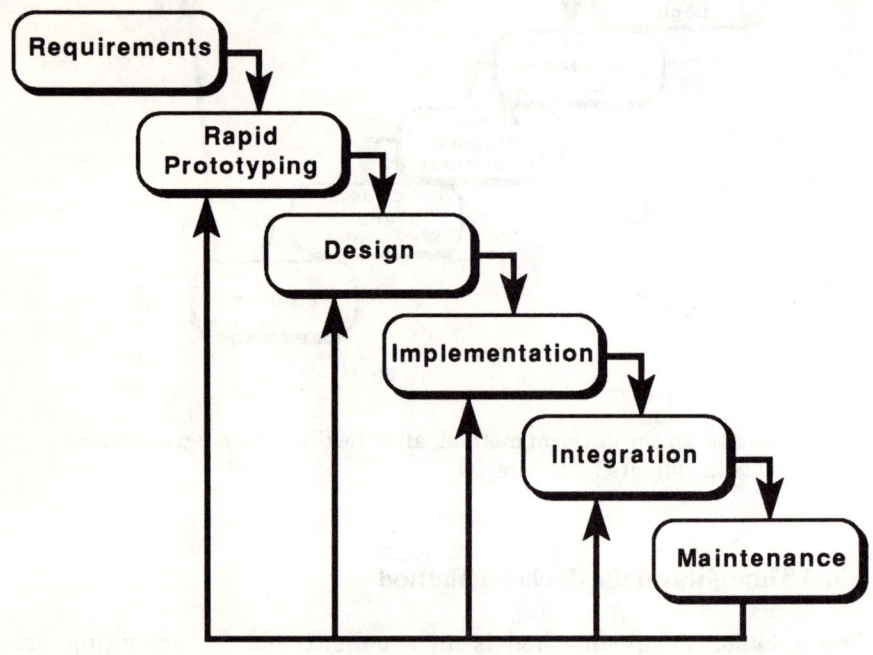

**Figure 3.26** The Rapid Prototyping method is a modification of the Waterfall method.

A rapid prototype is a functional equivalent of the actual product. The rapid prototype must perform all of the basic functions required of the final product. But, there is generally no error checking, file updating, or data isolation. It is not even important that the software be reliable for long periods of time. If the software crashes frequently, then so be it. The primary use of the rapid prototype is to assure that the developer fully understands the requirements set by the customers. Therefore, it need only run long enough to demonstrate the major software functions. Rapid prototypes are also particularly useful in developing user interfaces.  Since little time is spent making the interface fancy, you can spend  more time with the customer determining favored approaches.

There are six major phases in the Rapid Prototyping method of software development:  requirements, rapid prototyping, design, implementation, integration, and maintenance.

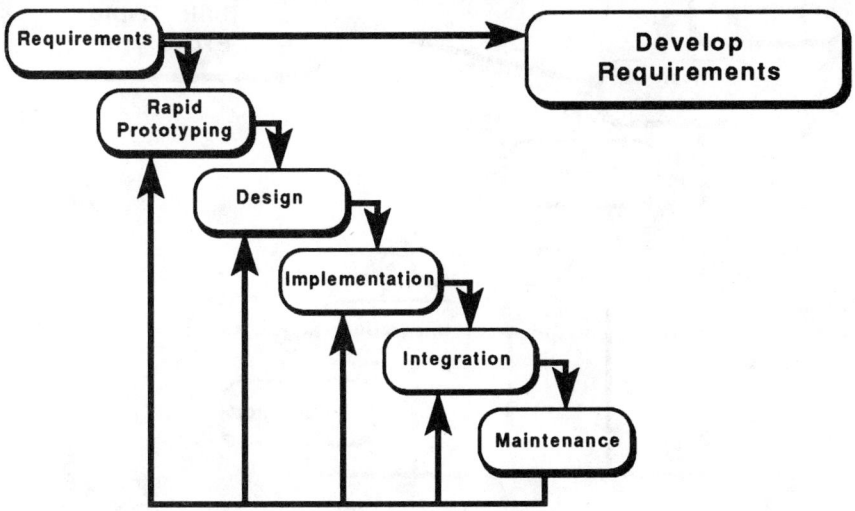

**Figure 3.27** The requirements phase of the Rapid Prototyping method involves developing a working set of system requirements.

### Requirements

The requirements phase of the Rapid Prototyping method is used to develop system and software requirements (see Figure 3.27).  The standard questions concerning the overall function of the system, what platform and software are preferred, system response time, and the general look and feel of the program must be asked.  In addition, you must be more specific than you have been in previously studied software development methods.  You must obtain enough information to develop the rapid prototype in the next phase, paying particular attention to information concerning the user interface. The closer you are with the first cut of the Rapid Prototype of the user interface, the less time you will spend modifying it to please the customer.

## Rapid Prototyping

The second stage of the Rapid Prototyping method is the rapid prototyping phase (see Figure 3.28). In this phase, the rapid prototype is
developed using the requirements set up in the requirements phase.

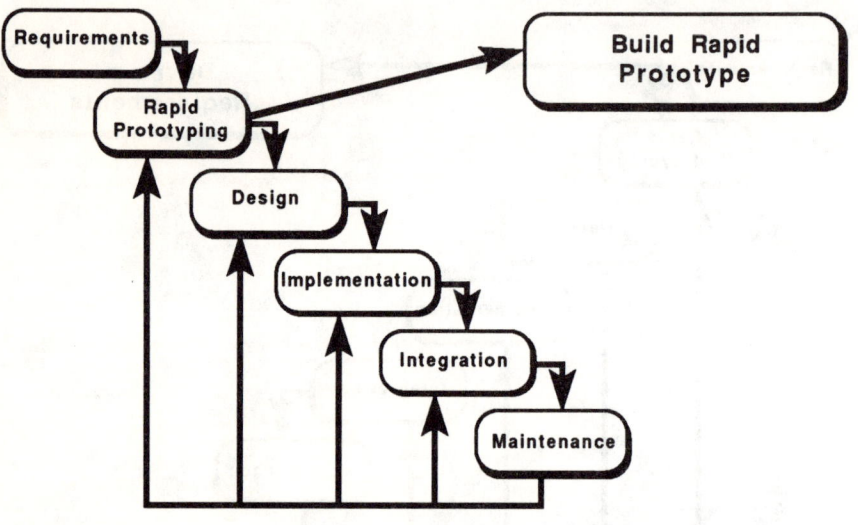

**Figure 3.28** In the rapid prototyping phase, a functional prototype is
developed.

The key to the rapid prototype is the word rapid. You will want to
get a working prototype up and running as quickly as possible. To
accomplish this you may need to use a rapid prototyping language.
A rapid prototyping language is usually a graphical programming
environment that does most of the actual grunt programming
(behind the scenes programming such as setting up windows and
handling events) for you. The major disadvantage of rapid prototyping languages is speed, or rather the lack of it. Rapid prototyping
languages will be covered in great depth in Section 3 of this book.
Don't concern yourself with any form of error checking or any other
cleanup details. Your main goal should be to get back to the customer as quickly as possible with a functional prototype.

Close interaction with your customers is absolutely essential in
the rapid prototyping phase. Once you have a working prototype,
demonstrate it to your customers or potential users for feedback.
More than likely, the prototype will cause a rethinking of the system

requirements. It will almost certainly require several iterations of reworking the prototype and demonstrating it to your users before all system requirements are agreed upon. Once you have reached that point, don't waste time writing up formal system specifications. The rapid prototype actually becomes the system specification and will be used to design the software in the next phase.

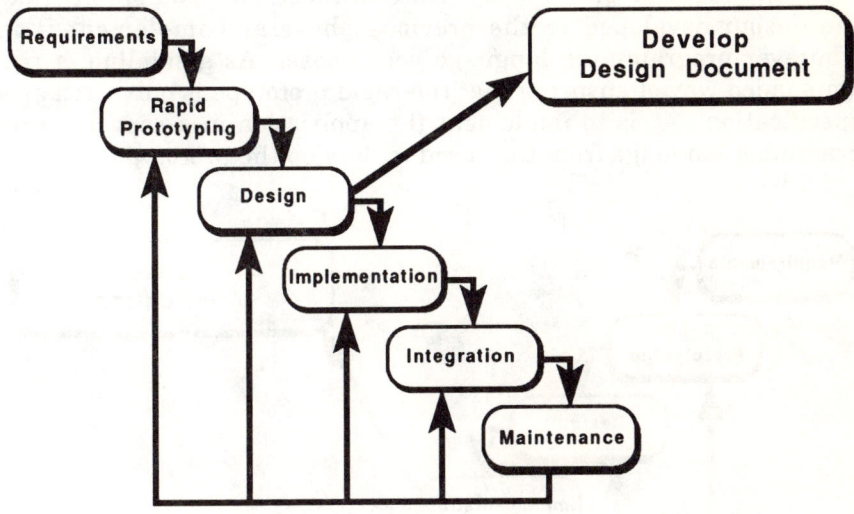

**Figure 3.29** During the design phase of the rapid prototyping method, a design document is created.

## Design

In the design phase of the Rapid Prototyping method, you will develop a design document using the rapid prototype developed in the previous phase as a software specification (see Figure 3.29). There will be a temptation to use the rapid prototype as a baseline system design; unless your application is extremely small, this is a mistake. According to the Rapid Prototyping method, the correct use of the rapid prototype is as a clarification of the system requirements. The rapid prototype itself should not be added to or modified in any way to transform it into the deliverable application. Instead, you should examine and dissect the rapid prototype to create a design document. First, break the functionality of the prototype into as many modules as necessary. Then, break down the functionality of those modules. Continue the abstraction process until the entire system is designed down to the lowest level.

## Implementation

The result of the implementation phase of the Rapid Prototyping method is a coded application (see Figure 3.30). This phase is exactly like the code phase of the Waterfall method. You simply take the design developed in the previous phase and implement it in whatever programming language you choose. As a sideline, a recommended way of ensuring that the rapid prototype is only used as a specification tool is to implement the application in a separate programming language from that used to develop the prototype.

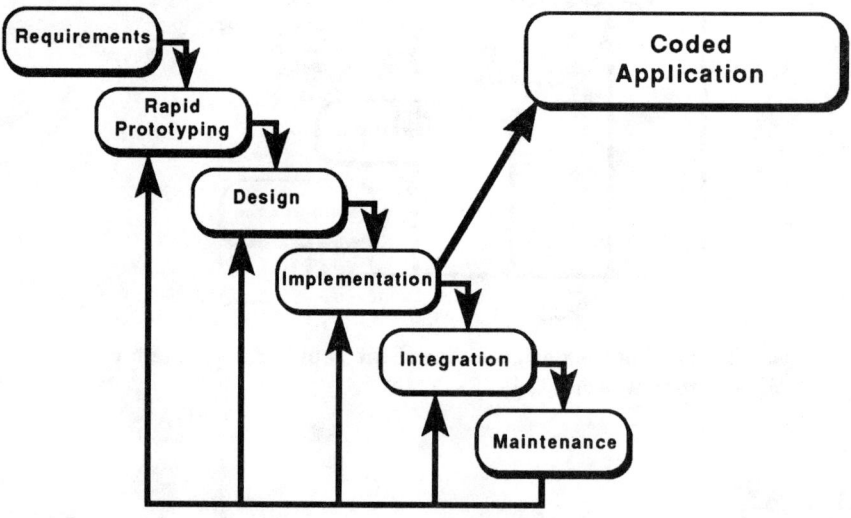

**Figure 3.30** The result of the implementation phase of the rapid prototyping method is a fully coded application.

There are several guidelines you should follow to develop readable, understandable, and maintainable code. The guidelines are:

1.  Always aim for simplicity and clarity.
2.  Use meaningful variable names.
3.  Use consistent formatting conventions.
4.  Use short headers to describe each module.
5.  Establish commenting conventions.

6.  Simplify your statement construction and program layout.
7.  Code all I/O for ease of data transfer and error checking.
8.  Strive for efficient code.

At this point, you should review the code to assure that it is traceable to the design document. The code must accurately reflect the intent of the design. If possible have someone else look at the code and evaluate it for readability and understandability. Once you are satisfied that the design has been properly implemented, you can go on to the next phase—integration.

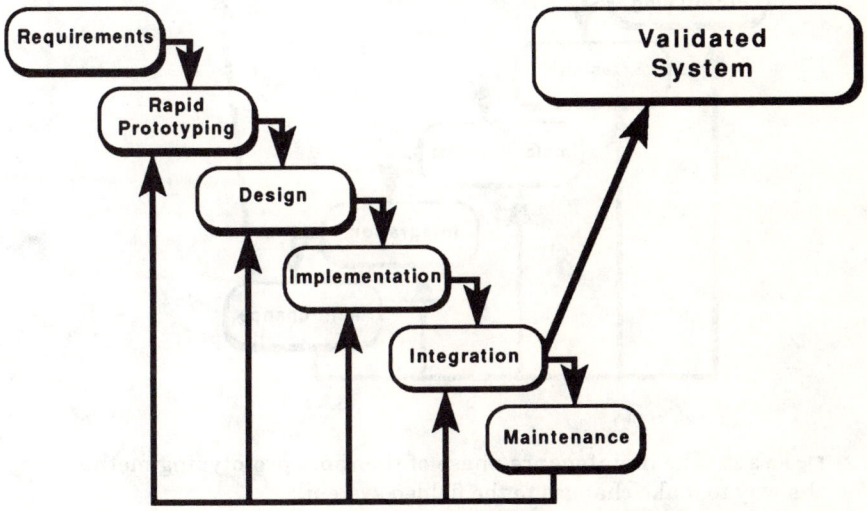

**Figure 3.31** The result of the integration phase of the rapid prototyping method is a complete system ready to be fielded.

### Integration

The integration phase of the Rapid Prototyping method actually involves two steps: system integration and testing. Once these two steps are finished, then the system is considered validated and is ready to be fielded (see Figure 3.31). The system integration step involves piecing together all the software modules into one software entity. Then the application is run on the hardware platform for which it was designed. After the application is running, complete system testing takes place. Testing should be based upon two things: making sure that there are no system errors and ensuring that the system requirements are met. Correcting system errors is done in the same fashion as with the other software development methods. With the Rapid Prototyping method, the best way to ensure that all requirements are met is to refer to the functionality of the rapid prototype. When you are satisfied that the testing is complete, the system is ready to be fielded.

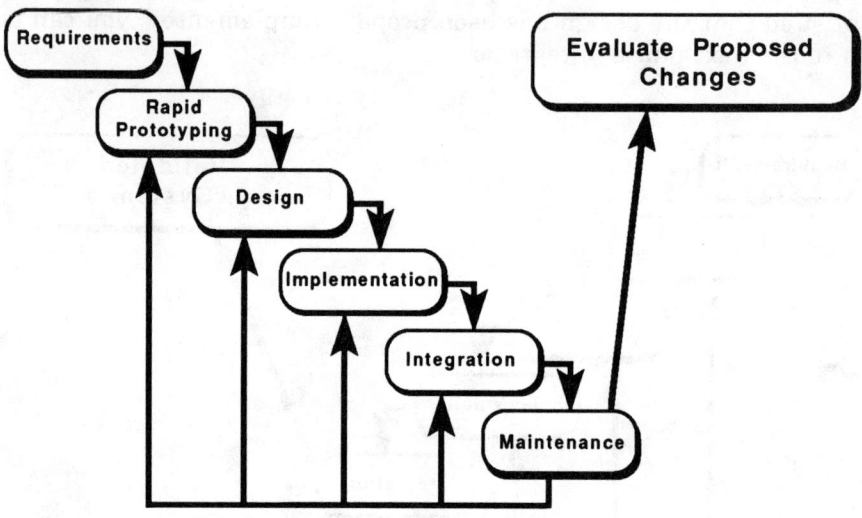

**Figure 3.32** The maintenance phase of the rapid prototyping method is the way to make changes to the fielded system.

## Maintenance

The maintenance phase of the Rapid Prototyping method centers around evaluating proposed changes to the system (see Figure 3.32). If you determine that it is desirable to make a specific change to the system and the change involves the functionality of the system (i.e., the change is not simply a new algorithm to accomplish the same task), you should first incorporate the change into the rapid prototype to determine its impact. After review of the altered prototype, if you still desire to make the change, then continue with the rest of the Rapid Prototyping method as before.

### Final Thoughts on the Rapid Prototyping Method

The Rapid Prototyping method is an excellent mix of two well established methodologies. It gets its overall flavor primarily from the Waterfall method. This gives the Rapid Prototyping method the advantages of a complete life-cycle method: requirements traceability, testability, and maintainability to name a few. To this it adds the concept of the rapid prototype. The Rapid Prototyping method provides several advantages. Among these advantages are increased user interaction, confirmation of requirements, reduced paperwork (remember, the rapid prototype serves as the system specification), and better maintenance. The better maintenance comes from being able to experiment with changes on the rapid prototype to determine their impact before implementing the change on the actual system.

## THE SPIRAL METHOD

Sometime in the late 1970s it had become apparent that a new software development process must evolve to handle particularly large (read government) projects. The primary area that was lacking was risk analysis. For very large projects there must be a risk analysis to determine if all parties wish to continue or desire to cancel the project all together. In response to this need, the Spiral method was developed. In the Spiral method of software development, there are four distinct cycles of the spiral as shown in Figure 3.33. For the purpose of explanation, these cycles will be referred to as concept, requirements, design, and implementation.

### Concept

The concept cycle of the Spiral method begins at the innermost ring of the spiral on the commitment partition. Overall objectives of the system are determined and many alternative approaches are examined. A risk analysis is performed and prototypes are developed to help resolve the identified risks. The final part of the first cycle is the development of an overall life-cycle plan. At the end of the concept cycle (on the commitment partition), a review is held to determine if there is a willingness to continue with the development.

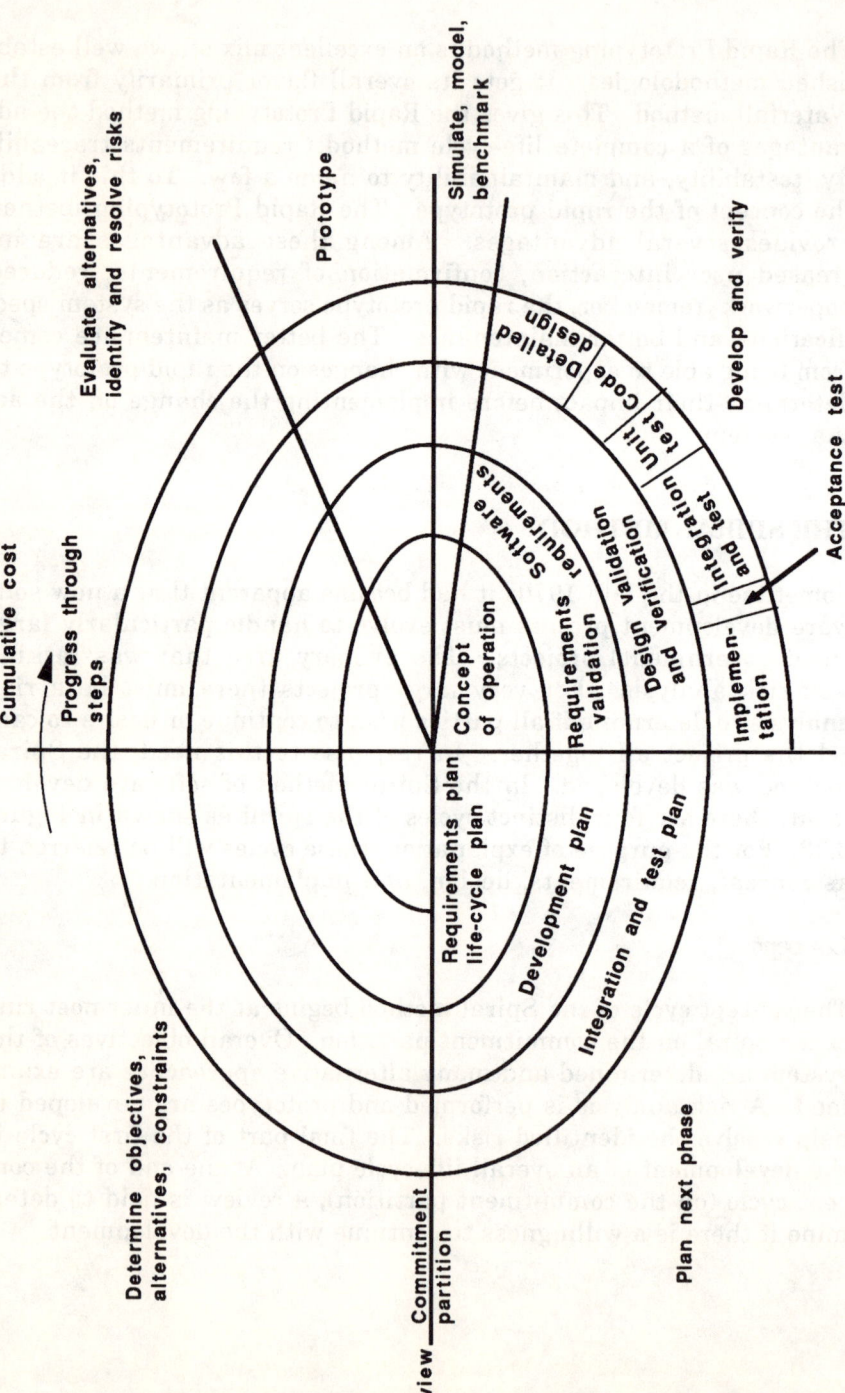

**Figure 3.33** The Spiral method.

## Requirements

The Requirements cycle begins with a reevaluation of the overall objectives. New alternatives and potential system constraints are identified. Then another risk analysis is performed with respect to the life-cycle plan developed in the previous cycle. Prototypes with their associated simulations, models, and benchmarks are again developed to support the risk resolution. Software requirements are then completely defined and validated. Finally, a software development plan is drawn up in anticipation of the next cycle. At the end of the requirements cycle, a review is held to clarify any requirements ambiguities and obtain complete agreement on the development plan.

## Design

The third cycle of the Spiral method of software development is the design cycle. As with all the cycles, the design cycle begins with an evaluation of the system objectives, alternatives, and constraints. The cycle then moves into the resolution of risk quadrant. Once all risks are resolved or accepted, the software is designed. This high-level design is then validated and verified. At the end of the design cycle, an integration plan and a test plan are created. A review is held at this point to determine if it is feasible to continue with full scale development of the software.

## Implementation

The final cycle of the Spiral method is the implementation cycle. The first key distinction in this cycle is the prototype. In the implementation cycle, the prototype is a fully functional, operational prototype which is used as a software specification. This is followed by a detailed design based on the operational prototype. The software is then coded, tested and integrated with the final hardware configuration. Finally, just prior to fielding the system, acceptance testing is performed.

## Final Thoughts on the Spiral Method

The Spiral method of software development is extremely valuable in developing large scale projects. It is designed around four distinct quadrants:

1. Determine objectives, alternatives, and constraints.
2. Evaluate alternatives; identify and resolve risks.

3.  Develop and verify the next level product.
4.  Plan the next phase.

As the developer progresses through the quadrants moving outward from the center of the spiral, the cumulative cost of the project increases. At the end of each round of the spiral, there is a review with the primary people in the involved organizations. The primary objective of these reviews is to determine if all concerned parties are committed to the next phase.

While the Spiral method seems highly desirable, there are two distinct problems: smaller projects and maintenance. Running the Spiral method for small projects would lead to an unbelievable amount of unjustifiable overhead. Therefore, for small projects the Spiral method must be tailored to meet the needs of the individual project. If you examine the Spiral method closely, you will find that in tailoring you will be left with either the Waterfall method or the Rapid Prototyping method. If this is the case, then why use the Spiral method. Unless you feel there is a need to perform extensive risk analysis, another software development method is recommended. The second problem is maintenance. It is not addressed in the graphical model and there is no clean way of entering the Spiral method halfway through. The implication is that a maintenance action would be treated as a complete software effort. This could lead to incredible expense for a potentially minor change and may be a contributing factor as to why government software is so expensive to maintain.

## THE PARALLEL METHOD

Anytime you are about to develop software (outside of a few lines of code for your personal use), you should consider using a software development method. However, it is certainly not mandatory that you use one of the previously described methods. Consider, though, that all of the described methods are tailorable to your own application. Select one of the methods that most closely fits your needs and then customize it to fit your needs exactly. This is what has been done in creating the Parallel method of software development. The needs of the Hypermedia domain have been examined and the Rapid Prototyping method has been modified to meet those needs (see Figure 3.34). There are six sequential phases and one parallel phase in the Parallel method. The six phases are requirements, rapid prototyping, design, implementation, integration, and maintenance. The parallel phase of the Parallel method is designated the modify user interface phase.

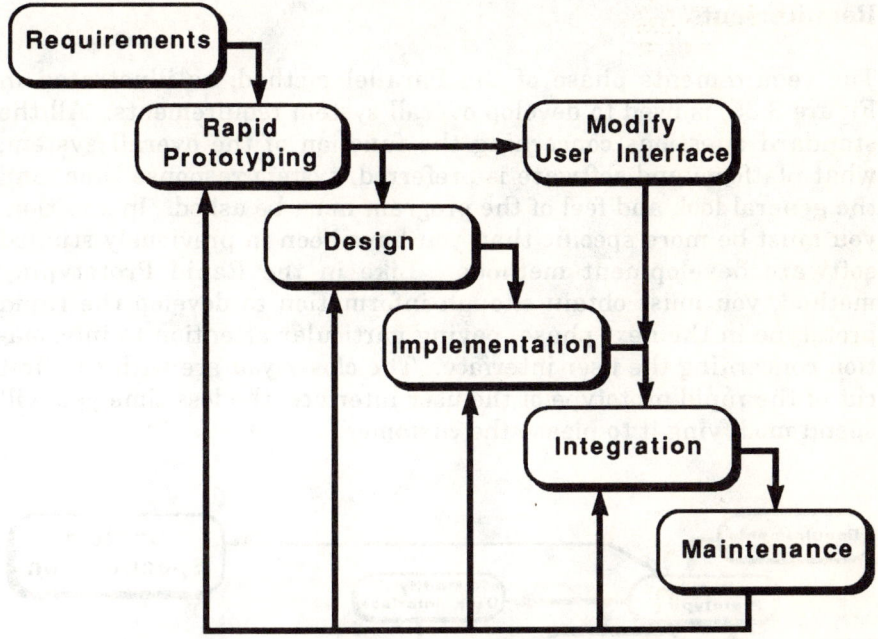

**Figure 3.34** The Parallel method is a modification of the Rapid Prototyping method.

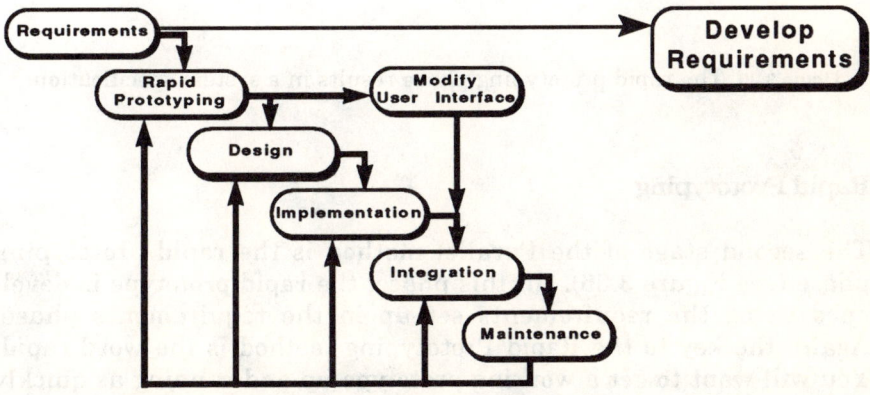

**Figure 3.35** In the Requirements phase of the Parallel method, system requirements are developed.

## Requirements

The requirements phase of the Parallel method, as illustrated in Figure 3.35, is used to develop overall system requirements. All the standard questions concerning the function of the overall system, what platform and software is preferred, system response time, and the general look and feel of the program must be asked. In addition, you must be more specific than you have been in previously studied software development methods. Like in the Rapid Prototyping method, you must obtain enough information to develop the rapid prototype in the next phase, paying particular attention to information concerning the user interface. The closer you are with the first cut of the rapid prototype of the user interface, the less time you will spend modifying it to please the customer.

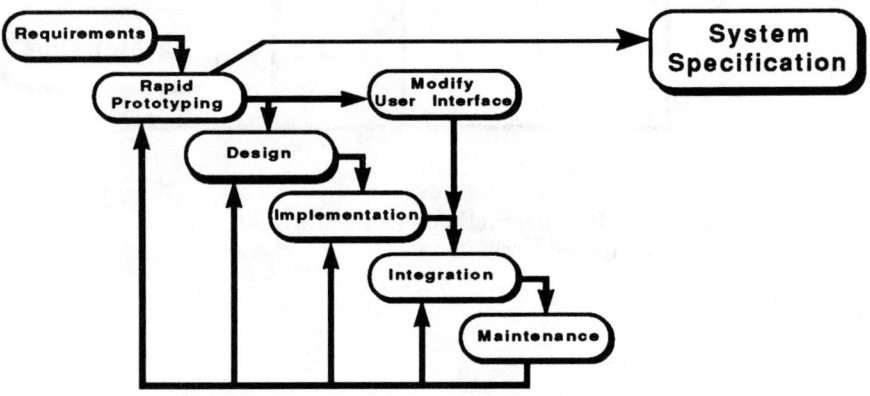

**Figure 3.36** The rapid prototyping phase results in a system specification.

## Rapid Prototyping

The second stage of the Parallel method is the rapid prototyping phase (see Figure 3.36). In this phase, the rapid prototype is developed using the requirements set up in the requirements phase. Again, the key to the Rapid Prototyping method is the word rapid. You will want to get a working prototype up and running as quickly as possible. Don't concern yourself with any form of error checking or any other cleanup details. Your main goal should be to get back to the customer as quickly as possible with a functional prototype.

Close interaction with your customers is absolutely essential in the rapid prototyping phase. Once you have a working prototype, demonstrate it to your customers or potential users for feedback. More than likely, the prototype will cause a rethinking of the system requirements. It will almost certainly require several iterations of reworking the prototype and demonstrating it to your users before all system requirements are agreed upon. Pay particular attention to the user interface again. Attempt to establish a complete understanding of what the customer wants in a user interface. Once you have reached that point, don't waste time writing up formal system specifications. The rapid prototype actually becomes the system specification and will be used to design the software in the next phase.

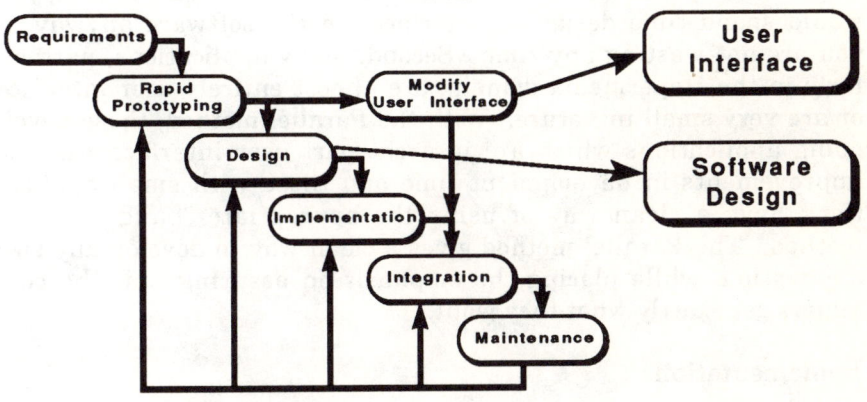

**Figure 3.37** The design phase results in a complete software design while the modify user interface phase builds upon the prototype.

## Design and Modify User Interface

At this point, the Parallel method veers in content from the Rapid Prototyping method (see Figure 3.37). The design is still drawn directly from the rapid prototype, but first, the user interface is broken cleanly from the rest of the prototype. This is done by examining the user interface and establishing function calls or subroutine calls to the levels below the user interface. The application then moves in two directions. The user interface, which has already been established as good by the user, is cleaned up while maintaining The application then moves in two directions. The user interface, which has already been established as good by the user, is cleaned up while maintaining the established interface with the rest of the program. Meanwhile, the remainder of the application goes through the standard design process like any of the previously described software development methods while also maintaining its linkage to the user interface. You must be especially aware of establishing and maintaining the interface between the user interface and the rest of the program or you will run into problems at integration time.

At first glance, this part of the Parallel method seems to fly in the face of the standard thinking on software development. A "build and fix" approach is almost never recommended except in very small applications. However, there are two major advantages to the Parallel method. First, you have already developed a user interface that the customer likes in the rapid prototyping phase. There is no reason to spend time redesigning the rapid prototype user interface only to end up with something that looks exactly the same. And, you would spend time designing interfaces in the software anyway so you are not wasting any time. Second, many applications, particularly in the Hypermedia domain, are almost entirely user interface or are very small in nature. With the Parallel method, those developing applications which are in great part user interface will see improvements in development time and those with small applications have a clean way of using the appropriate "build and fix" method. The Parallel method gives a clean way to develop any size application, while placing the emphasis on assuring that the customers get exactly what they want.

### Implementation

In the implementation phase, that part of the application which is not the user interface is coded based on the design that was developed in the previous phase (see Figure 3.38). As in other software development methods, there are several guidelines you should follow to develop readable, understandable, and maintainable code. The guidelines are:

1. Always aim for simplicity and clarity.
2. Use meaningful variable names.
3. Use consistent formatting conventions.
4. Use short headers to describe each module.
5. Establish commenting conventions.
6. Simplify your statement construction and program layout.
7. Code all I/O for ease of data transfer and error checking.
8. Strive for efficient code.

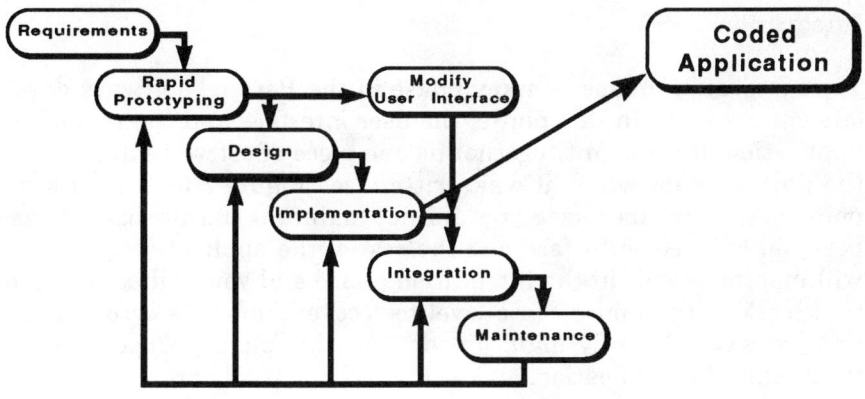

**Figure 3.38** In the implementation phase, the application is coded.

At this point, you should review the code to assure that it is traceable to the design document. The code must accurately reflect the intent of the design. If possible have someone else look at the code and evaluate it for readability and understandability. Again, it is absolutely imperative that you maintain the established linkage between the user interface and the rest of the application. Once you are satisfied that the design has been properly implemented, you can go on to the next phase—integration.

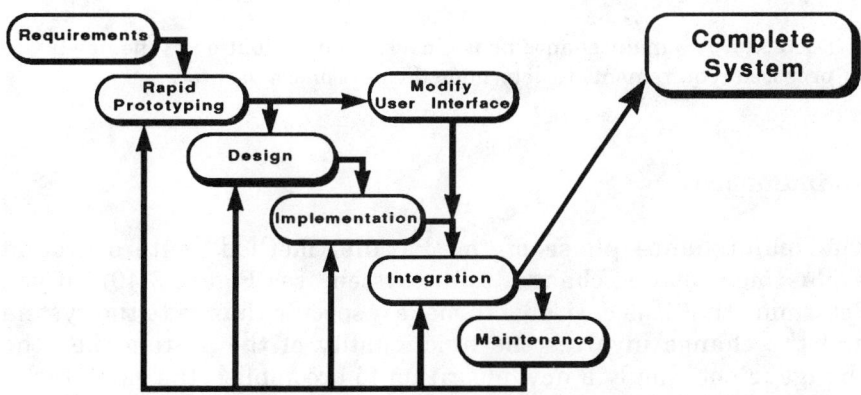

**Figure 3.39** The integration phase brings the user interface together with the application on the specified hardware.

## Integration

The integration phase is a key phase in the Parallel software development method. In this phase, the user interface and the rest of the application are brought together as one piece of software and run on the hardware for which it was written (see Figure 3.39). If at some point in a previous phase you did not maintain the precise linkage between the user interface and the rest of the application, the error will manifest itself in the integration phase and you will be forced to backtrack to the appropriate level to recover from this error. If the linkage was faithfully maintained, then this phase is used strictly for testing the application.

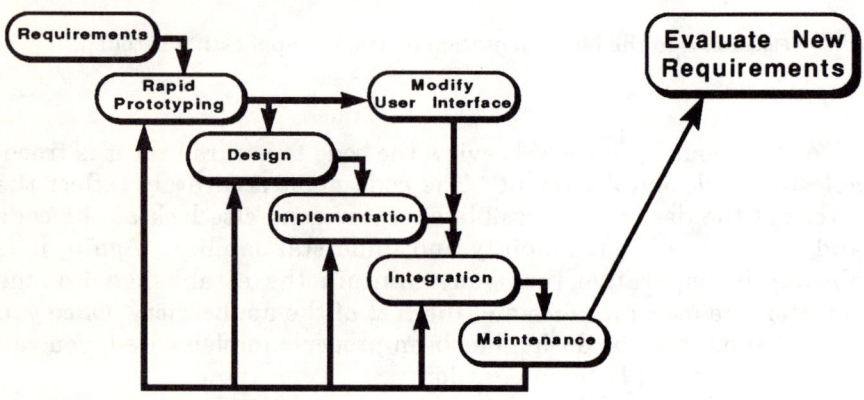

**Figure 3.40** The maintenance phase involves an evaluation of the newly proposed requirements to determine the next phase to enter.

## Maintenance

The maintenance phase of the Parallel method centers around evaluating proposed changes to the system (see Figure 3.40). If you determine that it is desirable to make a specific change to the system and the change involves the functionality of the system (i.e., the change is not simply a new algorithm to accomplish the same task), you should first incorporate the change into the prototype to determine its impact. After review of the altered prototype, if you still desire to make the change, then continue with the rest of the Parallel method as before. If the change is only to the user interface with the same underlying functionality, then you can simply modify the user interface, integrate it with the rest of the application, and test the resulting program.

### Final Thoughts on the Parallel Method

The Parallel software development method is a hybrid of the Rapid Prototyping method and the age old "build and fix" method. As such, it combines the extreme, but appropriate in some cases, simplicity of the "build and fix" model with the powerful, user-oriented Rapid Prototyping method. The resulting software development method is an extremely versatile model. Small, simple applications are kept simple by using the parallel branch and concentrating on development of the user interface. And, the development cycle for large, complex programs is significantly shortened because the customer approved user interface is not redesigned. With any size application though, the Parallel method places the emphasis on customer interaction and satisfaction.

The rest of Section 2 is devoted to a more in-depth examination of the Parallel method and its utilization in Hypermedia application building.

# 4

# Requirements and Specifications

Now that we are all familiar with several different software development methods, it is time to investigate one of those methods more closely and apply it directly to the Hypermedia domain. Of course, anytime you are going to develop software (outside of a few lines of code for your personal use), you should use some form of a software development method. The recommended software development method is, naturally, the Parallel method.

As illustrated in Chapter 3, the advantage of understanding many different software development methods is in knowing that all of them can be modified to some extent to meet the specific needs of your application. While the Parallel method could be used with great success on any software project, it was created with Hypermedia applications in mind. In general, Hypermedia applications concentrate on the user interface. Quite often there is little or no processing below that level. And, even when there is a great deal of processing that is invisible to the user, the emphasis is still on the user interface. Since the goal of any software development method is to organize the development process in order to ultimately save time and money, the method you choose in developing your Hypermedia application should take into account the previous statements. The Parallel method (see Figure 4.1) results from examining the specific needs of the Hypermedia domain.

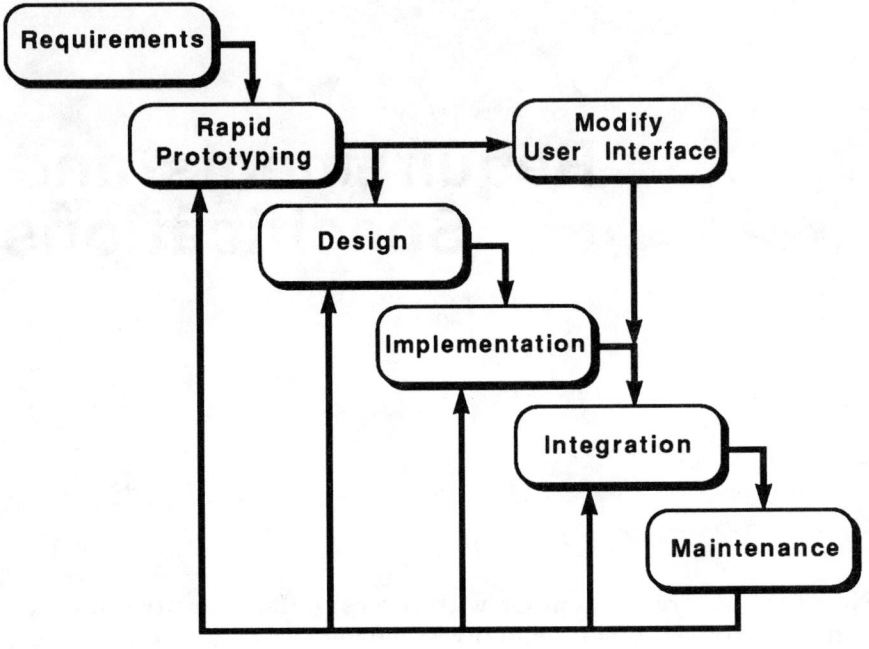

**Figure 4.1** The Parallel method was created with the needs of Hypermedia applications in mind.

As should be obvious from the illustration, the Parallel method is a hybrid of the Rapid Prototyping method and the simplistic "build and fix" model. The strength of the Rapid Prototyping method is in its emphasis on user interaction and time savings in the specification phase. Maximum user interaction is demanded in the rapid prototyping phase to assure that all system requirements are understood. And because of the use of a rapid prototype, writing a formal software specification is unnecessary. The strength of the "build and fix" model is in its simplicity. However, it is only recommended for very small applications. When the two methods are combined, the strengths of both are magnified. The design can be drawn directly from the rapid prototype, thus eliminating the need for a formal software specification. And, the user interface, which was blessed by the customer in the rapid prototyping phase, is simply cleaned up, thus eliminating the unnecessary repetition of rewriting the user interface. There are six sequential phases and one parallel phase in the Parallel method. The six phases are requirements, rapid prototyping, design, implementation, integration, and maintenance. The parallel phase of the Parallel method is designated the modify user interface phase.

The Parallel software development method will be examined in depth in the remainder of Section 2. In addition, the Parallel method will be used to develop two sample Hypermedia applications. This chapter is devoted to the first two phases of the Parallel method: requirements and specifications. The system and software requirements are set up in the requirements phase and the system and software specifications are set up in the rapid prototyping phase.

## REQUIREMENTS

The purpose of the Requirements phase (see Figure 4.2) of the Parallel method is to establish an understanding between the users (or potential users) of the software and the software developers concerning the exact function of the software. The final result of this phase is a set of system and software requirements.

There are, naturally, many different ways to determine these requirements. One of the most common and preferred ways is direct interaction with the customer. Of course, this only works if the developers have access to a specific customer. If not, then the developers will have to use some alternative method. Some alternative methods are questionnaires, sample groups acting as customers, and the developer acting as the customer. The best way to please your customers, though, is by determining their needs through face to face contact. Once you have established a method of customer interaction, you can attempt to establish the system requirements.

### System Requirements

Once you have determined a method of obtaining the requirements, you must concern yourself with what information to gather. At first, you should concentrate on system requirements. System requirements refer to what the overall system is to accomplish  It is helpful, at this point, to fall back on the who, what, when, where, why, and how approach.

The most important of these questions is "what." You must determine from your interaction with the customer the system functions and the inputs and outputs of the system. It often helps to actually draw out, in diagram form, the system functions. You should not get too specific here. Simply establish the broad functions. The rapid prototype in the next phase will be used to establish the specifics.

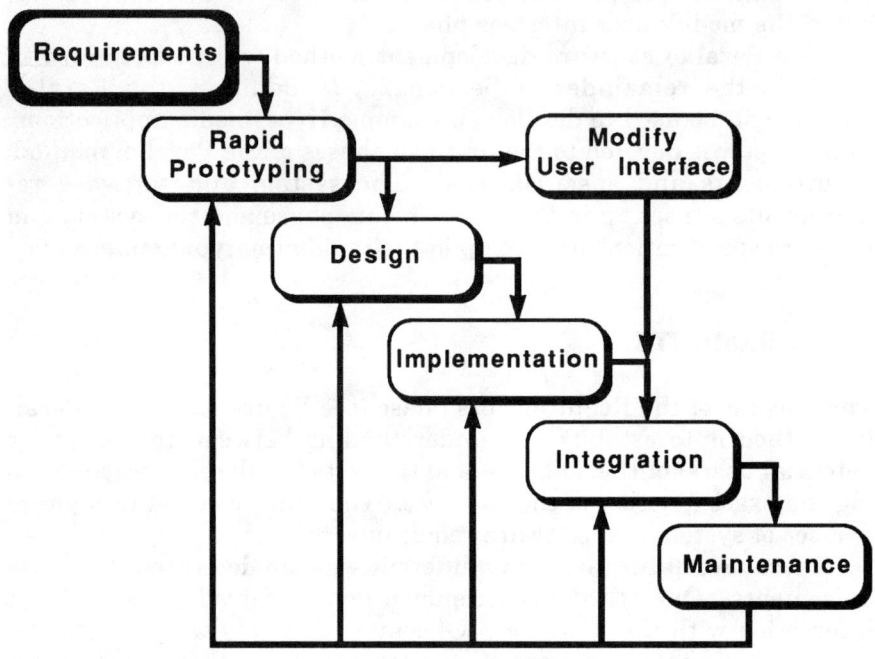

**Figure 4.2**  The requirements phase of the Parallel method is used to set system and software requirements.

The next question to consider is "who." It can be extremely valuable, particularly in developing the user interface, to know what type of person will be using the system. Try to establish whether the system will be used by engineers, clerical workers, managers, etc. It is possible that the system could be used by a combination of the listed types. Another related point is how much training, if any, the user will receive.

A point that is associated with the first two questions is "why." Often when developing software, the big picture is forgotten. If you are to develop software that will be beneficial to your customers, then you must understand why they want the system in the first place. Establish what need the customer is trying to satisfy.

Once you have settled on the first three rather broad questions, you can get a little more specific by examining "where." This actually has two components:  physical location, and hardware platform. The physical location of the system comes particularly into play when there are specific constraints on the system.  For example, there could be special security measures to consider.  Or, the system could be physically exposed to the elements and would therefore need special protection.  The second component of "where" refers to where the software will run.  There are two possibilities here.  The customers may want you to develop the software to run on a platform they already own or they might buy whatever platform is required to run the software.  In the first case, you must determine if it is feasible to run the described system on the prescribed hardware.  In the second situation, you must determine what type of hardware platform to utilize based on the needs and resources of the customer. Some guidelines for making these decisions are provided in Section 3 of this book.

The "when" consideration should be evaluated in conjunction with the second part of the "where" question. The "when" actually deals with system response time. How fast the system is expected to perform has a direct relationship to what hardware and software selections must be made.

The final question is "how." This "how" does not refer to how the software will be written, but rather to how the user interface will look.  Try to pin your customers down on the general "look and feel" that they expect out of the system.  Do they want it to be menu-driven, purely graphical, or a combination of the two?  This information will be extremely valuable in developing your rapid prototype.

Now that you have all the necessary information, it would be helpful to have it in one document for later reference.  One sample layout for a requirements document follows:

1.0     Customer
     1.1     Management points of contact
     1.2     Technical points of contact
     1.3     Other personnel involved in requirements setup
     1.4     Persons who will be using the system
     1.5     Persons who will maintain the system
2.0     System Description
     2.1     The overall purpose of the system
     2.2     Narrative of system operation
     2.3     Flow diagram
     2.4     Types of media utilized
     2.5     System inputs

After you have written up the requirements document, you should return to your customers and review the document. This will assure that both the customer and the developer understand and agree upon the major functions of the system, the hardware and software to be used, and the system constraints. Once the review is complete, you are ready to go on to the rapid prototyping phase.


## SPECIFICATIONS

The purpose of any system specification is to further refine the system requirements. System requirements sometimes tend to be a little vague. And, often there are some potential problem areas which do not arise until you begin to evaluate exactly how the system is to accomplish its requirements. In the normal engineering cycle, software specifications are acquired by identifying and allocating software tasks to the hardware. The only problem with this is that everything is on paper and there is little to show the customer except that you have been faithful to the paper requirements. One of the primary advantages of the Parallel method of software development is its utilization of the rapid prototype. Since the entire application is implemented in the rapid prototyping phase, there is a much greater chance that all potential problem areas will be identified. This aspect gives the developer the opportunity to identify and resolve any high-risk areas early in the development cycle. Also, the rapid prototype gives the customer something concrete to examine as early as possible so that any changes will have minimal impact from a cost and schedule point of view.

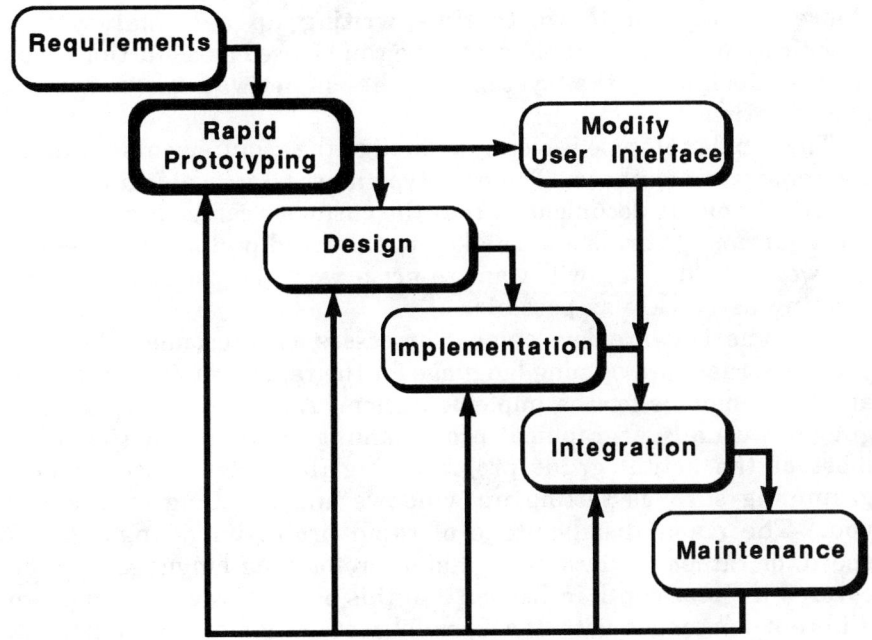

**Figure 4.3** The rapid prototyping phase is used to confirm the requirements and results in a system specification.

## Rapid Prototyping

In the rapid prototyping phase of the Parallel method, you will develop a prototype for the purpose of confirming the requirements established in the requirements phase (see Figure 4.3). A rapid prototype is a functional equivalent of the actual product. The rapid prototype must perform all of the basic functions required of the final product. But there is generally no error checking, file updating, or data isolation. It is not even important that the software be reliable for long periods of time. It is okay if the software crashes frequently. The primary use of the rapid prototype is to assure that the developer fully understands the requirements set by the customers. Therefore, it need only run long enough to demonstrate the major software functions. Rapid prototypes are also particularly useful in developing user interfaces. Since little time is spent making the interface fancy, you can spend more time with the customer determining favored approaches. Another key advantage of the rapid prototype is that it serves as the system specification. There is no need to waste time writing up a formal system specification when the rapid prototype can be used as a starting point in the design of the system in the same way as a system specification.

The rapid prototype is closely related to the requirements set up in the requirements phase. The prototype must be traceable directly to the requirements document so that the customer can be assured that all requirements are met. The key to the rapid prototype concept is the word rapid. You will want to get a working prototype up and running as quickly as possible.

In some software development processes, it is recommended that you use a rapid prototyping language for the rapid prototype and then another language for the implementation. A rapid prototyping language is usually a graphical programming environment that does most of the actual grunt programming (behind the scenes programming such as setting up windows and handling events) for you. The major disadvantage of rapid prototyping languages is speed, or rather the lack of it. Rapid prototyping languages will be covered in great depth in Section 3 of this book. However, using two different languages with the Parallel method is not recommended. Decide on either a graphical environment or a traditional high–order language based on the information presented in Section 3 and then use your selection for both the rapid prototype and the implementation. This will simplify things greatly in the implementation and maintenance of the system. The Parallel method calls for you to break the user interface developed in the rapid prototyping phase from the rest of the application and then to work on the two sections in parallel. It will be much easier at integration time if both sections are written in the same language. Also, the maintainer of the system will not be required to know two programming languages in order to make changes to the system.

Don't concern yourself with any form of error checking or any other cleanup details in developing the rapid prototype. Your main goal should be to get back to the customer as quickly as possible with a functional prototype. Close interaction with your customers is absolutely essential in the rapid prototyping phase. Once you have a working prototype, demonstrate it to your customers or potential users for feedback. More than likely, the prototype will cause a re-thinking of the system requirements. It will almost certainly require several iterations of reworking the prototype and demonstrations to your users before all system requirements are agreed upon. Once you have reached that point, don't waste time writing up formal system specifications. The rapid prototype actually becomes the system specification. And, according to the Parallel method, the prototype will be broken into two distinct entities for further development. The user interface will be modified to meet the standards of a finished product and the rest of the application will go through the standard design and implementation process. The two separate entities will meet again during the integration phase and undergo testing as a single unit.

## EXAMPLES

Starting here and continuing through the rest of Section 2, two Hypermedia applications will be developed. The purpose of developing these applications is to give you a complete understanding of how to use the Parallel method to develop Hypermedia related software. While the applications chosen to be developed are not exceedingly complex, they are representative of two different types of applications that are generally in great demand: training aids and databases. They are also representative of two different aspects of application building: having a customer upfront, and development for self-use with the potential for later sales. The companies and individuals referred to are purely fictitious. There is no intended relationship between the named companies and individuals and any actual company or person, living or dead. During the development, you will be supplied with as much information as possible.

## EXAMPLE 1—A Training Aid

The first example is one that is extremely common in the business world. The application itself is not very complex, but it is typical of the type of Hypermedia application that could be requested by a medium- to large-sized corporation. Also, this application could be modified to include much more information about the company, thus becoming considerably more complex.

## Background

For the purpose of developing this example, assume that a freelance software developer has been approached by the assistant to the CEO at a fair-sized manufacturing firm who has been placed in charge of training for junior executives. She explains, at the first meeting, that the company has a desire for all junior executives to be completely aware of the overall hierarchy of the corporation. While this alone could be done on a single sheet of paper, there is also a desire to relate names, faces, and voices to the individual positions. Because of the general nature of the problem, it is identified as one that is begging a Hypermedia solution.

## Set Requirements

The software developer asks the assistant to the CEO to set up a meeting with all the persons necessary to establish the requirements of the system. He/she explains that it is important to have a broad range of the corporate hierarchy present to set requirements, but also that the number of people should be kept to a minimum. There must also be someone present with the authority to approve the requirements. The following week, a meeting is set up with the following people:

1.  The assistant to the CEO
2.  Two mid-level managers
3.  Two junior executives
4.  The head of the office automation department

At the beginning of the meeting, explain the entire software development process as well as what part the individuals present play in that process. Ask pertinent questions about the system. After obtaining all the appropriate information, proceed to write up a requirements document. Ask that another meeting be set up in one week with the same people present to review the requirements. One week later, return with the following document:

**Requirements
for the
Junior Executive Hierarchy Trainer
(JEHT)**

1.0   **Customer**
      Noname Manufacturing Corporation

1.1    **Management points of contact**
Jane Doe, Assistant to the CEO, ext. 1111
1.2    **Technical points of contact**
Darlene Landry, Head of Office Automation, ext. 8462
1.3    **Other personnel involved in requirements setup**
Bob Jones, Director of Marketing, ext. 5375
Veronica Hayes, Credit Manager, ext. 9521
Jack Smith, Assistant Sales Manager, ext. 2376
Connie Fredrick, Assistant Manager for Engineering Research and Development, ext. 3475
1.4    **Persons who will be using the system**
The system is to be designed for junior-level executive training. Since Noname Manufacturing Corporation is such a broad company, its junior executives come from a wide variety of backgrounds. All junior executives have, as a minimum, a bachelors degree. In addition, all junior executives are expected understand or learn on their own time whatever computer skills are necessary to accomplish the job.
1.5    **Persons who will maintain the system**
Someone, as yet undetermined, from the Office Automation department will be resposible for maintenance of the system. This person will learn whatever is necessary to make and distribute changes to JEHT. This person will receive no formal training on the system and, therefore, must have a sufficient technical background to be able to understand how to modify the JEHT without detrimentally impacting existing functions.
2.0    **System Description**
2.1    **The overall purpose of the system**
As part of their training program, the company wishes that all junior executives be completely aware of the overall hierarchy of the corporation. The junior executives must be able to relate names, faces, and voices of individuals to the positions they hold within the company. Persons in the corporate hierarchy are constantly being refered to by name, listened to in meetings, and spoken to on the telephone by these junior executives. It is management's feeling that the sooner the junior executives have a firm grip on who is responsible for what in the corporate hierarchy, the sooner they will become productive members of the corporate team.
2.2    **Narrative of system operation**
The Overview/Title screen will have a drawing of the corporate hierarchy. By clicking on any of the levels, the user will be presented with a picture of the person who holds that

position and some information on that person and the position. Some mechanism will be provided to hear the voice of the selected person. The system must be designed so that changes in corporate personnel will not result in major changes to the software. Drastic changes in the corporate structure are not anticipated, and therefore, need not be considered.

2.3   **Flow   diagram**

From a software flow point of view, the JEHT system is trivial and therefore, a flow diagram is not seen as necessary.

2.4   **Types of media utilized**

The JEHT system will utilize drawings, pictures, text, and sound. A drawing of the corporate structure and the pictures and voices of individuals within that structure will be provided to the developer by Noname Manufacturing Corporation.

2.5   **System   inputs**

From a user's point of view, the system inputs will be a series of mouse clicks which will be used to navigate around the application. From a maintainer's point of view, files will exist that the system will draw upon to obtain the most current personnel information.

2.6   **System   outputs**

The only outputs of the system will be screen oriented. No printed output requirement exists at this time.

2.7   **Look  and  feel  of  the  system**

There will be no formal training on the JEHT provided to the users. Therefore, the software should be intuitive in nature with a great emphasis on an easy to use, graphical user interface. Menu functions as necessary may be utilized.

3.0   **Hardware**

3.1   **Type of computer system**

Noname Manufacturing Corporation has an extensive network of Apple Macintosh computers. Since they wish to utilize their existing equipment, the software will be targeted to the Macintosh personal computer. Most of the computers are equipped with color monitors, but there are some with only black and white monitors. There are approximately 50 systems which will run the software. An approximate breakdown of the system types is as follows:

```
10  –   Macintosh Plus
12  –   Macintosh LC
17  –   Macintosh IIsi
11  –   Macintosh IIci
```

The software must be able to run with any configuration. All systems are equipped with hard drives and a minimum 4MB of RAM.

3.2     **Necessary peripherals or add ons**

Due to the rapidly changing personal computer market, Noname Manufacturing Corporation does not wish to expend any more funds on hardware of any type at this time. The software must be able to run on existing systems as described in Sec. 3.1 without the purchase of additional peripheral devices.

3.3     **Special purpose hardware**

For development and maintenance purposes, some sort of an image scanning device and some sound recording equipment must be purchased. These are one time purchases to be retained after development by the designated maintainer of the system. Individual user systems will not be required to have these devices.

4.0     **Software**

4.1     **Operating system**

The JEHT software will run under Macintosh operating system version 6.0.7. Precautions will be made to assure that the anticipated transition to Macintosh operating system version 7.0 will not have adverse affects on the software.

4.2     **Off-the-shelf software**

No special purpose off-the-shelf software will be purchased for the user systems. The JEHT application must be standalone with no requirements for support software to execute. However, for development and maintenance purposes there must be made available off-the-shelf software for scanning pictures and recording sounds.

4.3     **Programming language**

No preference in programming language is made by Noname Manufacturing Corporation. The developer is free to choose the development language and environment.

5.0     **System constraints**

5.1     **Available resources**

Sufficient resources are available or can be made available by Noname Manufacturing Corporation to assure full development and deployment of the JEHT. Also, the developer either currently possesses or will acquire the resources necessary to develop and provide short term support and training for the JEHT.

5.2     **Security needs**

At the present time, the security needs of the JEHT are met by the security precautions already in place for the existing network of personal computers.

5.3    **Size limits**

Since the JEHT will use existing computer resources, size limits are not applicable.

5.4    **Physical location of the system**

The physical locations of the systems will not be such that special precautions must be made. The systems will be located in a standard, environmentally controlled office complex.

5.5    **Acceptable system response time**

There should be a minimum of delay between an action taken by the user and a response by the system. The customer understands that this is a vague requirement and that this issue will be explored in further depth during the rapid prototyping phase.

5.6    **Special reliability needs**

The JEHT software should not fail because of any software error. The customer understands that failures due to faults in the Macintosh operating system are unavoidable.

5.7    **Special power requirements**

There are no special power requirements at this time.

5.8    **Other**

There are no other considerations at this time.

6.0    **Other Information**

6.1    **Diagrams and drawings**

Figure 4.4 is a drawing of the corporate hierarchy of Noname Manufacturing Corporation.

6.2    **Sounds, pictures, etc.**

The developer shall have access to pictures of the necessary persons. Also, those designated persons will be available to have their voices recorded at the convenience of the developer.

6.2    **Other information**

There is no other necessary information at this time.

At the follow-up meeting, the requirements document is presented to the same group that set the requirements. The group determines that the there is sufficient information present to create a prototype in the next phase and the assistant to the CEO gives authorization for the next phase to begin.

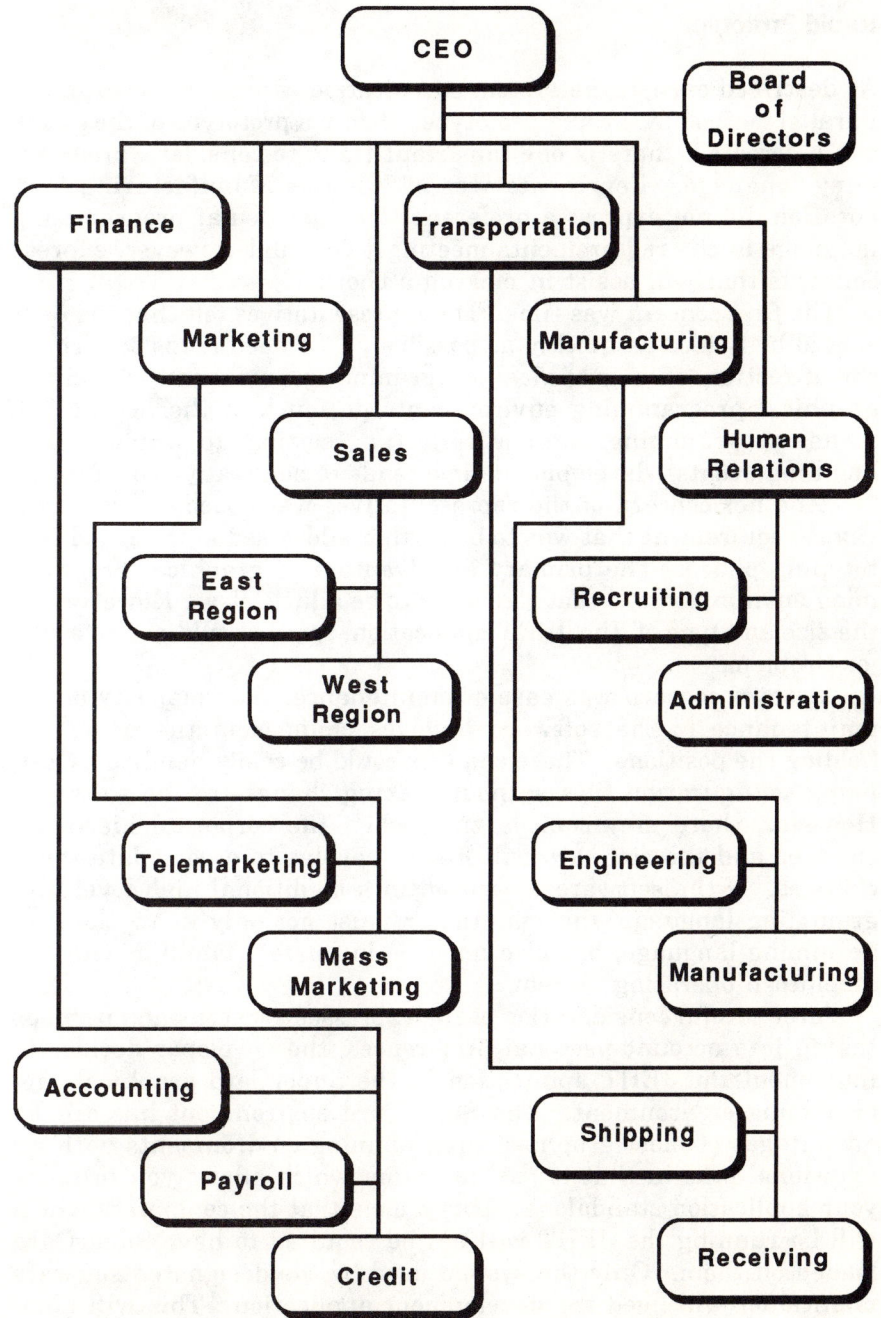

Figure 4.4 A diagram of the corporate hierarchy of Noname Manufacturing Corporation.

**Rapid Prototype**

As described earlier, the system specifications are established in the Parallel method by a rapid prototype. Before a prototype of the JEHT can be created, there is one important thing to consider: programming language. Representatives of Noname Manufacturing Corporation did not express a preference for a particular programming language in the requirements meeting. They did, however, express concerns that will assist in making a choice.

The first concern was time. The representatives felt that the Jeht should be fielded as quickly as possible. This need tends to push in the direction of a graphical programming environment. Since graphical programming environments do much of the behind the scenes programming automatically (i.e., setting up windows and handling events), development time tends to be greatly reduced.

Another concern of the representatives was speed. This was a vague requirement that was to be further addressed in the rapid prototyping phase. The primary disadvantage of graphical programming environments is that they tend to be a little slow. However, for the size and type of the JEHT application, speed should not be a major problem.

A third concern was ease of maintenance. The majority of the maintenance to the software involves changes in the personnel holding the positions. These changes could be easily handled by utilizing configuration files without making changes to the software. However, there may come a time when the corporate hierarchy changes and the software will have to evolve to accomodate these changes. If the software is written in a traditional high-level programming language, the maintainer must not only know the programming language, but also must be intimately familiar with the Macintosh operating system.

After careful consideration of the expressed concerns and perhaps taking into account personal preferences, the developer decides to implement the JEHT application in the SuperCard graphical programming environment. The SuperCard environment has all the advantages of most graphical programming environments with an additional plus in that it has an option which allows you to make your application standalone. This means that the computers which will be running the JEHT will not be required to have SuperCard loaded on them. Only the system used by the designated software maintainer will need the development application. This will eliminate the need for any unnecessary software purchases.

Now that the question of programming language has been decided, move on to actually creating the rapid prototype. Your first concern in creating the rapid prototype should be faithfullness to the requirements. Beyond that, your next concern should be speed of development. Don't worry about making the application fancy. Skip the colors and the flash and simply make the prototype perform the bare bones requirements.

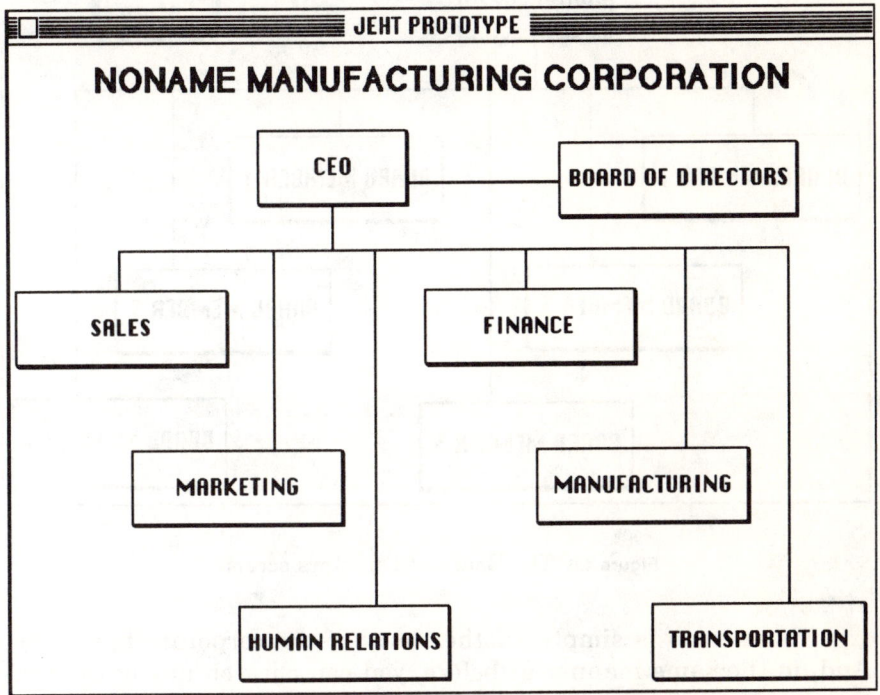

**Figure 4.5** The title screen for the JEHT prototype.

In creating the prototype for the JEHT, it was determined that the hierarchy for Noname Manufacturing Corporation was a little too busy for the title screen. To resolve this problem, the hierarchy was broken down into several levels. Figure 4.5 is a reduced screen dump of the title screen for the JEHT prototype. Each of the boxes on the title screen is actually a button which, when clicked on, will take the user to the next screen. The next screen will give more detail on the corporate hierarchy or more information on a specific person within that hierarchy. For example, when the Board of Directors button is clicked on, the screen shown in Figure 4.6 comes into view giving information concerning the layout of the Board of Directors.

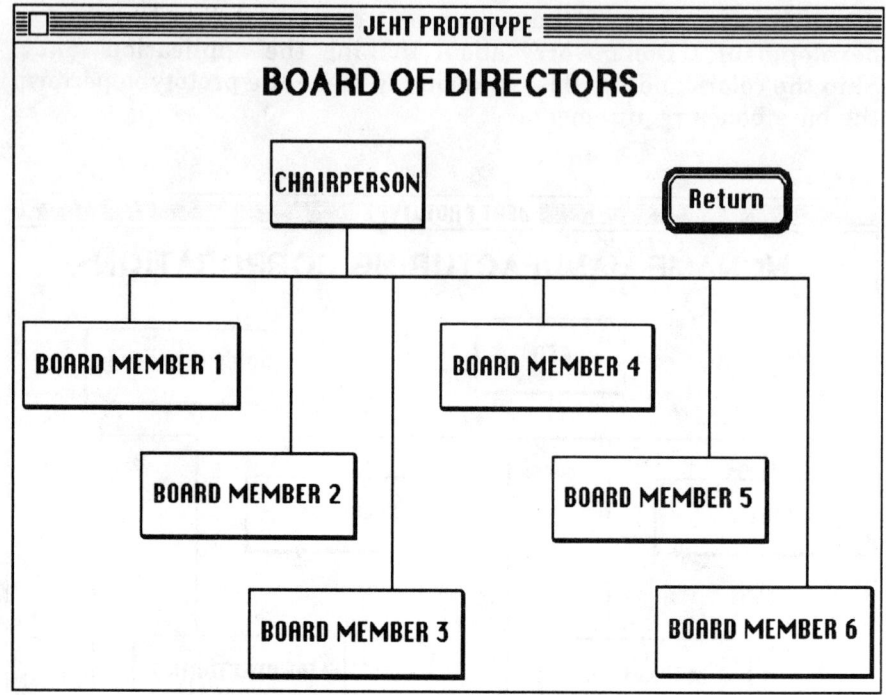

**Figure 4.6** The Board of Directors screen.

This screen is simply another level of the corporate hierarchy. And, in the same manner as before, you can click on any of the buttons and receive more information about specific persons on the Board of Directors. If you click on the Chairperson button, for example, the screen in Figure 4.7 comes into view.

The Chairperson screen is an example of a screen containing only information about a single person. Notice that for the purpose of a rapid prototype, no actual information concerning any person is on the card. Since the purpose of the rapid prototype is to verify and clarify the requirements and to establish a baseline user interface, it is not necessary to waste any time placing authentic information in the application. It is sufficient to simply put placeholders, as in Figure 4.7, in place of data such as pictures, names, titles, and personal information. This will give the customers enough of a feel for the application that they will be able to give you valuable input as to what changes should be made.

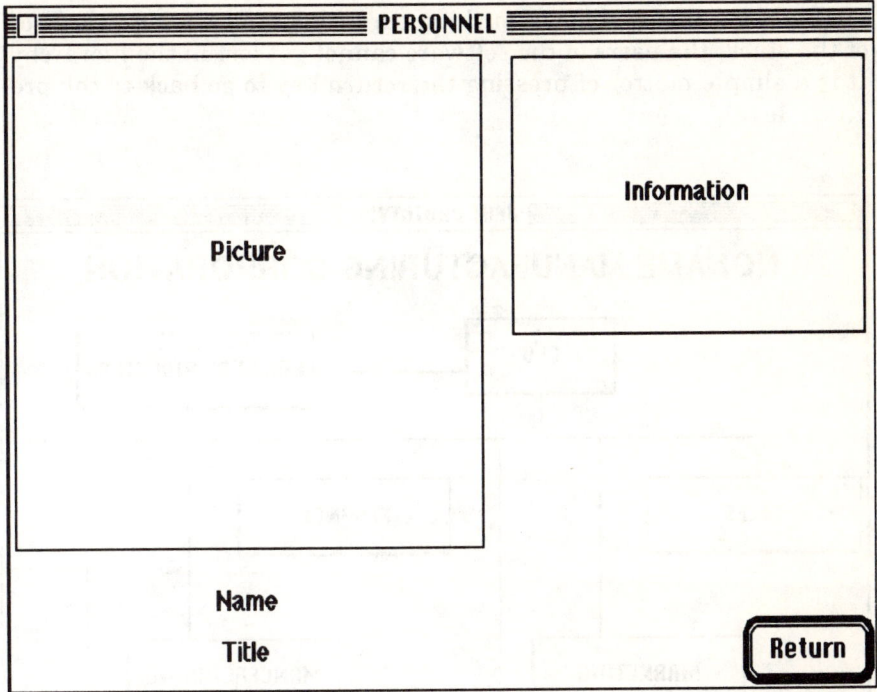

**Figure 4.7** The Chairperson screen.

You may have noticed the bold outlined return button on every screen but the title card. First, the bold outline around the button is a standard convention for a default button. This means that the same action will occur whether you click on the button or if you simply press the return key on the keyboard. If this button is clicked on or if the return key on the keyboard is pressed, the user will be returned to the previous screen in the corporate hierarchy. The JEHT prototype was created to work like a last-in first-out (LIFO) stack. For example, when you go from the title card to the Board of Directors card, the title card is pushed onto a stack. If you click on the return button at that point, the title card is popped off the stack and becomes the current card. But, if, from the Board of Directors card, you click on the Chairperson button, then the Board of Directors card is pushed onto the stack on top of the title card. Now, if you press the return key from the Chairperson card, the last card in is popped off the stack and you will go back to the Board of Directors card. And, if you press the return key again, you will return to the title card shown again in Figure 4.8.

By using this scheme of pushing cards onto and popping cards off of the stack, the users of the software cannot get lost in the hierarchy. It is a simple matter of pressing the return key to go back to the previous level.

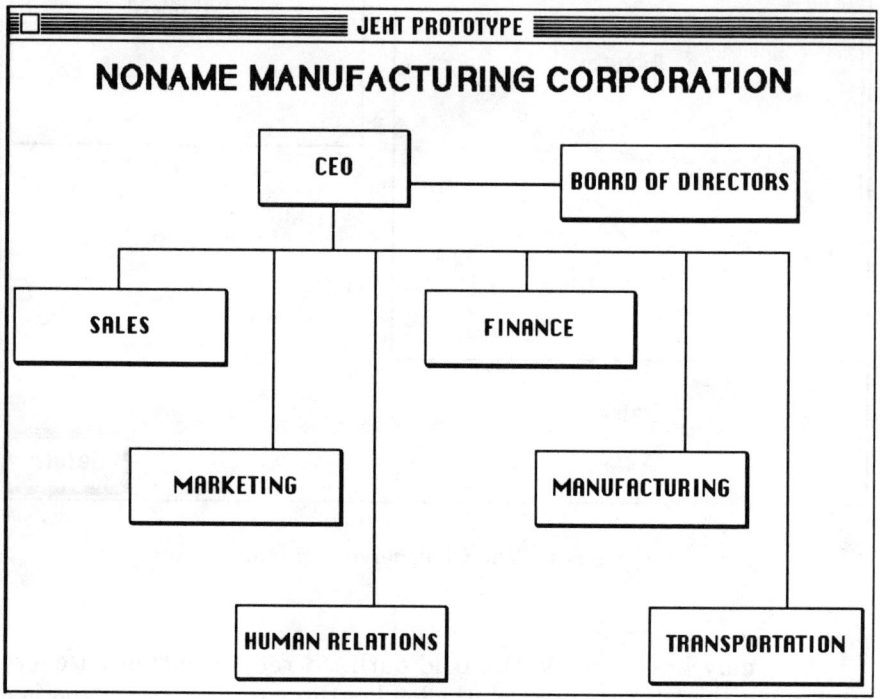

**Figure 4.8** The title screen for the JEHT prototype.

Now, to further explain the layout of the JEHT prototype, refer to the title card shown in Figure 4.8. Clicking on the CEO button will bring up a card similar to the Chairperson card we examined earlier. Therefore, to avoid unnecessary repetition, do not examine that particular path. However, if you were to click on the Sales button, the card shown in Figure 4.9 would come to the forefront.

This card actually serves two purposes. It provides information about a specific person in the corporate hierarchy. In this case, that person is the Director of Sales. And, it is a gateway to deeper levels of the hierarchy. The two buttons labeled East Regional Manager and West Regional Manager are the keys to the gateway. If you click on one of the two buttons, say the East Regional Manager button, you will be presented a card similar to the previously examined

Chairperson card. The only difference would be that the information on the card, once it is put in, will be specific to the person who is the East Regional Manager.

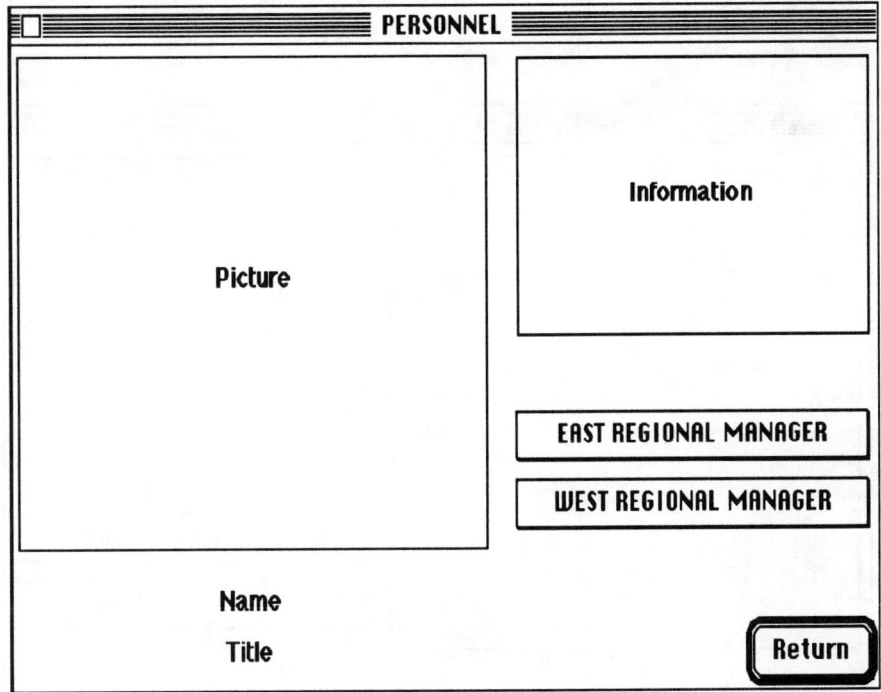

**Figure 4.9** The Sales card for the JEHT prototype.

Notice again that no information outside of the details of the corporate hierarchy are included in the rapid prototype. Up to this point, sound has not been addressed. Obviously, for the rapid prototype, we do not want to take the time to record sounds. But, to show the customers how the sound would be incorporated into the application, they must be included in the prototype. If the user clicked on the picture, the voice of the person in the picture could be heard. To save time in the prototype, play any sound, in this case a car starting, when any picture field is clicked on. In this manner, the functionality of sounds can be illustrated to the customer without taking the time to record specific voices.

Backing up a bit, if you click on the Marketing button from the title card, the Marketing card (Figure 4.10) comes into view. This card is similar to the Sales card we just examined, except that the picture and other information, when included, will be that of the Director of Marketing. The path down the hierarchical ladder, in this case, leads to the Telemarketing Manager and the Mass Marketing Manager. Everything else on the card is identical including the functionality of the Return button and even the car sound which is played when the picture is clicked on.

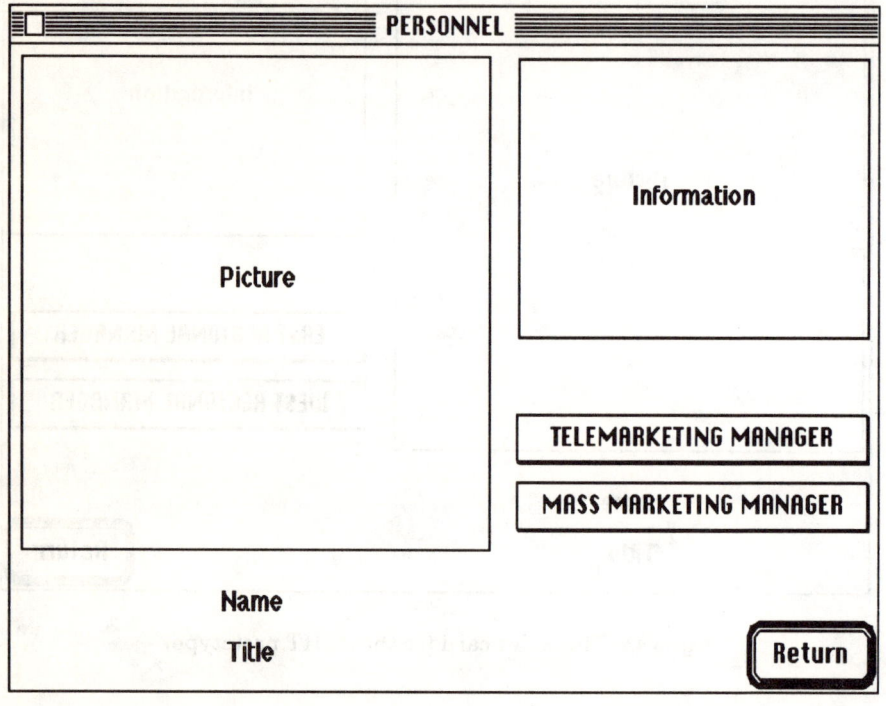

**Figure 4.10** The Marketing card for the JEHT prototype.

There are four unique cards left to examine. They are all similar to the last two cards we have looked at except for the layer of hierarchy in which they exist. Figure 4.11 shows the Human Relations card with a gateway to the Recruiting Manager and the Administration Manager. In Figure 4.12, the Director of Finance is shown to be in charge of the Accounting Manager, the Payroll Manager, and the Credit Manager. Figure 4.13 is an illustration of the Manufacturing card and its links to the Engineering Manager and the Manufacturing Manager. And finally, the Transportation card (see Figure 4.14) shows the link between the Director of Transportation and the Shipping and Receiving Managers. All of these cards have the same functionality as the previous cards we have examined.

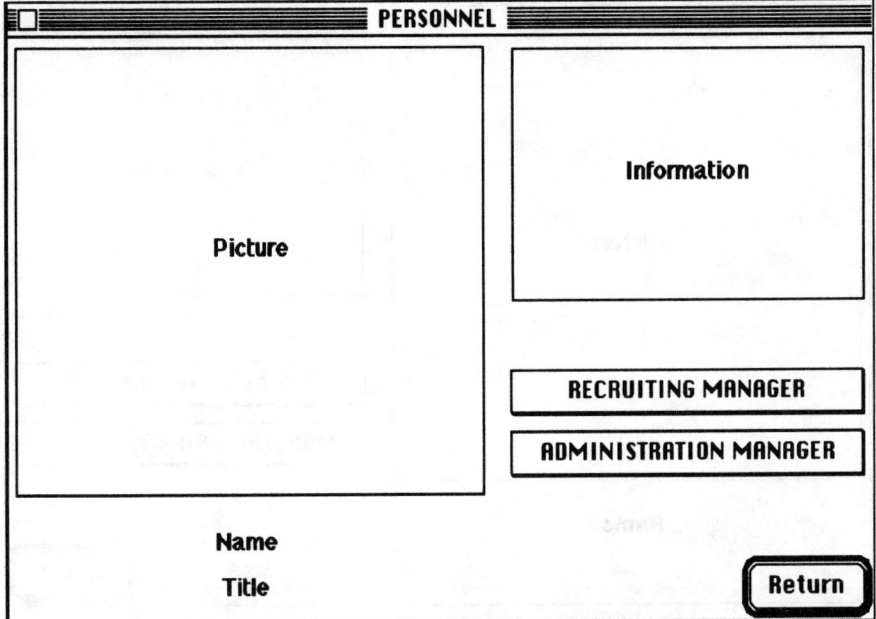

Figure 4.11 The Human Relations card.

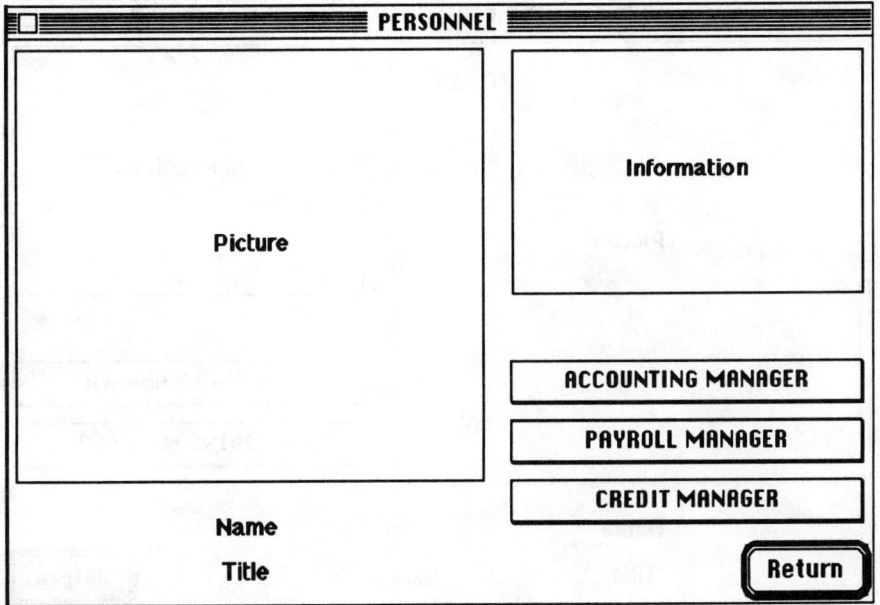

Figure 4.12 The Finance card.

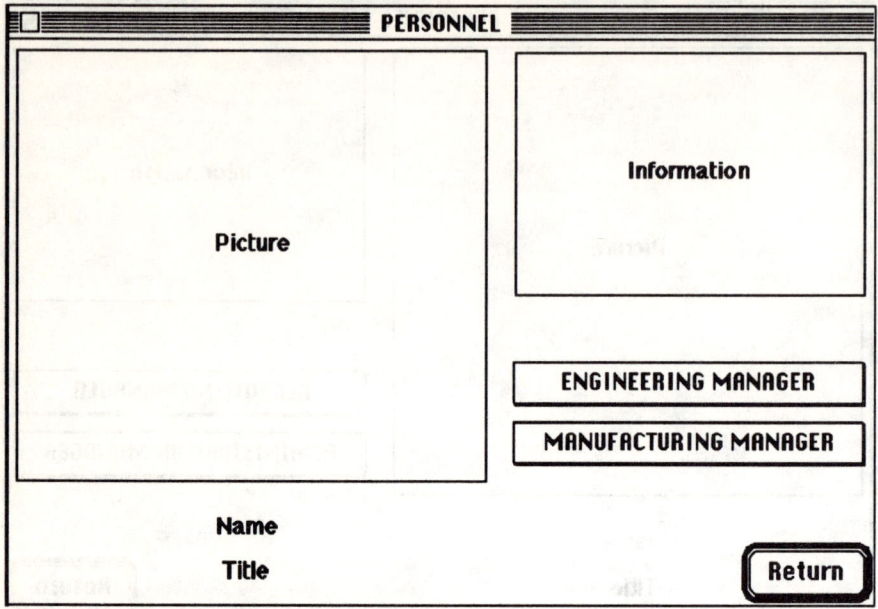

Figure 4.13 The Manufacturing card.

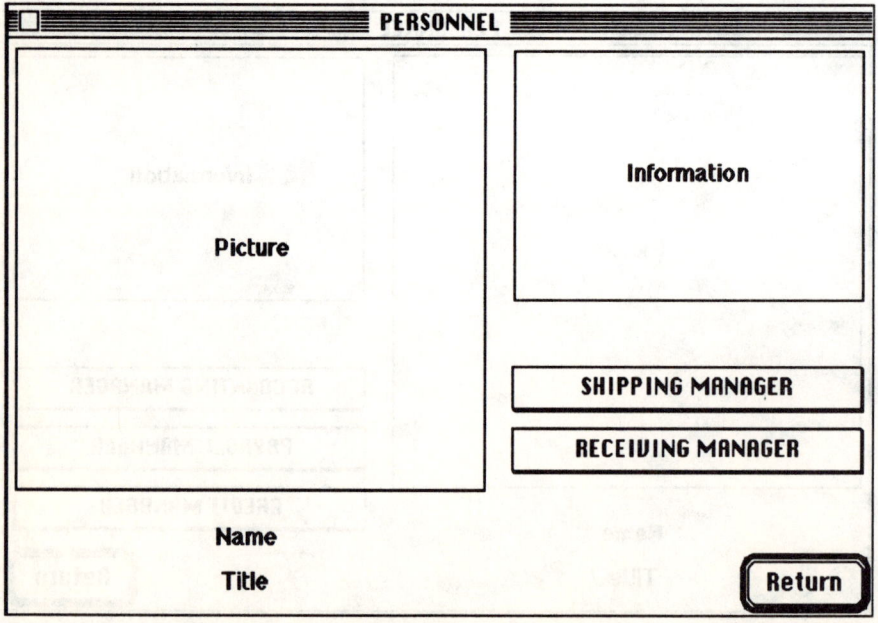

Figure 4.14 The Transportation card.

The rapid prototype is now complete. But, there is one thing left to do before going on the the design phase. Call Jane Doe, the CEO's assistant, and ask her to set up yet another meeting, a specification review, with the requirements group. At this meeting, demonstrate the rapid prototype to the group. You must explain, before the demonstration, the purpose of the rapid prototype. There will always be individuals who, in their ignorance of the software development method you are using, expect the intial prototype to be a finished product. Therefore, to avoid embarassment on both sides, be sure to preface your demonstration with a reemphasis of the purpose of the meeting. As an example, a specification review might consist of the following phases:

1. Welcome—thanks for coming again
      led by the customer
2. Reintroduction of the people involved
      led by the customer
3. Review of management objectives
      led by the customer
4. Examination of the requirements document
      led by the developer
5. Explanation of the purpose of the rapid prototype
      led by the developer
6. Demonstration of the rapid prototype
      led by the developer
7. Formal feedback session
      led by the developer
8. Formal identification of action items
      led by the developer
9. Conclusion—establish a time frame for the next meeting
      led by the developer

This is the format used for the JEHT specification review. Steps 1, 2, and 3 are a general introduction and review of the JEHT project. These steps were performed by the CEO's assistant, Jane Doe. The rest of the steps were led by the developer. Step 4 is an examination of the requirements document. Since the rapid prototype is based on the requirements document, it is wise to refresh everyone's memory. Step 5, the explanation of the purpose of the rapid prototype, is a critical step for reasons already explained.

The conclusion of Step 5 ended the preliminaries. After a short break, proceed with Step 6: the actual demonstration of the prototype. Demonstrate the prototype on the slowest of the target machines so that the question of system response time can be addressed adequately. The key to the demonstration is to explain the functionality of the prototype. Encourage questions, but, only those that clarify the functionality of the software as it currently exists. Defer any questions concerning the relationship of the software to the requirements document until the next step.

Step 7 is the formal feedback session. Step 7 is the appropriate time for questions concerning the relationship of the software to the requirements document. Everyone must agree that the full functionality described in the requirements document is achieved by the prototype. If there are shortcomings in the prototype, they should be brought up and discussed at this time. There is one thing that you cannot allow at this stage:  requirements creep. Often times, customers will ask for more than was in the original requirements. And, if you give in to the request, they will ask for something else. Quickly, you will find that you can't keep up with the constantly changing requirements and the schedule will begin to slip. The key to avoiding requirements creep and pleasing the customers at the same time is to stick to the original requirements, but retain some flexibility.  You should consider including minor enhancements that do not alter the overall functionality of the system. But don't allow major changes at this time.

As an example, one of the attendees suggested inserting links to the corporate charter and possibly to the charters for each of the individual groups.  It was even suggested that documentation on the manufactured products and the way each division affects the final product be included.  While these are all excellent ideas and would result in all corporate documentation being in an easy access, Hypermedia format, they had to be turned down based on the fact that they were far out of the original scope of the project.  These ideas should be brought up with management as future additions to the JEHT once it has been fielded.

Steps 8 and 9 are the concluding steps.  During Step 8, the problems related during the feedback of Step 7 are formally identified and given priorities.  If there were no problems identified, then there is no reason to meet again.  The developer simply moves on to the design phase.  If there are problems, then Step 9 is utilized to establish a time frame for the next meeting.

For the JEHT application, no major changes were identified. Therefore, the Specification phase is considered finished and you should move on to the design phase of the Parallel method.

## EXAMPLE 2—A Database Application

In the first example, you had a concrete customer.  In this second example, to illustrate a slightly different point of view, there will be no

predefined customer. This is probably one of the most common occurrences in software development. People, and often corporate
software developers, are always developing software, either for their
own use or with the idea that they might be able to find customers to
purchase the final product. This approach almost always involves
more risk as there is no guarantee that anyone will buy the software
you develop. However, the premiss you must go on is that in developing software for yourself, you do have a predefined customer: you.
And, hopefully, other people will like what you like. The particular
application developed in this example is not exceedingly complex,
but it is a good example, for the small developer, of how a rather
mundane database application can be made interesting and more
versatile by simply adding some drawings.

You may be wondering at this point, why, if you are developing for
yourself, do you need to use any software development method. This
is a common fallacy among individual programmers. The ten-
dency is to avoid the cumbersome software development methods
and start coding right off. You will find that, like many other tasks,
time spent upfront organizing and planning is not time wasted. In
fact, it will save you time in the overall life-cycle of your application. Don't be in awe of any software development method.
Almost all of them, in their basic form, are relatively easy to
understand and modify in order to meet your own needs.

## Background

You can assume, for the purpose of developing this example, that an
individual has an idea for a software project. The idea is a rolodex
with a slightly different angle. In his/her job, the individual has
contacts all over the United States. When referencing these contacts, it is usually by the state or region in which they are located. A
standard software rolodex usually gives you basic database functionality: you can add things to the database, take things out of the
database, and look things up in the database. The individual may
desire to create a software rolodex with a graphical interface to meet
his/her specific needs. It is believed that there are possibly others
who have a similar problem who may wish to purchase this application. But the goal is to create an application that will enhance productivity.

## Set Requirements

Since this application is being developed for personal use, there is
obviously no need to have a meeting with anyone else. So, simply sit

down for an hour with the requirements document outline and fill
in the blanks.  The result is as follows:


**Requirements
for
RoloMap**

**1.0    Customer**
Self
    **1.1    Management  points  of  contact**
    N/A
    **1.2    Technical  points  of  contact**
    N/A
    **1.3    Other  personnel  involved  in  requirements  setup**
    N/A
    **1.4    Persons  who  will  be  using  the  system**
    Unknown, besides self.
    **1.5    Persons  who  will  maintain  the  system**
    The software must be standalone and self-maintainable.
**2.0    System  Description**
    **2.1    The  overall  purpose  of  the  system**
    As part of his/her daily work, the developer contacts clients
    and/or colleagues.  He/she remembers these people based on
    their geographic location.  The goal of Rolomap is to provide
    a graphical interface to a rolodex that will assist in day to
    day activities.
    **2.2    Narrative  of  system  operation**
    The Overview/Title screen will have a drawing of the
    United States.  By clicking on any particular region, the
    user will be presented with a larger version of that region.
    Then, by clicking on a specific state, a list of points of con-
    tact for that state will appear.  Some mechanism will be pro-
    vided to add and subtract items from the list.
    **2.3    Flow  diagram**
    From a software flow point of view, Rolomap is nearly triv-
    ial and therefore, a flow diagram is not seen as necessary.
    **2.4    Types  of  media  utilized**
    Rolomap will utilize drawings, and text.  An appropriate
    drawing of the United States must be obtained.
    **2.5    System  inputs**
    From a user point of view, the system inputs will be a series
    of mouse clicks which will be used to navigate around the

application. There will also be user input in the form of additions to and removals from the database.

2.6    **System outputs**
The primary outputs will be screen oriented. However, there will be options for printed output .

2.7    **Look and feel of the system**
Initially, there will be no associated documentation. Rolomap is expected to be completely intuitive. Menu selections may be utilized as necessary.

3.0    **Hardware**

3.1    **Type of computer system**
The software will be targeted to the Macintosh personal computer. Because marketing the finished product is a possibility, assure that the software will be able to run on any of the following Macintosh system types:

| | |
|---|---|
| Macintosh Portable | Macintosh SE 30 |
| Macintosh Plus | Macintosh IIsi |
| Macintosh Classic | Macintosh IIcx |
| Macintosh SE | Macintosh IIci |
| Macintosh LC | Macintosh IIfx |

The software must be able to run with any configuration. All systems are expected to have a minimum 2MB of RAM.

3.2    **Necessary peripherals or add ons**
The software must be able to run on standard systems as described in Sec. 3.1 without the purchase of additional peripheral devices.

3.3    **Special purpose hardware**
No special purpose hardware is necessary either for development or for normal software maintenance. It is possible that future enhancements will require some development hardware.

4.0    **Software**

4.1    **Operating system**
The Rolomap software will be developed under Macintosh operating system version 6.0.7. Precautions will be made to assure that the software will also run under Macintosh operating system version 7.0.

4.2    **Off-the-shelf software**
No special purpose off-the-shelf software will be required to run Rolomap. The Rolomap application must be standalone with no requirements for support software to execute.

4.3    **Programming language**

The developer's personal preference is the SuperCard graphical programming environment.

5.0    **System constraints**

    5.1    **Available resources**

    Sufficient resources are available to assure full development of Rolomap.

    5.2    **Security needs**

    N/A

    5.3    **Size limits**

    N/A

    5.4    **Physical location of the system**

    N/A

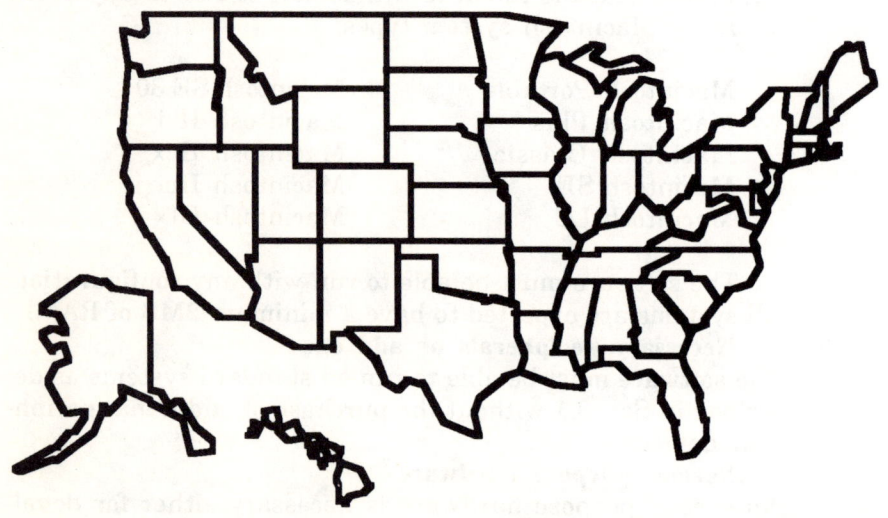

**Figure 4.15** The baseline drawing for Rolomap.

    5.5    **Acceptable system response time**

    There should be a minimum of delay between an action taken by the user and a response by the system. This is a vague requirement and will be examined in greater detail during the rapid prototyping phase.

    5.6    **Special reliability needs**

    The Rolomap software should not fail because of any software error. Macintosh operating system errors are, of course, unavoidable.

    5.7    **Special power requirements**

N/A
5.8    **Other**
There are no other considerations at this time.
6.0    **Other Information**
6.1    **Diagrams and drawings**
Figure 4.15 is the drawing that will be used as a baseline for Rolomap.
6.2    **Sounds, pictures, etc**
N/A for now.
6.2    **Other information**
There is no other necessary information at this time.

After finishing the requirements document, set it aside for a day. Then, review it to determine whether there is sufficient information present to create a prototype. Determine that all the necessary information is there and move on to the specification phase.

## Rapid Prototype

As described earlier, the system specifications are established in the Parallel method by a rapid prototype. Your first concern in creating the rapid prototype should be faithfullness to the requirements. Beyond that, your next concern should be speed of development. Don't worry about making the application fancy. Skip the colors and the flash and simply make the prototype perform the bare-bones requirements.

A common problem encountered when developing applications for yourself is trying to make the prototype a finished product. Remember that the rapid prototype is a tool for confirming requirements and building user interfaces. Put some thought into it, but, don't waste too much time. There should not be any actual information in the prototype other than what is necessary to explain the software functionality. For example, in the case of Rolomap, a map for the application had to be selected, but, it was not necessary to put actual phone numbers and addresses into the database. It is sufficient to simply put placemarkers in place of the actual data. These placemarkers should be self-explanatory (i.e., names go here, phone numbers go there).

Another common problem in creating prototypes is attempting to optimize. At this point, it is not important to write good code. What is important is making the software functional. If you are using a graphical programming environment, you will have a little more time to consider how to implement the prototype so that the design phase will go smoothly. But, if you are using a traditional high-order language, you have a great deal of code to write to implement any sort of a graphical user interface. Whip something up quickly. Pay little attention to coding standards or commenting the code beyond what is absolutely necessary. In fact, at this time, you can hard code everything. The key is to get a prototype running that contains the functionality in the requirements document. With the Parallel method, you will be doing a complete design of everything except the user interface. And, the user interface will be cleaned up to reflect quality coding standards.

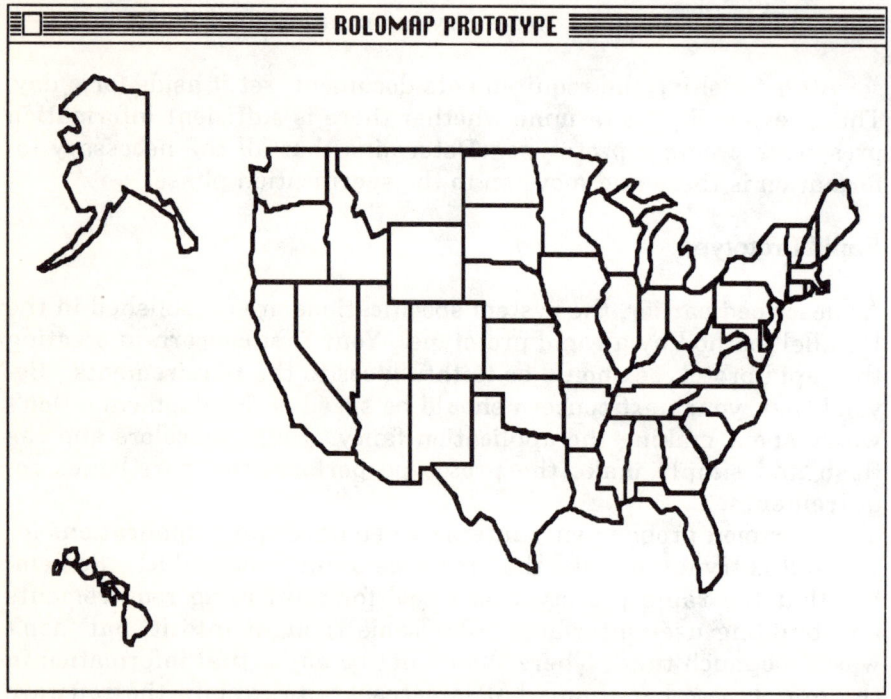

Figure 4.16 The title card for the Rolomap prototype.

The title screen for Rolomap is very simple (see Figure 4.16). It contains a map of the United States and nothing else. Originally, it was intended for the user to be able to directly select a state from this map. But, after looking at the size of some of the states when the map was sized to fit on the lowest common denominator screen, it was determined that this was not feasible. The active area on some of the smaller states was so small that it would have been difficult to click on them. To solve this problem, the map of the United States was broken into six distinct sections: Northwest, Southwest, North Central, South Central, Northeast, and Southeast. The SuperCard polygon button tool was used to create odd-sized buttons that would encompass the entire region of interest. This type of problem is one of the prime reasons for using prototypes. In some instances, there is no way of knowing exactly how parts of the program will work until you actually try to code them. This is particularly true of the user interface. Often, something that seems to make perfect sense conceptually will look horrible on the computer screen. And, upon seeing that blunder, you will envision a new way for the program to look that you may not have thought of before.

If, from the title screen, you click on the portion of the map that is designated as the Northwest, you will be presented with the screen shown in Figure 4.17.

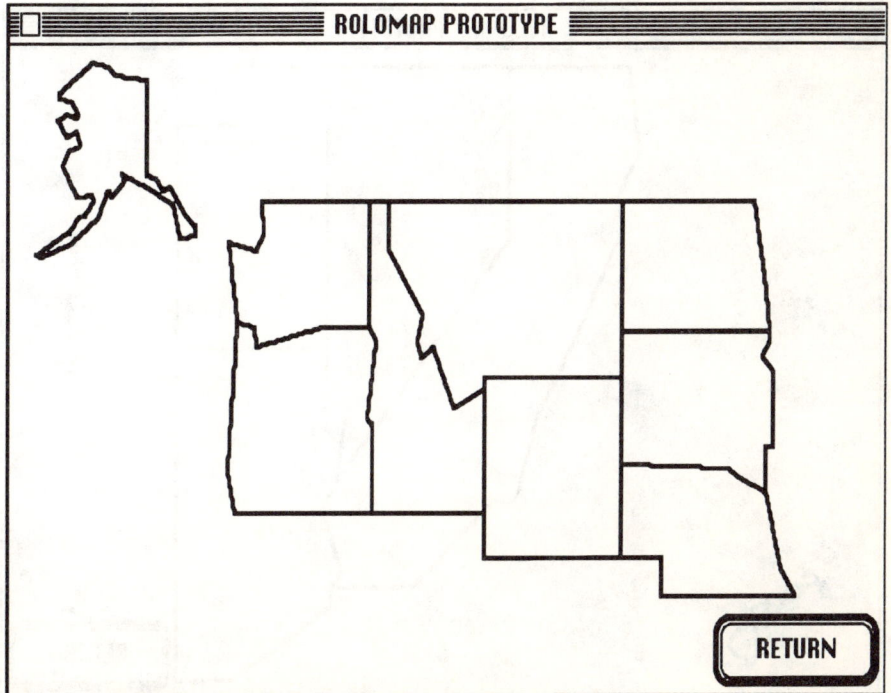

**Figure 4.17** The Northwest card for the Rolomap prototype.

This screen is a blowup of the Northwest section of the title screen. The Northwest region encompasses the states of Alaska, Washington, Oregon, Idaho, Montana, Wyoming, North Dakota, South Dakota, and Nebraska. The reason for this blowup will become more apparent when we examine the Northeast section with all of the small states that are prevalent in that area. From this screen, you can click on a specific state. Again, the SuperCard polygon button tool was used to create buttons that are approximately the size and shape of the individual states. Each of these buttons, when clicked upon, will highlight themselves before any action is taken to indicate which button was selected. If the cursor is moved off the button before the mouse button is released, no action occurs. Using this scheme, you can recover easily from a misplaced mouse click without having to return from another card.

Going back to the title screen, if you click and release the mouse button anywhere in the lower-left corner of the map you will be presented with the screen in Figure 4.18.

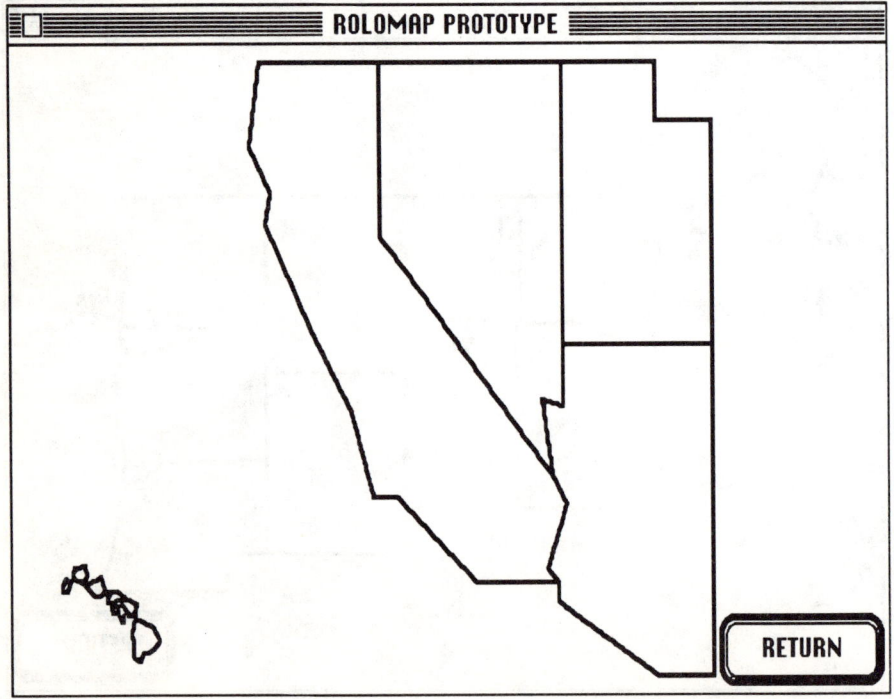

**Figure 4.18** The Southwest card for the Rolomap prototype.

This is a blowup of what has been designated as the Southwest region. As defined, the Southwest region contains the states of Hawaii, California, Nevada, Utah, and Arizona. In functionality, this screen is identical to the last card we examined.

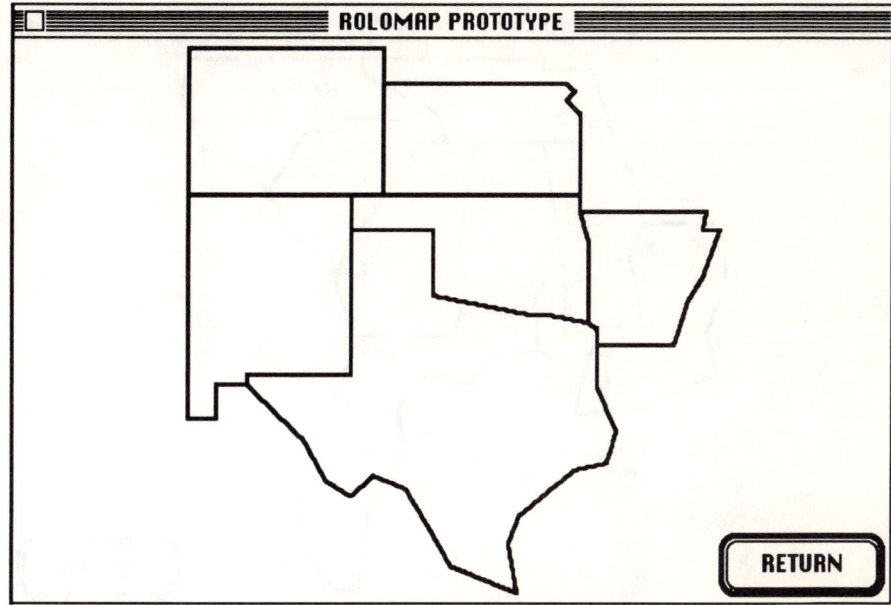

**Figure 4.19** The South Central card for the Rolomap prototype.

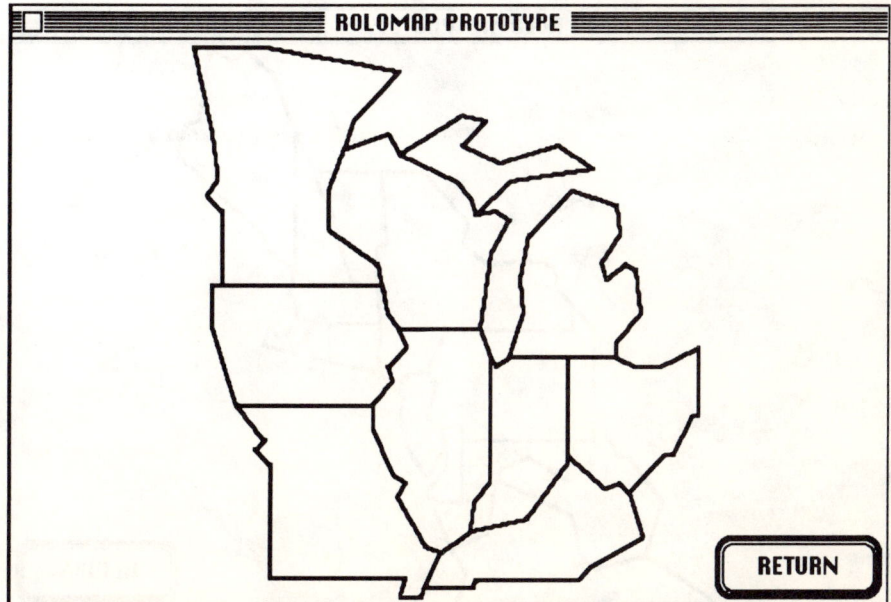

**Figure 4.20** The North Central card for the Rolomap prototype.

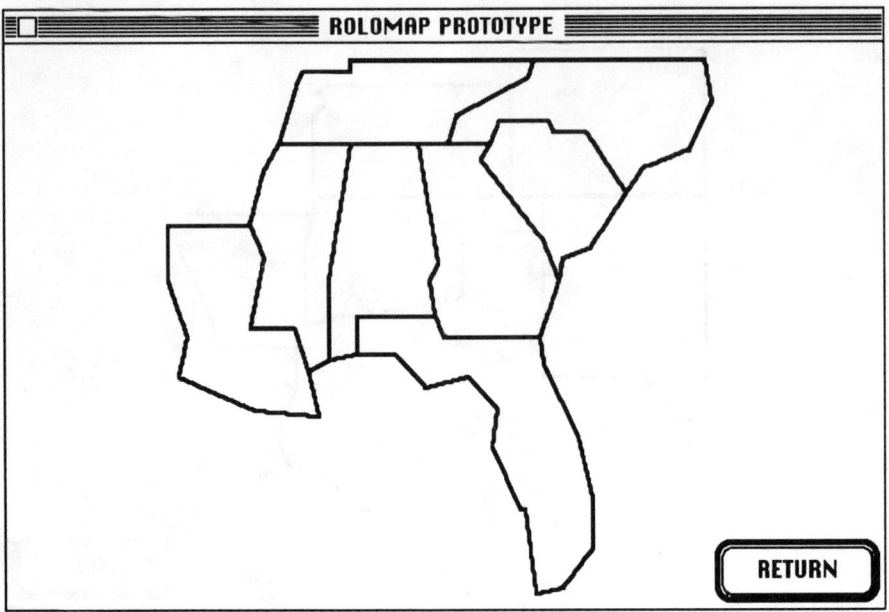

**Figure 4.21** The Southeast card for the Rolomap prototype.

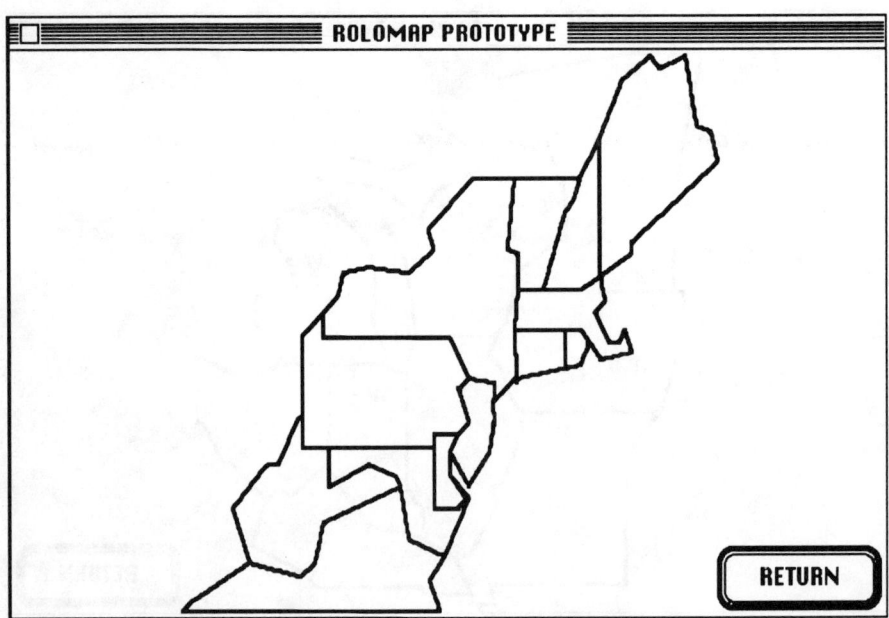

**Figure 4.22** The Northeast card for the Rolomap prototype.

Figures 4.19, 4.20, 4.21, and 4.22 are screen dumps of the South and North Central, and South and Northeast cards, respectively.   In Figure 4.19, the South Central region is defined to contain the states of Colorado, New Mexico, Kansas, Oklahoma, Texas, and Arkansas.   From Figure 4.20 it is obvious that the North Central region consists of Minnesota, Wisconsin, Michigan, Iowa, Illinois, Indiana, Ohio, Missouri, and Kentucky.   In Figure 4.21, the Southeast region is defined to contain Tennessee, North Carolina, South Carolina, Georgia, Alabama, Mississippi, Louisiana, and Florida. And Figure 4.22 represents the Northeast region as Virginia, West Virginia, Maryland, Delaware, Pennsylvania, New Jersey, New York, Connecticut, Rhode Island, Massachusetts, Vermont, New Hampshire, and Maine.

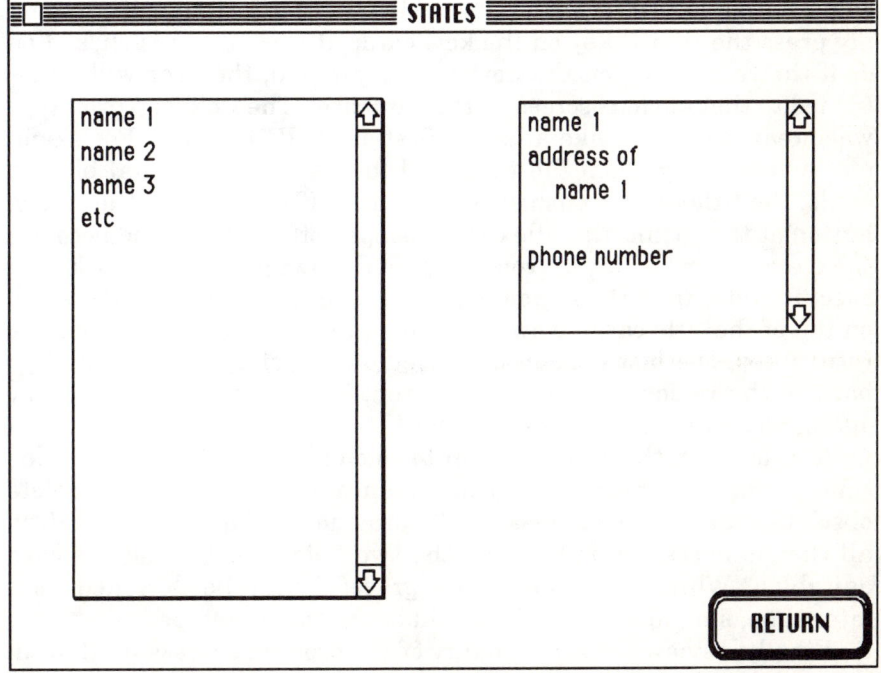

**Figure 4.23** The Address card for the Rolomap prototype.

Each of these cards is identical in functionality to the first two we examined.   You can click on the specific state which contains the point of contact you wish to have more information on.   The same button highlighting scheme is also used on this card to allow the user to gracefully recover from a misplaced mouse click.

Now that the regional cards have been completely described, let's move on to the next level. If you do click on a particular state you will be presented with the card shown in Figure 4.23. This card contains two fields. The list on the left of the card contains the names of the individuals in the state you selected that are entered in the database. As a default, the top name will be highlighted. If you click on any name in the list, the address and phone number corresponding to that person will be displayed in the field on the right. Notice that for the purpose of the prototype there are no actual names, addresses, or phone numbers in either of the lists.

You may have noticed the bold outlined return button on every screen but the title card. First, the the bold outline around the button is a standard convention for a default button. This means that the same action will occur whether you click on the button or if you simply press the return key on the keyboard. If this button is clicked on or if the return key on the keyboard is pressed, the user will be returned to the previous screen in the database. The Rolomap prototype was created to work like a last-in first-out (LIFO) stack. For example, when you go from the title card to one of the regional blowup cards, the title card is pushed onto a stack. If you click on the return button at that point, the title card is popped off the stack and becomes the current card. But, if, from a regional blowup card, you click on a specific state, then the regional blowup card is pushed onto the stack on top of the title card. Now, from the Address card, if you press the return key, the last card in is popped off the stack and you will go back to the regional blowup card. And, if you press the return key again, you will return to the title card.

At this point, the only thing left to do on the prototype is to provide some means by which to enter new names and addresses and delete obsolete names and addresses. To provide the basic functionality, all that is necessary is to make the two fields on the Address card editable. While something more graceful may be designed at a later time, simple editable fields will do for the prototype.

Finally, review the functionality of the prototype to assure that all the requirements are met. This done, the specification phase for Rolomap is complete and you are ready to move on to the design phase.

# 5

# Design and Implementation

In Chapter 4, the requirements and specifications phases of the Parallel method were examined. Then, after the examination, we applied the concepts presented to two different applications. The requirements for both of the applications were obtained in a different manner. For the Junior Executive Hierarchy Trainer (JEHT), a job training example, there was a specified customer for the software. However, for the Rolomap application, a database example, there was no customer. Different methods were explored both for obtaining requirements and developing specifications. The final result of the example section of Chapter 4 were working prototypes for both examples which directly reflected the intent of the requirements document.

Now, we will move on to the next phases of the Parallel method: design and implementation. Actually, in the Parallel method, the design phase consists of a preparation phase followed by two parallel phases. The preparation phase breaks the application into two parts: the user interface, and the remainder of the software. From there, the user interface goes to the modify user interface phase while the rest of the software goes through the standard design phase. Once

the design is completed, it is implemented in whatever programming language is selected by the developer.

This chapter will completely examine the multifaceted design
phase and the implementation phase of the Parallel method. Then,
both applications, JEHT and Rolomap, will be used to clarify the
presented concepts. The final result of this chapter, for the examples, will be completely designed and implemented software that is
ready to be integrated and tested as a unit.

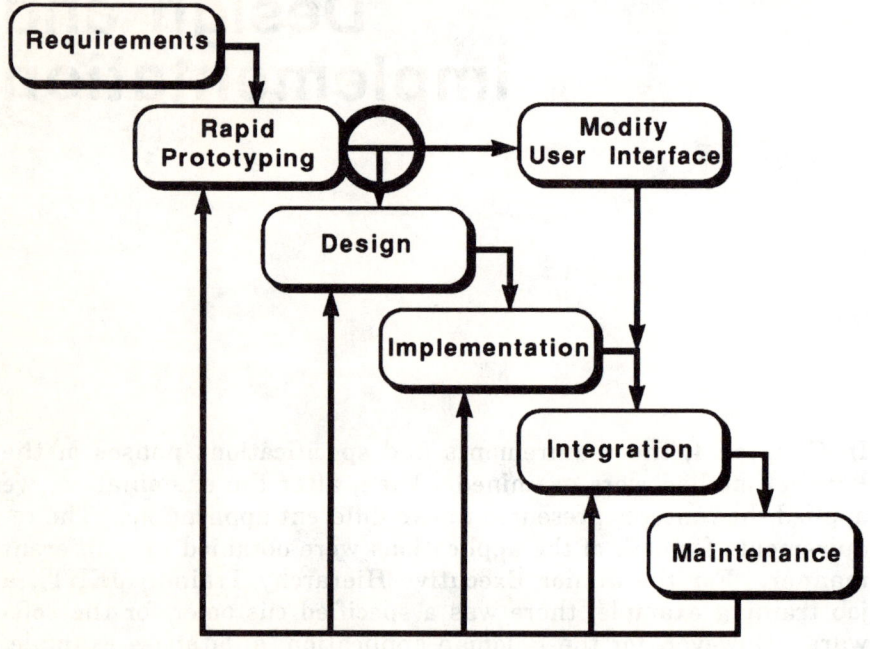

**Figure 5.1** The preparation phase of the Parallel method occurs at the
intersection where the process becomes parallel.

## DESIGN WITH THE PARALLEL METHOD

What is normally considered the design phase is actually three
distinct sub-phases in the Parallel method. First, there is a preparation phase which is followed by the parallel phases, design and modify user interface.

## Preparation

The preparation sub-phase of the Parallel method occurs at the point where the parallel branches begin (see Figure 5.1). The purpose of this sub-phase is to break the user interface cleanly from the rest of the application. Once this is accomplished, we can continue the development in a parallel fashion. The meat of the application will go through a standard design phase and the user interface will be modified to reflect good coding style and a fancier look.

The key to breaking the application apart is knowing where to draw the user interface line. How can you tell the difference between user interface and regular code? For Hypermedia, the following rules usually apply:

1. If the action is related to navigation through the information, then it is user interface.
2. If there are buttons not related to navigation, then the buttons themselves are user interface and the code which performs the action is regular code.
3. If the action involves entering new information or deleting obsolete information, then the object which initiates the action is user interface and the code to perform the action is regular code.
4. For menus, the menu items are user interface and the code to perform the designated actions is regular code.

It is extremely important to use common sense when applying these rules. An action may be regular code by the rules. But, if you know that the code to implement the action is trivial, then classify it as user interface. There is no point in going through a formal design process for a trivial piece of code. One of the main reasons for the parallel branch is to save time and effort in the development process. But, it will only work well if you give it a chance.

Once you have established which parts of the application are user interface and which parts are regular code, you must formalize an interface scheme between the two parts. Every piece of code (outside of initialization) is launched by something in the user interface. Each action that is not user interface must be formally (i.e., in writing) identified and specified. A sample of this identification is:

For each action list:

1. Launching user interface item
2. Description of required action
3. Calling protocol

　　4.　Parameters
　　5.　Return values

　　It is imperative that you do not change anything about these items once they are established. If the specifications are adhered to, the integration phase will go smoothly. If they are not maintained, then much time will be wasted during integration as the changed functions and subroutines will not work.

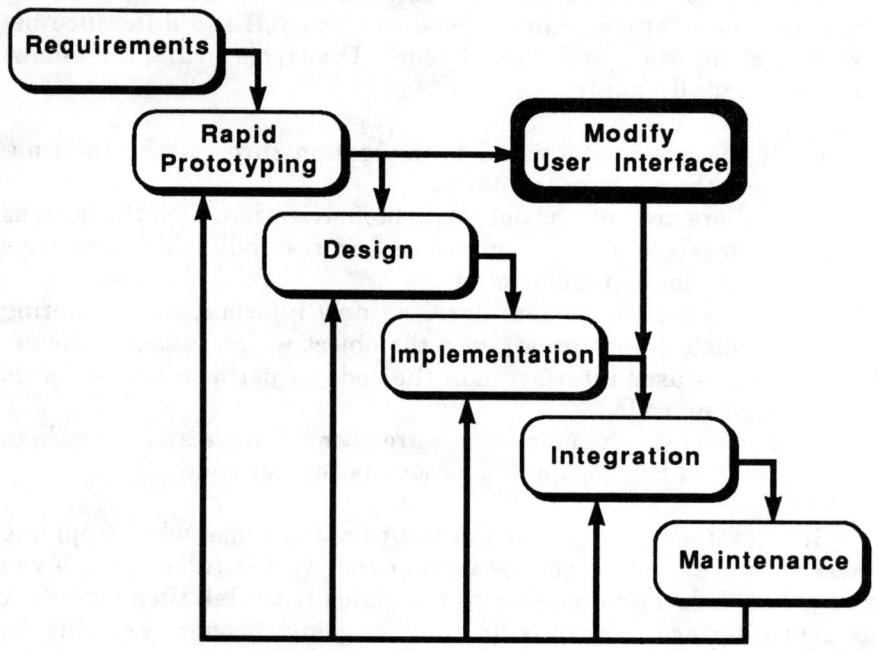

**Figure 5.2** The modify user interface phase of the Parallel method.

　　Once all of the actions which are not designated user interface are formally specified, you are ready to move on to the design and modify user interface phases. As you can see from Figure 5.1, the design and modify user interface phases can be accomplished in parallel. In fact, if you have a team working on the project, you can literally work in parallel. But, since this book is serial in nature, the Modify User Interface phase will be discussed first.

**Modify User Interface**

The modify user interface phase, as illustrated in Figure 5.2, is what gives the Parallel method its name. While the overall process will save time in development, there can be a great deal of time savings if there is a team working on the software. The team can be split up and the software can be literally developed in parallel. The purpose of the modify user interface phase is to take the user interface, which has already been approved by the users, and fine tune it to meet good programming standards. Also, during this phase, you can develop creative buttons and integrate colors and patterns to make the application more aesthetically pleasing. While these items are certainly not mandatory, they can sometimes make your users feel more comfortable using the application.

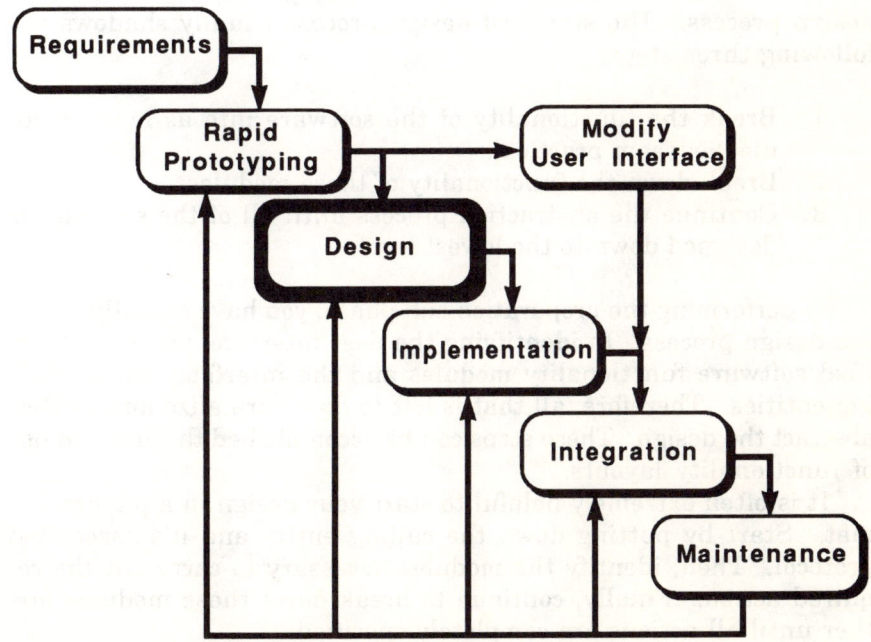

**Figure 5.3** The design phase of the Parallel method.

Absolute care must be taken to assure that the interfaces which were established in the preparation sub-phase, are maintained in the modify user interface phase. If these interfaces are not maintained, you will lose all the time you saved in the previous phases. Problems associated with not maintaining the interfaces will surface during the integration phase. Navigation testing should take place before moving on to the integration phase. If the application is small enough, test every navigation path. If this is not feasible then select typical navigation paths that are representative of all types of navigation present in the application and test them thoroughly. Once this testing has been accomplished, you are ready to go on to the integration phase.

## Design

The next phase of the Parallel method to consider is the design phase (see Figure 5.3). In this phase, the part of the application that was not identified as part of the user interface undergoes a typical software design process. The standard design process usually shadows the following three steps:

1. Break the functionality of the software into as many modules as seem practical.
2. Break down the functionality of those modules.
3. Continue the abstraction process until all of the software is designed down to the lowest level.

By performing the preparation sub-phase, you have actually begun the design process. In identifying the user interface, you have specified software functionality modules and the interfaces to the calling entities. Therefore, all that is left to do is formalize and further abstract the design. These steps can be accomplished through the use of functionality layouts.

It is often extremely helpful to start your design in a picture format. Start by putting down the calling entity and it's associated protocol. Then, identify the modules necessary to carry out the required action. Finally, continue to break down these modules further until all actions are completely specified.

Figure 5.4 illustrates an example of that type of functionality breakdown. At the top level, identify the routine, what entity calls it, and the calling protocol. Then, if necessary, break down the routine into as many steps as you deem necessary. In this case, routine X consists of Steps 1, 2, and 3. Step 1 is broken down into three sub-steps, two of which are sufficiently broken down. The first of the three sub-steps is itself made up of two distinct sub-steps. Step 2 is made up of two sub-steps that are both broken down sufficiently.

And finally, Step 3 only has one sub-step which is made up of two distinct parts.

Once you have completed the functionality diagrams for each of the required actions, you are ready to write pseudocode. Pseudocode is essentially English formatted as you would format a computer program.

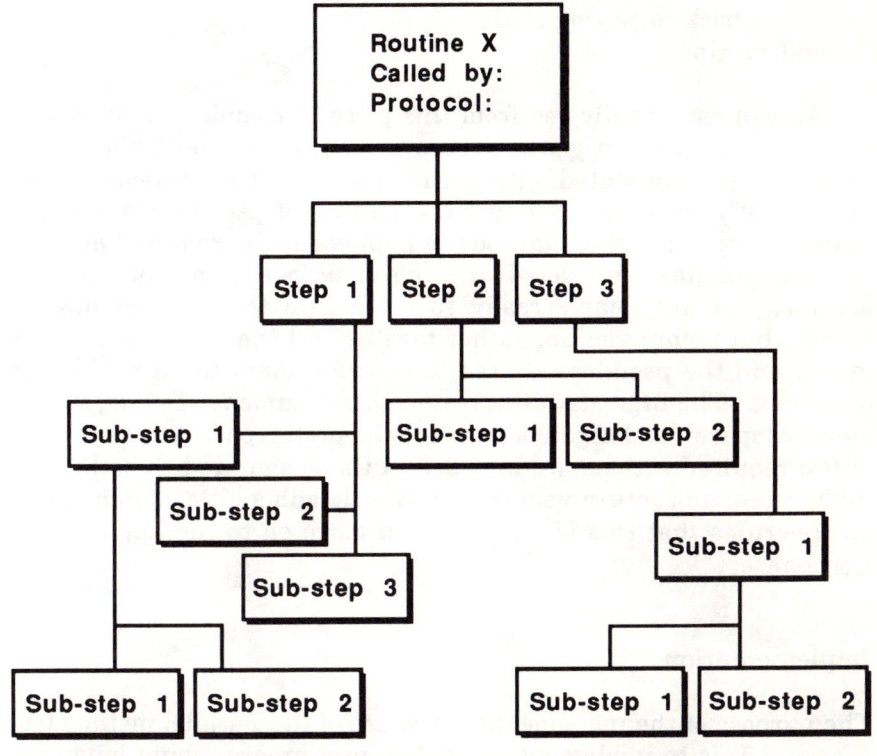

**Figure 5.4** An example functionality layout for one called routine.

The following is a short example of pseudocode:

when the SAVE AS option is selected
    show the SAVE AS dialog box

    on return

        check to see if the specified file already exists
        if it does then

```
            check to see if the user want to replace it
            if the user does then
                    save the file to disk
            end if
        end if

    end return

    go back to editing mode
end routine
```

As you can readily see from this piece of pseudocode, it is very easy to identify exactly what you are required to do. This pseudo code will be translated into actual code in the implementation phase. Of course, in most cases, each line of pseudocode may require several lines of actual code to implement the required action.

Once you have completed writing pseudocode for all the specified actions, you are nearly ready to move into the implementation phase. but before you do, gather together all the functionality diagrams and the pseudocode used to describe them to form a design document. The final step is to review this document. During the review, compare the design document to the prototype to assure that all of the required actions are included in the design and that the calling protocol and return values were strictly adhered to. After the review verifies that this is true, you can move on to the implementation phase.

## Implementation

The purpose of the implementation phase of the Parallel method (see Figure 5.5) is to implement the design in a programming language. If the design has been properly done, this is a relatively simple process. You just take the pseudocode and write actual code to perform the required statements. Often, it will take several lines of code to implement one line of pseudocode.

If your code is to be readable, understandable, and maintainable, you should use good coding style. There are eight guidelines to developing good code. The guidelines are:

1.  Always aim for simplicity and clarity.
2.  Use meaningful variable names.
3.  Use consistent formatting conventions.
4.  Use short headers to describe each module.
5.  Establish commenting conventions.

6. Simplify your statement construction and program layout.
7. Code all I/O for ease of data transfer and error checking.
8. Strive for efficient code.

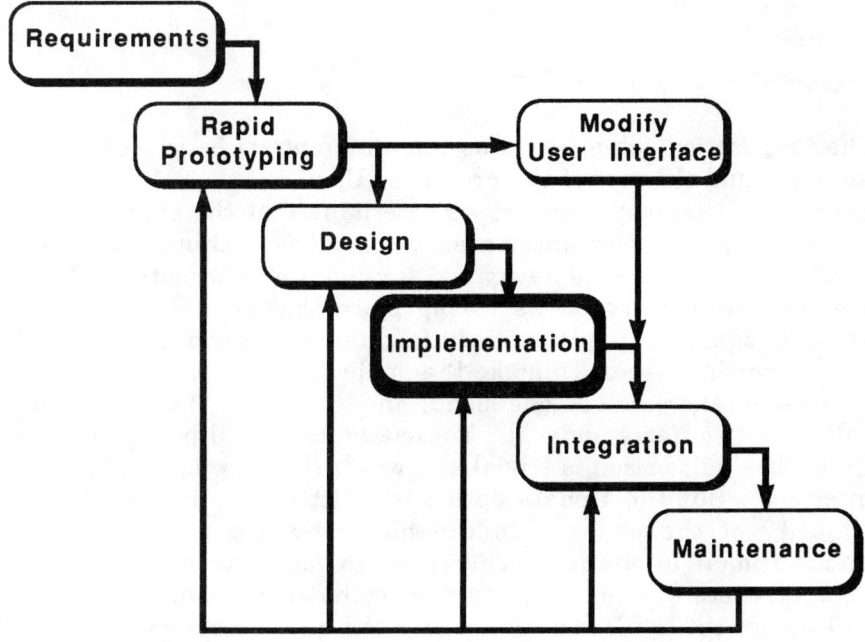

**Figure 5.5** The implemetation phase of the Parallel method.

Once the functionality of the pseudocode has been translated into a programming language, some form of unit testing should be done. This testing should verify that there are no syntax errors and that the code appears to perform the intent of the design. Absolute care should be taken to assure that the interfaces to the user interface are maintained. After unit testing, the code is ready to be integrated with the user interface.

## EXAMPLES

In this part of the chapter, the two sample applications will be taken through the Preparation sub-phase and the design, implementation, and modify user interface phases of the Parallel method. In explanation of the Parallel method, these phases will be illustrated as much as possible.

## EXAMPLE 1 – Junior Executive Hierarchy Trainer (JEHT)

### Preparation

The Preparation sub-phase is used to differentiate between the user interface and the rest of the program. Upon analysis of the Junior Executive Hierarchy Trainer, we determine that the application is almost entirely user interface. Nearly everything about the application is related to navigation through the information. There are few buttons or actions taking place that require significant amounts of code to implement. In fact, there is only one item which is not user interface. To make the application as easy to maintain as possible, there will be one menu: the File menu. This File menu will have two items under it. These two items will be Update and Quit. The quit option is trivial and will be kept as part of the user interface. But the Update option is a little more involved. The majority of the changes to the hierarchy are expected to be informational in nature. Therefore, to facilitate ease of maintenance, there will be an Update file for the JEHT. This Update file will be an ASCII file containing only the data necessary to update the information fields in the Personnel window. With this in place, when a common change occurs to the information field (such as age, years with the company, marital status, etc.), the maintainer will not have to change the application. He or she will only have to place the information into a file in the proper format and distribute a simple ASCII file to the users either on a floppy disk or over the network. Of course, if a physical change of personnel occurs, the maintainer will have to make changes to the application. A complete description of the Update menu option is as follows:

1. **Launching user interface item**
   Menu:      File
   Item:      Update
2. **Description of required action**
   Determine where the Update file is located and update the appropriate fields with the information in the file.
3. **Calling protocol**
   UPDATE
4. **Parameters**
   None

5. **Return values**
   None

## Modify User Interface

Since it was determined that nearly the entire application is user interface, we will need to assure that nothing is left out during the modify user interface phase. To accomplish this, use the following list:

1. Initialize
   create menu items
   install menu items
   other miscellaneous initialization
2. Clean up
   remove any unnecessary hardcodings
   optimize performance where possible
   put in the actual information
   enhance the look, if desired
3. Test
   test all navigation possibilities if feasible
   if not then test an appropriate sample

Concerning the first item, one menu was created and two were installed. The Apple menu did not have to be created. It is a standard Macintosh convention and is identified from within Super-Card as the "apple" menu. As shown in Figure 5.6, the Apple menu gives the user access to all loaded desk accessories while the application is running. The File menu, also shown in Figure 5.6, is the one created for the JEHT application. It contains the Update and Quit menu items. Each of these menu items has its own script. A script is a program written in the SuperTalk programming language.

The SuperTalk language is very similar to English and allows manipulation of all objects and data within the SuperCard environment. Generally, there is one script attached to each action item. However, a single script can be launched by more than one object if the author of the application desires. This is commonly done when the author has several buttons, or other objects, that perform the same operation on slightly different data. The particular data can be passed to a common script to have the operation performed upon it. The Script for the Update menu item is as follows:

```
on itemSelect
```

```
        UPDATE
    end itemSelect

    on UPDATE

    end UPDATE
```

The way it is written now, nothing will happen when the Update item is selected.  But, after the Update action finishes with the design and implementation phases, the Update script will be placed in between the "on Update" and the "end Update" in the Update menu item script.

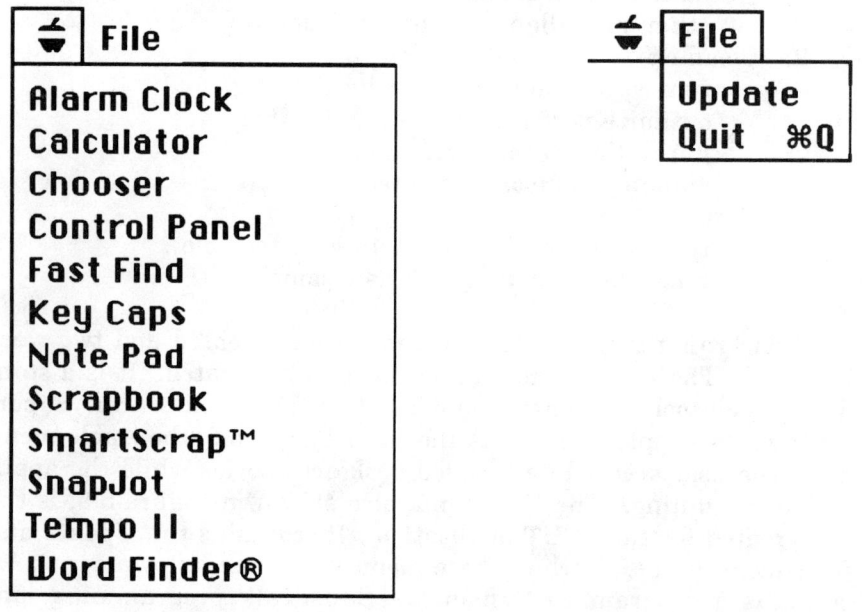

**Figure 5.6** The Apple and File menus of the JEHT application.

The Quit menu item will be explained in a moment.  First let's discuss the SuperCard hierarchy.  SuperCard is oriented toward objects and events.  There are nine objects in SuperCard:  menus, menu items, buttons, fields, graphics, cards, backgrounds, windows, and projects.  These objects and their relative positions in the SuperCard hierarchy are shown in Figure 5.7.

Menus and menu items generate an event when they are selected. Generally, scripts to handle menu events are attached to the menu item. Buttons, fields, and graphics generate events when they are clicked on. Again, most of the time scripts to handle events generated by these objects are handled at the object level. However, if there are events that are common to several low-level objects, the script can be placed at the card level. If there is a script common to several, but not all, of the cards in a window, then the script could be placed in a background common to the appropriate cards. If the script is common to all cards within a window, then it can be located in the window script. And finally, if the script is common throughout the entire project, it can be placed in the project script.

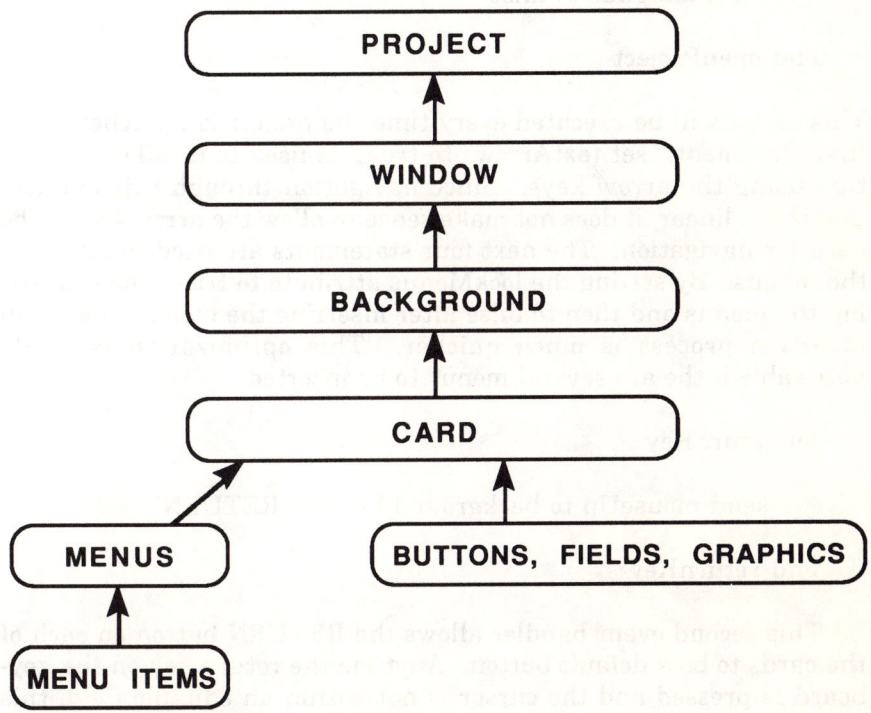

**Figure 5.7** The SuperCard hierarchy of objects.

If an event is generated at any level of the SuperCard hierarchy and there is no event handler at that level, then the event is passed on to the next higher level. This continues until either an event handler is found for the event or it is determined that there is no event handler.

Upon finishing the initialization and clean up step of the list, you will find that you have four unique event handlers in the project script. The first of the four handles the openProject event as follows:

```
on openProject

    set textArrows to true

    set lockMenus to true
    insert menu "apple"
    insert menu "File"
    set lockMenus to false

end openProject
```

This script will be executed every time the project is launched. The first statement, "set textArrows to true," is used to disallow navigation using the arrow keys. Since navigation through this application is not linear, it does not make sense to allow the arrow keys to be used for navigation. The next four statements are used to establish the menus. By setting the lockMenus attribute to true before inserting the menus and then to false after inserting the menus, the menu insertion process is much quicker. This optimization is easily noticeable if the are several menus to be inserted.

```
on returnKey

    send mouseUp to background button "RETURN"

end returnKey
```

This second event handler allows the RETURN button on each of the cards to be a default button. Anytime the return key on the keyboard is pressed and the cursor is not within an editable field, this handler will execute. The script has the effect of simulating a mouse button release while the cursor is over the RETURN button.

```
on closeBox

    close all windows

end closeBox
```

This third event handler closes all the windows within the project. This has the effect of quitting the application. This handler could execute after either one of two events takes place. The first potential event is the action of clicking on the close box of a window. The other event is selecting the Quit menu item from the File menu. The Quit menu item script simply sends the event "closeBox" to the project script to execute the handler.

```
on mouseUp

    put the name of the target into LONG_TARGET_NAME

    if word 1 to 2 of LONG_TARGET_NAME = "card button"
    then

        push card
        put the short name of the target into CARD_NAME
        go card CARD_NAME of window "PERSONNEL"

    else if word 2 of LONG_TARGET_NAME = "field" then

        put the short name of this card into THE_SOUND
        play THE_SOUND

    end if

end mouseUp
```

This is the final event handler in the project script. It is used to eliminate hard coding and to reduce redundancy in coding. The RETURN button on each card has it's own event handler. Therefore, this script will not execute upon clicking on the RETURN button. This one script handles nearly all the navigation within the application. The first two lines establish that a card button was clicked on. If so, then the present card is pushed onto the stack and the user is sent to the card with the same name as the button which was clicked upon. If the clicked on object was a graphics field, then the sound with the same name as the field is played.

All that is left to accomplish now is the testing of the user interface. With an application as small as JEHT, it is feasible to test every navigation path in a reasonable amount of time. Once this is done, wait for the rest of the application to finish the design and implementation phases.

## Design

In the Preparation sub-phase we determined that there was only one item that needed to go through the design phase: the Update menu item. There are two things to consider in the design of the Update menu item. These things are the Update software and the Update file.

The Update file will take on the following format:

```
***BEGIN***
Button you would click on to get to the changed card

    this is the new information on the specified person
    this is the new information on the specified person
    this is the new information on the specified person
***NEXT***
Button you would click on to get to the changed card

    this is the new information on the next person
    this is the new information on the next person
    this is the new information on the next person
    this is the new information on the next person
***NEXT***
Button you would click on to get to the changed card

    this is the new information on the next person
    this is the new information on the next person
    this is the new information on the next person
***END***
```

There is nothing mandatory about this particular format. It was chosen because it provides all the data needed to update single or multiple information fields within the application. If there was only one information field to update, the file would contain the following:

```
***BEGIN***
Button you would click on to get to the changed card
this is the new information on the specified person
this is the new information on the specified person
this is the new information on the specified person
***END***
```

For the Update file, the "***NEXT***" indicates that there is another item to update and the "***END***" indicates that there are no more items in the file.

Now, we must consider the software to accomplish the update. The functionality diagram, in this case, contains only one step:  update the application.  Since the functionality diagram is so simple, there is no point in formally drawing it out.  We will move on to write the pseudocode.  The pseudocode for the Update action is as follows:

UPDATE

    Get the location of the Update file
    Put the file contents into a local field
    Repeat until all fields are updated
        Put information into the correct fields
    end Repeat

    end UPDATE

Notice that the pseudocode completely describes the actions that must take place for the Update action to occur.  However, it does not go into the specifics of how the action should be implemented.  Each of the pseudocode lines may translate into one or several lines of actual code.  The specific details of the code will be taken care of in the Implementation phase.  For now, it is only important to identify all of the actions that must occur and to maintain the calling protocol established in the preparation sub-phase.

Completion of the pseudo-code indicates that the design phase is over.  The Update routine is now ready to go on to the implementation phase.


**Implementation**

What follows is the actual SuperCard script used to implement the pseudocode.  The coding guidelines established earlier were followed whenever possible.  The number placed in front of each code segment is not part of the SuperCard script.  They were placed in order to make it easy to reference the segments in explanation of the code.

    on UPDATE

1   --   Get the location of the Update file from the user

```
2        put getFile("Select the Update File") into FILE_NAME

3        if FILE_NAME is empty then
             exit UPDATE
         end if

--    Put the file contents into a local field

4        set the cursor to "watch"
         set the lockScreen to true

5        open file FILE_NAME
         read from file FILE_NAME for 65000
         close file FILE_NAME

6        put it into card field "TEMP FIELD" of card "title" of
             window  "JEHT"

7        put lineOffset("***BEGIN***", card field "TEMP FIELD"
             of card "title" of window "JEHT") into THE_LINE

8        if THE_LINE is zero then
             exit UPDATE
         end if

9        delete line THE_LINE of card field "TEMP FIELD" of card
             "title" of window "JEHT"

--    Repeat until all fields are updated
--        Put information into the correct fields
--    end Repeat

10       put "FALSE" into LAST_UPDATE
         repeat while LAST_UPDATE = "FALSE"

11           put lineOffset("***NEXT***", card field "TEMP
                 FIELD" of card "title" of window "JEHT") into
                     THE_LINE

12           if THE_LINE is zero then
                 put lineOffset("***END***", card field "TEMP
                     FIELD" of card "title" of window "JEHT") into
                         THE_LINE
                 put "TRUE" into LAST_UPDATE
             end if
```

13          put line 1 of card field "TEMP FIELD" of card "title" of
            window "JEHT" into THE_CARD

14          put line 3 to THE_LINE - 1 of card field "TEMP FIELD"
            of card "title" of window "JEHT" into background
            field "INFORMATION" of card THE_CARD of
            window "PERSONNEL"

15          delete line 1 to THE_LINE of card field "TEMP FIELD"
            of card "title" of window "JEHT"

        end repeat

16      set the lockScreen to false
        set the cursor to "hand"

    end UPDATE

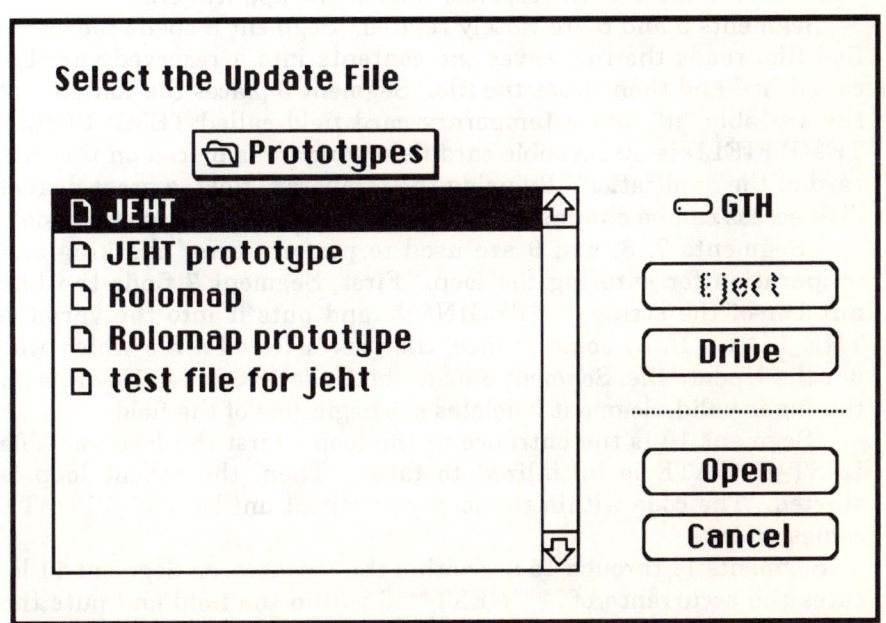

**Figure 5.8** The getFile dialog box.

Segment 1 illustrates a common commenting convention. The pseudocode itself is used to comment the code. Most of the time, this is sufficient to explain the purpose of the following code. But, if you use a programming construct that may be difficult for someone to understand, you should take a little more time to explain what you are doing.

Segment 2 puts the dialog box shown in Figure 5.8 on the screen for user input. The user simply locates the file and opens it. If the user selects a file, the path to that file is stored in the variable FILE_NAME. However, if the user chooses to click on the Cancel button, then nothing will be returned. Segment 3 provides the utility behind the cancel button on the dialog box. If FILE_NAME comes back empty, then the Update routine is exited.

Segment 4 accomplishes two things. First, the cursor is replaced by a watch icon. This tells the users that something is going on in the background and prevents them from becoming concerned when they click on something and nothing happens. The second line keeps the screen from being updated. This will allow the CPU to concentrate solely on the tasks to follow and not be concerned with screen update. Locking the screen from updates in this manner will improve the overall response time of the application.

Segments 5 and 6 are closely related. Segment 5 opens the specified file, reads the file, saves the contents into a reserved variable called "it," and then closes the file. Segment 6 places the contents of the variable "it" into a temporary card field called TEMP FIELD. TEMP FIELD is an invisible card field which was placed on the title card of the application. By using the temporary field, a great deal of disk access can be eliminated to further speed up the response time.

Segments 7, 8, and 9 are used to perform error checking and preparation for entering the loop. First, Segment 7 finds the line number of the string "***BEGIN***" and puts it into the variable THE_LINE. If, by some chance, the user selected a file which was not the Update file, Segment 8 exits the Update routine. However, if the file is valid, Segment 9 deletes the begin line of the field.

Segment 10 is the entrance to the loop. First the loop variable LAST_UPDATE is initialized to false. Then, the repeat loop is started. The code within the loop will repeat until LAST_UPDATE comes up true.

Segments 11 through 15 are within the repeat loop. Segment 11 locates the occurrence of "***NEXT***" within the field and puts the line number into the variable THE_LINE. If that action returns a zero, then there must be only one field left to update and Segment 12 puts the line number of the string "***END***" into THE_LINE. Also, since this is the last field to update, the variable LAST_UPDATE is set to true. The first line of the temporary field is now the name of the card to be modified. This value is placed into the variable THE_CARD in Segment 13. Segment 14 places the information into the appropriate card field. And finally, Segment 15 deletes the newly updated information from the temporary field. If this was the last item to be updated, the loop will be exited. If not, then the next card to be updated is at the top of the temporary field ready to go through the loop once again.

Segment 16 is used to return control of the application to the user. First, lockScreen is set to false allowing the screen to once again be updated. And then, the cursor returns to the shape of a hand indicating that the software has completed the update task.

All that is left now is to perform some unit testing to assure that the code is syntactically correct and that it performs the required tasks. Once this is accomplished, we are ready for the integration phase.

### EXAMPLE 2 – Rolomap

### Preparation

Like in JEHT, the Preparation sub-phase is used to differentiate between the user interface and the rest of the program. Upon analysis of Rolomap, we determine that the application is almost entirely user interface. Nearly everything about the application is related to navigation through the information. There are few buttons or actions taking place that require significant amounts of code to implement. In fact, there are only two items which are not user interface. To make the application as easy to maintain as possible, there will be one menu: the File menu. This File menu will have three items under it. These three items will be Add, Delete, and Quit. The quit option is trivial and will be kept as part of the user interface. But the Add and Delete options are a little more involved. Complete descriptions of the Add and Delete menu options are as follows:

### Add

1. **Launching user interface item**
   Menu:     File
   Item:      Add
2. **Description of required action**
   Put up a dialog box for the user to enter the new information. Extract the information from the dialog box and update the appropriate fields.
3. **Calling protocol**
   ADD_DATA
4. **Parameters**

A global variable called CARD_NAME containing the name of the card into which the information is to be placed must be initialized before going to the dialog box.

5. **Return values**
   None

## Delete

1. **Launching user interface item**
   Menu:     File
   Item:      Delete
2. **Description of required action**
   If an item is selected, delete the item and the information associated with it.
3. **Calling protocol**
   DELETE_DATA
4. **Parameters**
   None
5. **Return values**
   None

## Modify User Interface

Since it was determined that nearly the entire application is user interface, we will need to assure that nothing is left out during the modify user interface phase. To accomplish this, make a list of things that must be taken care of. A sample list is as follows:

1. Initialize
   create menu items
   install menu items
   other miscellaneous initialization
2. Clean up
   remove any unnecessary hardcodings
   optimize performance where possible
   put in the actual information
   enhance the look, if desired
3. Test
   test all navigation possibilities if feasible
   if not then test an appropriate sample

Concerning the first item, one menu was created and two were installed. The Apple menu did not have to be created. It is a stan-

dard Macintosh convention and is identified from within Super-
Card as the "apple" menu. As shown in Figure 5.9, the Apple menu
gives the user access to all loaded desk accessories while the application is running. The File menu, also shown in Figure 5.9, is the
one created for the Rolomap application. It contains the Add, Delete,
and Quit menu items. Each of these menu items has its own script
as described in a previous section.

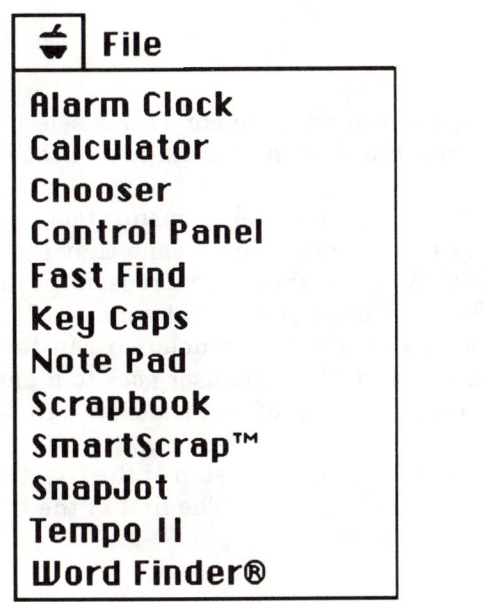
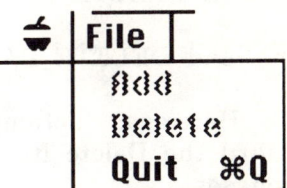

Figure 5.9  The Apple and File menus of the Rolomap application.

The Script for the Add menu item is as follows:

```
on itemSelect
      ADD_DATA
end itemSelect

on  ADD_DATA

end  ADD_DATA
```

The way it is written now, nothing will happen when the Add item
is selected. But, after the Add action finishes with the design and
implementation phases, the Add script will be placed in between the

"on ADD_DATA" and the "end ADD_DATA" in the Update menu
item script.

The script for the Delete menu item is as follows:

```
on itemSelect
    DELETE_DATA
end itemSelect

on DELETE_DATA

end DELETE_DATA
```

Here again, nothing will happen when the Delete item is selected
until the Delete item completes the design and implementation
phases.

You may have noticed that the Add and Delete menu items are
disabled as indicated by the gray shading. This means that these
items cannot be selected until they are enabled. The reason for doing this is common sense. The user must first select a piece of information to add or delete before the addition or deletion can take
place. The menu items will be enabled when the user goes to a part
of the application where a specific piece of information can be
selected.

Upon finishing the initialization and clean up step of the list, two
unique event handlers were found in the project. The first of the two
handles the openProject event as follows:

```
on openProject

    set textArrows to true

    set lockMenus to true
    insert menu "apple"
    insert menu "File"
    set lockMenus to false

    disable item "Add" of menu "File"
    disable item "Delete" of menu "File"

end openProject
```

This script will be executed every time the project is launched.
The first statement, "set textArrows to true," is used to disallow navigation using the arrow keys. Since navigation through this application is not linear, it does not make sense to allow the arrow keys to

be used for navigation. The next four statements are used to establish the menus. By setting the lockMenus attribute to true before inserting the menus and then to false after inserting the menus, the menu insertion process is much quicker. This optimization is easily noticeable if the are several menus to be inserted. The two inserted menu items are then disabled to disallow user selection until the appropriate time. The second event handler is as follows:

```
on returnKey

    send mouseUp to background button "RETURN"

end returnKey
```

This second event handler allows the RETURN button on each of the cards to be a default button. Anytime the return key on the keyboard is pressed and the cursor is not within an editable field, this handler will execute. The script has the effect of simulating a mouse button release while the cursor is over the RETURN button.

The next place to look for event handlers is in the window script of the graphics windows. That script is as follows:

```
on mouseUp

    push card
    put the name of the target into BUTTON_NAME

    if word 1 to 2 of BUTTON_NAME = "card button" then
        put the short name of the target into CARD_NAME
        go card CARD_NAME
    end if

end mouseUp
```

This script handles any mouse click on a card in the graphics windows. The current card is pushed onto the stack. Then, the name of the object that was clicked on was saved in a local variable. If the object that was clicked on was a button, then the user is sent to the card with the same name as the button.

The next location is the window script of the actual data window. There are two event handlers in the window script as follows:

```
on openWindow

    enable item "Add" of menu "File"
```

```
        enable item "Delete" of menu "File"

    end openWindow


    on closeWindow

        disable item "Add" of menu "File"
        disable item "Delete" of menu "File"

    end closeWindow
```

The openWindow script executes whenever the window is opened and the closeWindow script executes whenever the window is closed. These are the scripts which enable the Add and Delete menu items when the user enters the information window. When the user leaves the window, the items are again disabled.

The following script is located in the card script of the ADD ENTRY window.

```
    on returnKey

        send mouseUp to card button "OK"

    end returnKey
```

It was necessary to put this handler in the card script to intercept the returnKey system message before it got to the project script where the returnKey message is handled differently. Here, the handler allows the OK button to be a default button. If the user presses the return key on the keyboard, it will have the same result as if the OK button was clicked on.

Since the user will be entering the information, all that is left to accomplish is testing of the user interface. With an application as small as Rolomap, it is feasible to test every navigation path in a reasonable amount of time. Once this is done, we wait for the rest of the application to finish the Design and Implementation phases.


## Design

In the preparation sub-phase we determined that there were only two items that needed to go through the design phase: the Add and Delete menu items. We will attack these two items separately.

**Add**

There are two things to consider in the design of the Add menu item.
These things are the Add menu item software and the Add dialog
box.

The Add menu item software is the easiest, so we will start there.
We know that the software must pop up a dialog box for user entry.
And, that we must initialize a global variable to allow the user to
return to the correct location after entering the data.  The pseudocode
for the Add menu item is as follows:

on  ADD_DATA

      declare and initialize global variable
      pop up the dialog box

end  ADD_DATA

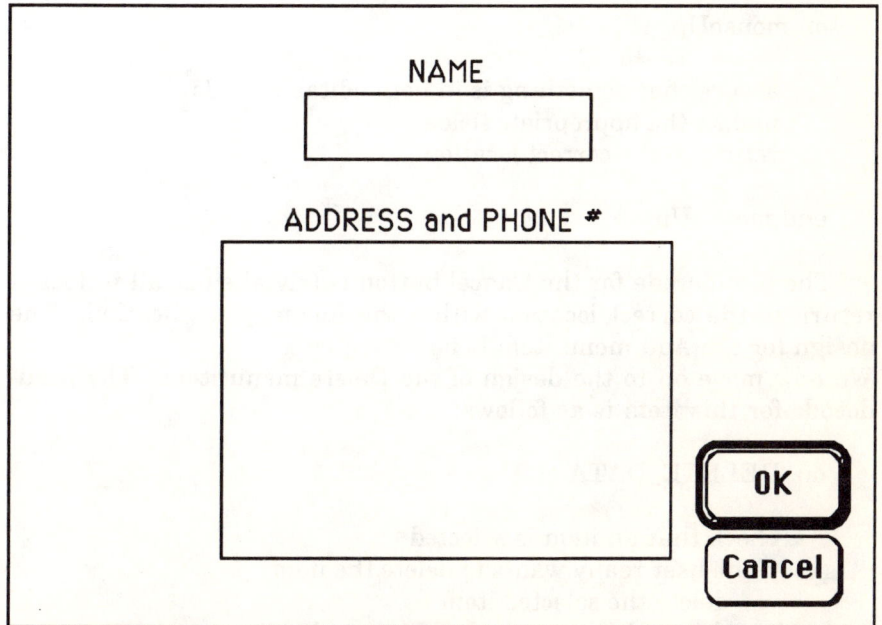

**Figure 5.10** The Add dialog box.

You may be wondering why the name was changed to
ADD_DATA.  Since "Add" is a SuperCard reserved word, the name

was changed to something else to avoid ambiguity. Notice that the pseudocode only describes the actions that must take place for the dialog box to pop up. The next thing to consider is the dialog box for the user to enter new information.

The dialog box for the Add menu item is shown in Figure 5.10. Before we continue, let me explain dialog boxes. A dialog box forces the user to accomplish a task. No other user inputs are allowed while the dialog box is in view. In this case, the user must select either OK to enter the data or Cancel to abandon the data. The fields under NAME and ADDRESS and PHONE # are editable fields in which the user will put, surprise, the name and address and phone number of the person to be added to the database. After the data is entered, the user has two options. If the information is correct and you wish to enter the information in the database, click on the OK button or press the Return key on the keyboard. If you changed your mind or selected the menu item by accident, click on the Cancel button and no changes will be made.

The pseudocode for the OK button is as follows:

    on mouseUp

        assure that something is in both editable fields
        update the appropriate fields
        return to the correct location

    end mouseUp

The pseudocode for the Cancel button is trivial since all it does is return to the correct location within the Rolomap application. The design for the Add menu item is now complete.

We now move on to the design of the Delete menu item. The pseudocode for this item is as follows:

    on DELETE_DATA

        check that an item is selected
        if the user really wants to delete the item
            delete the selected item
            delete the associated address and phone number
        end if

    end DELETE_DATA

Notice again that the pseudocode completely describes the actions that must take place for the Delete action to occur. However, it does not go into the specifics of how the action should be implemented. Each of the pseudocode lines may translate into one or several lines of actual code. The specific details of the code will be taken care of in the implementation phase. For now, it is only important to identify all of the actions that must occur and to maintain the calling protocol established in the preparation sub-phase. With the completion of the Delete design, we are ready to go on to the implementation phase.

### Implementation

What follows is the actual SuperCard script used to implement the pseudocode. The coding guidelines established earlier were followed whenever possible. There are actually three segments of code to implement: the ADD_DATA script, the script for the OK button on the ADD ENTRY card, and the DELETE_DATA script.

The script to implement ADD_DATA is as follows:

```
on ADD_DATA

    -- declare and initialize global variable
    global CARD_NAME
    put the short name of this card into CARD_NAME

    -- pop up the dialog box

    open window "ADD ENTRY"

end ADD_DATA
```

As a standard practice, it is helpful to use the pseudocode as a commenting device. The global variable CARD_NAME is declared and set to be the name of the current card so that the ADD ENTRY functions will know which card to modify and which card to return to when done. The open window statement pops up the dialog box in the foreground of the application. The user will now be forced to click on one of the two buttons on the Add card to return to the application.

For the OK button, a number was placed in front of each code segment. This number is not part of the SuperCard script. It was inserted to make it easy to reference the segments in explanation of the code. The script for the OK button is as follows:

```
      on mouseUp

      global CARD_NAME

         -- Assure that something is in both editable fields

1        put card field "NAME" into THE_NAME
         if THE_NAME is empty then

            close window "ADD ENTRY"
            exit mouseUp

         end if

2        put card field "ADDRESS" into THE_ADDRESS
         if THE_ADDRESS is empty then

            close window "ADD ENTRY"
            exit mouseUp
         end if

         -- Update the appropriate fields

3        put cr & THE_NAME after background field "NAME
            LIST" of card CARD_NAME of window "STATES"

4        put sortField(background field "NAME LIST" of card
            CARD_NAME of window "STATES") into background
            field "NAME LIST" of card CARD_NAME of
            window "STATES"

5        put cr & THE_NAME & cr & THE_ADDRESS after
            background field "ADDRESS LIST" of card
            CARD_NAME of window "STATES"

6        put cr & "******************" after background field
            "ADDRESS LIST" of card CARD_NAME of window
            "STATES"

         -- Return to the correct location

7        close window "ADD ENTRY"

      end mouseUp
```

The overall purpose of the OK button is to update the appropriate field in the application with the information contained in the dialog box. However, there are some other things that take place. First the global variable CARD_NAME is declared for this script. Then, in Segments 1 and 2, we make sure that there is something in the fields on the dialog box. If not, then simply close the window to return to the application.

In Segment 3, the name list is updated to include the information from the dialog box. And, in Segment 4, the name list of the appropriate card is sorted in alphabetical order. Segment 5 is used to update the address list with the corresponding address. And Segment 6 places a row of asterisks after the address as a designator of the end of that particular address. Finally, Segment 7 closes the window after the items are added and returns the user to the application.

Also for the DELETE_DATA script, a number was placed in front of each code segment. This number is not part of the SuperCard script. It was inserted to make it easy to reference the segments in explanation of the code. The script for DELETE_DATA is as follows:

```
on  DELETE_DATA

      -- check that an item is selected

1       put the hilitedLines of background field "NAME LIST" into
          LINE_NUM

      if LINE_NUM is not empty then

      -- if the user really wants to delete the item

2         answer "DELETE THIS ITEM?" with "YES" or "NO"

          if it is "NO" then
              exit itemSelect
          end if

      -- delete the selected item

3         put line LINE_NUM of background field "NAME LIST"
            into THE_NAME
          delete line LINE_NUM of background field "NAME
            LIST"
```

```
              --  delete the associated address and phone number

4             put lineOffset(THE_NAME, background field
              "ADDRESS LIST") into NAME_LINE

5             put lineOffset("*******", background field "ADDRESS
              LIST", NAME_LINE) into END_LINE

6             delete line NAME_LINE to NAME_LINE + END_LINE
              of background field "ADDRESS LIST"

       end if

    end DELETE_DATA
```

The overall purpose of the DELETE_DATA script is to delete the selected item and its corresponding data. To accomplish this task, we first check to see that an item is selected in Segment 1. If not, then the script is over. If an item is selected, then the user is asked if this is actually the item to delete. The dialog box for this code segment is shown in Figure 5.11. If it is not the correct item to delete, then the script is exited.

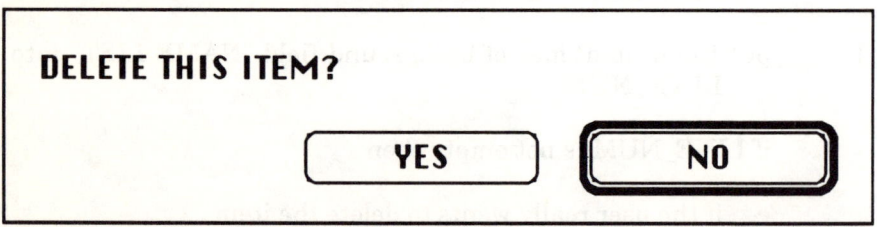

**Figure 5.11** A dialog box used to assure that the user wants the item deleted.

In Segment 3, the name is removed from the name list. Then, in Segments 4, 5, and 6, the associated address, phone number, and the row of asterisks used as an item delimiter are also removed.

All that is left now is to perform some unit testing to assure that the code is syntactically correct and that it appears to perform the required tasks. Once this is accomplished, we are ready for the integration phase.

# 6

# Integration and Maintenance

In Chapter 5, we examined the modify user interface, design, and implementation phases of the Parallel method. Then, after the examination, we continued the development of the two applications in order to apply the presented concepts. While the requirements for both of the applications were obtained in a different manner, the modify user interface, design, and implementation phases followed a similar track. Both applications, the Junior Executive Hierarchy Trainer (JEHT) and Rolomap, were determined to be almost entirely user interface. Because of that determination, the software development process was greatly speeded up. There was no necessity to redesign the user interface that was already approved by the user. So, only the portions of the applications that were software intensive went through the design and implementation phases. The rest of the applications went through the modify user interface phase where the user interface was cleaned up to reflect good coding standards. The final results of the example section of Chapter 5 was a fully developed user interface and fully implemented background code for both examples. All of the units have been tested to assure that they are syntactically correct and that they perform the required actions. Further testing will occur after the applications are integrated into one piece of software.

Now, we will move on to the final phases of the Parallel method: integration and maintenance. Actually, in the Parallel method, the integration phase envelops integration and testing. First, the two distinct parts of the application, user interface and background code, are brought together to form a single entity. Then two types of testing are performed on the newly formed application. Once the integration and testing are completed, the applications are ready to be fielded. The maintenance phase is used to introduce changes in the software throughout the rest of its life cycle.

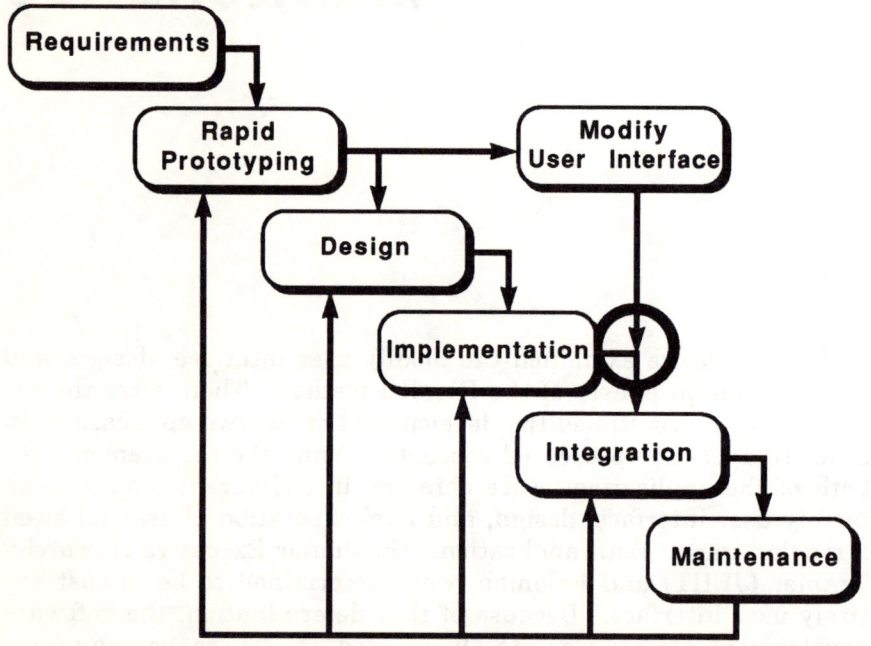

**Figure 6.1** The integration sub-phase of the Parallel method.

This chapter will completely examine the integration and maintenance phases of the Parallel method. Then, both applications, JEHT and Rolomap, will be used to clarify the presented concepts. The final result of this chapter, for the examples, will be complete Hypermedia applications that have been fielded and have a maintenance plan.

## INTEGRATION IN THE PARALLEL METHOD

The integration phase of the Parallel method of software development is actually two distinct sub-phases. First, there is a formal integration phase which is followed by a two step testing process to assure that the application is reasonably error-free and that it meets the user's requirements.

## INTEGRATION

As shown in Figure 6.1, the actual integration of the software takes place after the modify user interface and implementation phases are complete. The primary purpose of the integration phase is to reverse the preparation process that took place after the rapid prototyping phase. If you remember, the objective of the preparation sub-phase was to break the application into two separate entities: the user interface and the background code. In the integration phase, we will rejoin the user interface with the background code and run them on the target processor.

The key to the success of the integration phase is following the interface standards you established in the preparation sub-phase. These interface standards defined the interface between the user interface and the background code. As we defined it, the interface description should contain at least the following information:

1. Launching user interface item
   Description of which object within the application causes the code segment to execute.
2. Description of required action
   General description of what the code segment will do.
3. Calling protocol
   Formal description of how the code segment is called by the initiating object.
4. Parameters
   Description of any parameters that are passed to the code segment. The description should include any initialization or representative values for the parameters.
5. Return values
   Description of any value that is returned to the user interface by the background code.

Each of the background code segments that were to go through the formal design and implementation phases should have its associated interface description. If these interface descriptions were rigidly adhered to throughout the modify user interface, design, and implementation phases, the integration phase will go very smoothly.

If the interface standards have been maintained, the code assigned to the calling user interface object will look something like the following:

```
on SOME_EVENT

    PERFORM_THE_ACTION(User_Interface_Parameter)

end SOME_EVENT


on  PERFORM_THE_ACTION(Design_Parameter)

end  PERFORM_THE_ACTION
```

This code, of course, does nothing but simulate the code initiation and establish the interface description for the PERFORM-_THE_ACTION routine.  Once the background code completes the implementation phase, it should appear as follows:

```
on  PERFORM_THE_ACTION(Design_Parameter)

    Inserted here is the actual code that has gone through the
    design and implementation phases of the Parallel method.

end  PERFORM_THE_ACTION
```

The integration is as simple as taking the background code that has gone through the design and implementation phases and inserting it in the appropriate location.  After the insertion, sanity checks should be performed to assure that the actions that initiate the background code do not introduce errors in the calling process.  If they do, then the interface standards have not been followed and you will have to revisit a previous phase to correct the oversight.  Once you have completed the integration and the sanity checks have passed, you are ready to complete the formal integration phase.


## TESTING

Testing falls into the formal integration phase of the Parallel method illustrated in Figure 6.2.  Some basic unit testing has already been accomplished in the modify user interface and implementation phases.  But, this testing has only examined basic functionality and syntactical correctness.

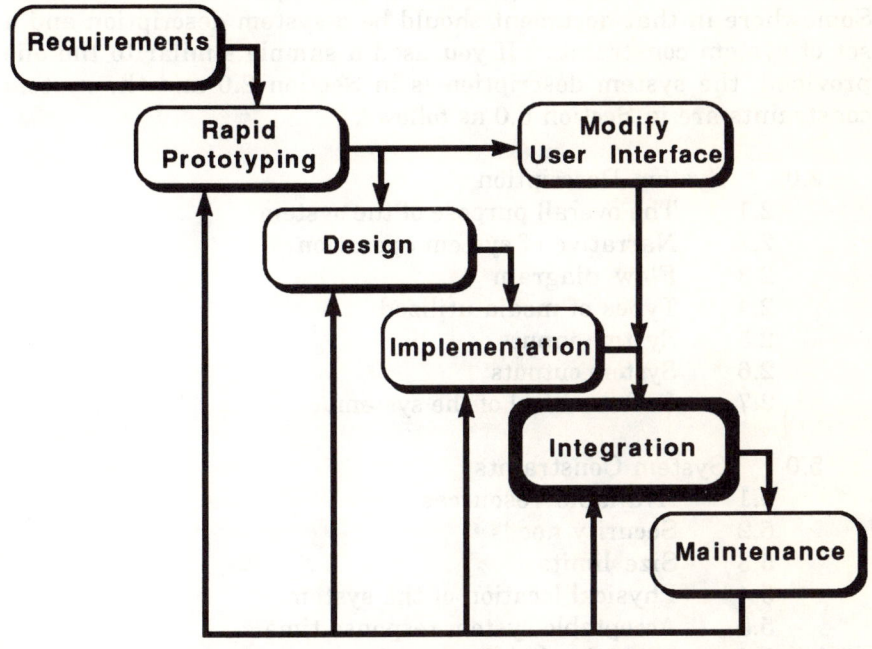

**Figure 6.2**  The integration phase of the Parallel method.

Obviously, there is a need to perform much more extensive testing on the integrated application before any product is fielded.  Some formal testing process should be defined to meet these needs.  There are many ways to break down the testing process.  However, for ease of understanding, you can break the testing process into two stages: requirements testing, and error testing.  These are sometimes referred to as black-box and white-box testing, respectively.  It is generally accepted that requirements testing should come first.  You have already established that the code is reasonably free of syntactical and navigational errors.  Therefore, you should move on to assure that all requirements on the software are met before going back to test for any obscure errors.

## Requirements Testing

The need for requirements testing is obvious. The software must perform at least what it is required of it. The easiest way to perform requirements testing is to go back to the requirements document. Somewhere in that document should be a system description and a set of system constraints. If you used a sample similar to the one provided, the system description is in Section 2.0 and the system constraints are in Section 5.0 as follows:

2.0     System Description
    2.1    The overall purpose of the system
    2.2    Narrative of system operation
    2.3    Flow diagram
    2.4    Types of media utilized
    2.5    System inputs
    2.6    System outputs
    2.7    Look and feel of the system

5.0     System Constraints
    5.1    Available resources
    5.2    Security needs
    5.3    Size limits
    5.4    Physical location of the system
    5.5    Acceptable system response time
    5.6    Special reliability needs
    5.7    Special power requirements
    5.8    Other

Most of the time, when performing requirements testing, you will not be modifying code or writing test drivers. Instead, the testing is usually by observation. From these two sections you can develop a testing document to assure that your tests cover all the appropriate areas. This testing document should cover all the essential areas from the requirements document without including unnecessary ones. A sample testing document could take on a format similar to the following:

2.0    System Description
    2.2    Narrative of system operation
           Observe the application to assure that it follows the narrative.
    2.3    Flow diagram
           Examine the application for compliance to the flow diagram.

2.5 System inputs
Were all the expected system inputs accounted for?
2.6 System outputs
Were all system outputs provided?
2.7 Look and feel of the system
Does the system look and feel as expected?

5.0 System constraints
5.2 Security needs
Are necessary security measures in place?
5.3 Size limits
Do the hardware and software fall within the required limits?
5.5 Acceptable system response time
Does the system respond as expected?
5.6 Special reliability needs
Are the reliability needs satisfied?
5.7 Special power requirements
If there are special power requirements, are provisions in place to handle them?
5.8 Other
Are all other constraints taken care of?

As you have noticed, the requirements document was followed exactly. The sections on the overall purpose of the system, types of media utilized, available resources, and physical location of the system were left out. All of these items are general information on the system and are not testable conditions. The sections that were left in, for the most part, are tested by observation. Exceptions to this rule are the system inputs, security needs, and reliability needs. Observing that all system inputs are accounted for is not enough. You must consider what will happen if one of the inputs is out of the expected range. If there are special security considerations, the security portion of the code should be physically tested. And, if there are special reliability needs, test drivers will need to be written to evaluate the reliability of the system.

Once you have completed the requirements testing and all found problems are fixed, you can be reasonably assured that the system performs as expected. Be particularly careful when fixing problems. Before making a change, evaluate it to assure that you will not be introducing any new errors into the system. All system requirements should now be satisfied and you are ready to move on to error testing.

## Error Testing

You are now sure that the software does what the customer expects it to do. But, you are unsure of the robustness of the software. Are the internal structures capable of withstanding long term use without failure? Error testing, if done properly, should give you that missing confidence in your software.

Proper error testing should utilize some testing principles. Four generally accepted testing principles are:

1.  Design your test cases with the object of uncovering errors in the software. Don't waste your time testing conditions that will never occur or code that is so simple it can't fail. Concentrate on searching for conditions and code structures where failures could occur.
2.  Design tests systematically. Don't rely solely on intuition, but don't rule it out either.
3.  The testing strategy starts at the module level.
4.  Record all test results and save all test cases for use during the maintenance phase.

Error-testing techniques assume that the developer is intimate with the software. To accomplish error testing, you should guarantee that all statements within a module are executed at least once, all logical decisions are evaluated on the true and false alternatives, all loops are executed at the boundaries and at nominal values, and all data structures are exercised to ensure their validity.

Loop testing is generally broken up into four cases: testing for simple loops, concatenated loops, nested loops, and unstructured loops. To adequately test simple loops, there are five steps to follow. The five steps (assume $n$ is the maximum loop counter value) are:

1.  Skip the loop entirely.
2.  Take one pass through the loop.
3.  Take two passes through the loop.
4.  Take $m$ passes through the loop, where $m < n$.
5.  Take $n-1$, $n$, and $n+1$ passes through the loop.

For nested loops, use the following four steps:

1.  Start at the innermost loop and set all other loops to minimum values.
2.  Perform the simple loop tests for the innermost loop.

3. Work outward, performing the simple loop test on the next loop while keeping outer loops at minimum values and inner loops at nominal values.
4. Continue until all loops are tested.

For concatenated loops there are two options. If the loops are independent of one another, use simple loop testing on each loop. If the loops are dependant upon one another, use the nested loop approach. Finally, for unstructured loops, you should redesign the loop using structured programming constructs.

The next step in the testing process is reviewing the testing strategy. When reviewing your strategy, the following questions should be answered:

1. Have test steps been identified and sequenced?
2. Are the tests traceable to the requirements?
3. Are major software functions demonstrated?
4. Is a test schedule defined?
5. Have available test resources and tools been identified?
6. Has a record keeping method been established?
7. Has work to develop test drivers been scheduled?
8. Have white- and black-box tests been specified?
9. Have all logic paths been tested?
10. Are all test cases listed with expected results?
11. Is error handling tested?
12. Are boundary values tested?
13. Are timing and performance tested?

Once the testing has been performed, you must fix whatever errors were encountered. Make sure that you carefully evaluate any changes you make to the software to fix errors. You could easily introduce more errors with your fix. Identify where you believe the change should occur, and then determine what other parts of the software will be affected by your proposed change. Once you are absolutely sure that your change will not have any adverse effects on other parts of the software, make the change and then retest the test that failed and any other tests that may have been affected by the change. Once all the errors have been fixed, you are ready to field the software.

## MAINTENANCE

The final phase of the first pass of the Parallel method to consider is the maintenance phase (see Figure 6.3). This is the first pass through the Parallel method because the software will remain in the maintenance phase throughout most of the rest of its life cycle. As you can see from the illustration in Figure 6.3, the maintenance phase acts like a router in directing the further development of the software to the appropriate phase of the Parallel method. There may be times in the life cycle of the software that will require some reworking of the product. The purpose of the maintenance phase is to first field the product and then, when changes need to be made, determine the appropriate phase of the Parallel method to initiate that change. There are three distinct stages in the maintenance phase. Those stages are: fielding the product, performing routine maintenance, and performing system upgrades. The flow of these stages is shown in Figure 6.4.

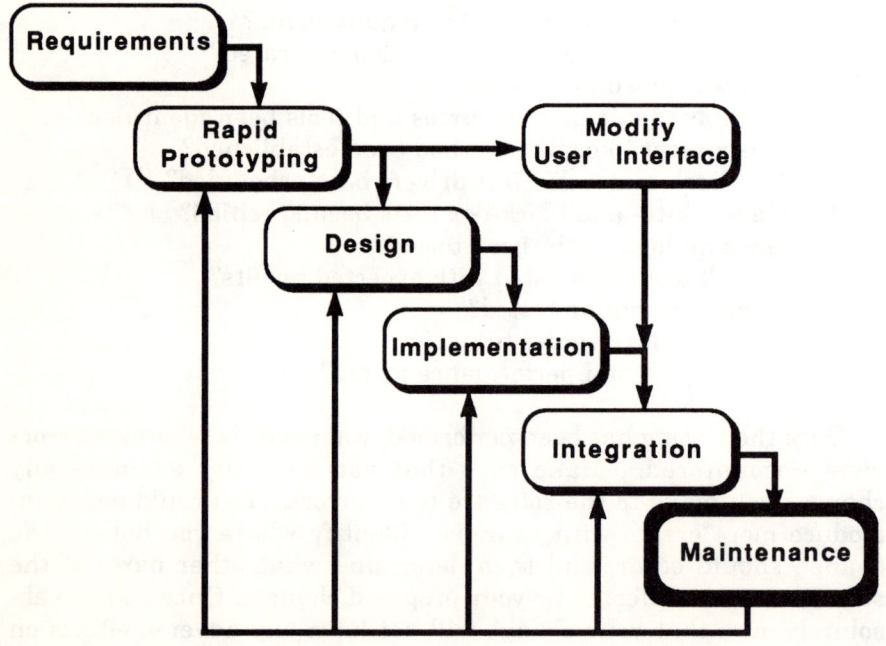

**Figure 6.3** The maintenance phase of the Parallel method.

### Fielding the Product

Fielding the product is the first stage of the maintenance phase. There are at least three keys to fielding a successful product:

maintaining a close relationship with your customer throughout the development, providing a means of customer feedback, and responding to that feedback in a timely manner.

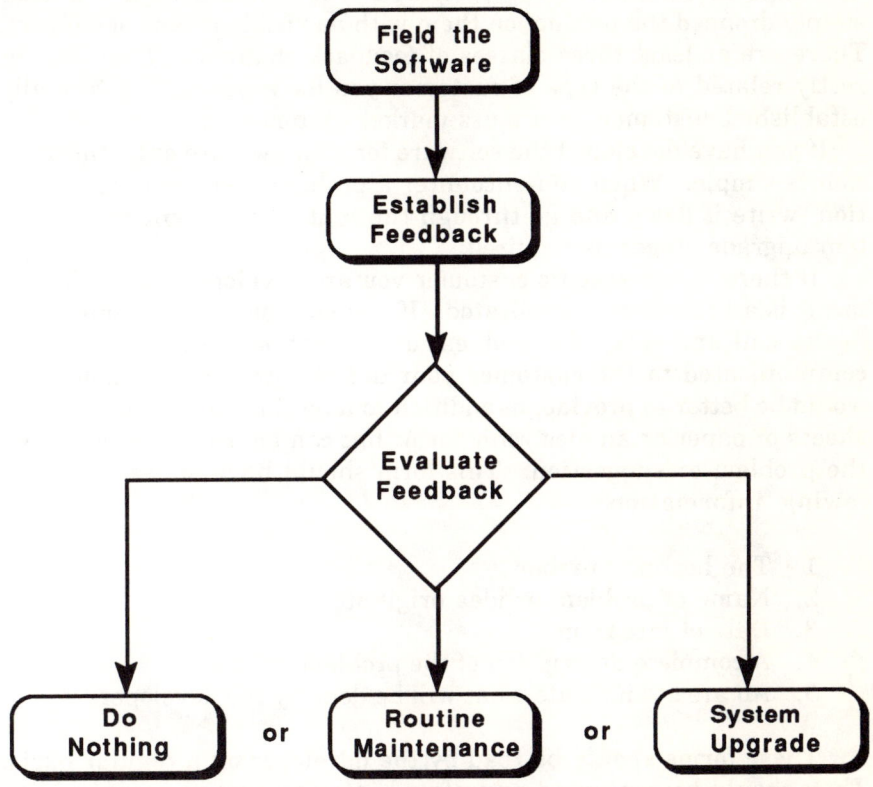

**Figure 6.4** The normal flow of the maintenance phase of the Parallel method.

Hopefully, you have established and maintained close ties with your customer throughout the development of the product. The Parallel method stresses continual communication with the potential users of the software. As a minimum, the customer should be included in a review at the end of every major phase of the Parallel method. This should eliminate any embarrassing surprises at delivery time. The actual delivery should be accompanied by any necessary training and some statement concerning the maintenance agreement. Both of these items were specified in the Requirements document, but they should be reemphasized upon delivery so that all parties understand how the software works and what their responsibilities are in the maintenance process.

Providing your customer with a method of giving you feedback on the software is vital to the success of your product. If you don't establish feedback channels, your customers will feel as though you have simply dropped the product on them with no visible means of support. There are at least three classes of feedback channels. They are directly related to the type of customer you have–yourself, a formally established customer, or a mass market customer.

If you have developed the software for your own use only, the solution is simple. When you encounter a problem or need a new function, write it down and go through the routine maintenance or system upgrade stages as required.

If there is one specific customer you are developing the software for, it is a little more complicated. If you only provide a phone number to call and relay the problem or suggestion, you will not have communicated to the customer your desire to receive feedback. It would be better to provide, in addition to a hotline for problems, a few sheets of paper or an electronic form that can be used to write down the problem or suggestion. This form should have at least the following information:

1. The hotline number
2. Name of problem or idea originator
3. Date of inception
4. A complete description of the problem or idea
5. An area to indicate what will be done by the developer

These forms should be read by the developer on a regular basis. They should be evaluated and placed into the routine maintenance or system upgrade process when appropriate. Whatever the resolution to the problem is, the developer should put it on the form and return it to the initiator. In doing this, you customers will know that their problems and ideas have been given consideration.

Finally, if you don't know your customers personally (mass market customers), all you can do is provide an address and a phone number and ask for feedback for feedback. Customers who genuinely like your product and want to see it improve will respond. When you receive feedback from customers in this way, be sure to acknowledge the feedback formally indicating what action you intend to take to resolve the problem or incorporate the idea. This will encourage further feedback and help you to make your software more desirable to a greater number of users. After the acknowledgement, classify the feedback as a routine maintenance action, a system upgrade action, or not feasible at this time and proceed to the appropriate stage.

## Routine Maintenance

Normally, the routine maintenance stage is used to fix errors discovered by the users of the software. These errors are identified through the use of the feedback process you set up in the first stage of the maintenance phase. Once a problem has been identified and classified as a routine maintenance action, you have to identify which phase of the Parallel method on which to accomplish the change. For routine maintenance, there are one of two places you will normally go: the Implementation phase or the rapid prototyping phase.

If the change is a fix of a problem in the background software or a new algorithm for accomplishing the same thing in a more efficient manner, you will usually go to the implementation phase. Once you have made the change, you will go to the integration phase and thoroughly test the application once again before fielding the new version.

If the problem is related to navigation through the application or to the user interface in general, you would go to the rapid prototyping phase. There, you will make the changes to the user interface, obtain some sort of approval from the user, and proceed to the modify user interface phase. There, you clean up the change and, again, move on to the Integration phase for complete testing before fielding the new version. If the reason for the change is to fix an error, be sure to modify your test procedures to look for the new class of errors. Most of the changes that fall into the routine maintenance category will follow one of these two paths. If the change is to complex for this, it should be considered a candidate for the system upgrade phase.

## System Upgrades

The primary use of the system upgrade phase is incorporating enhancements that add new functionality to the software. If the new functionality is simple enough, you may be able to reenter an intermediate phase. But, most of the time, a new software function should be treated as a new software requirement which you will take to the rapid prototyping phase. You would then proceed with the rest of the Parallel method as before culminating in a new release of the software upon reentering the maintenance phase.

## EXAMPLES

In this part of the chapter, the two sample applications will be taken completely through the integration and maintenance phases of the Parallel method. To help clarify the concepts that have been brought out, these phases will be illustrated as much as possible. The final result of these phases will be two complete applications that have been fielded and are poised to perform maintenance actions.

## EXAMPLE 1 – Junior Executive Hierarchy Trainer (JEHT)

In Chapter 5, the user interface and the background code of the JEHT application were brought completely through the modify user interface and design and implementation phases respectively. The application is now ready to come together and form one software unit.

## INTEGRATION

Since the key to the success of the integration phase is following the interface standards established in the preparation sub-phase, the standards established for the JEHT application will be repeated here.

1. **Launching user interface item**
   Menu:      File
   Item:        Update
2. **Description of required action**
   Determine where the Update file is located and update the appropriate fields with the information in the file.
3. **Calling protocol**
   UPDATE
4. **Parameters**
   None
5. **Return values**
   None

These interface standards define the interface between the user interface and the background code. Since we adhered to the interface standard, we simply need to inset the background code into the calling objects script. In this case, the calling object is a menu item. The complete script for the Update menu item is as follows:

```
on itemSelect
   UPDATE
end itemSelect

on UPDATE

-- Get the location of the Update file from the user

   put getFile("Select the Update File") into FILE_NAME
   if FILE_NAME is empty then
       exit UPDATE
   end if

-- Put the file contents into a local field

   set the cursor to "watch"
   set the lockScreen to true

   open file FILE_NAME
   read from file FILE_NAME for 65000
   close file FILE_NAME

   put it into card field "TEMP FIELD" of card "title" of
       window "JEHT"

   put lineOffset("***BEGIN***", card field "TEMP FIELD"
       of card "title" of window "JEHT") into THE_LINE

   if THE_LINE is zero then
       exit UPDATE
   end if

   delete line THE_LINE of card field "TEMP FIELD" of card
       "title" of window "JEHT"

-- Repeat until all fields are updated
--     Put information into the correct fields
-- end Repeat

   put "FALSE" into LAST_UPDATE
   repeat while LAST_UPDATE = "FALSE"

       put lineOffset("***NEXT***", card field "TEMP
           FIELD" of card "title" of window "JEHT") into
               THE_LINE
```

```
        if THE_LINE is zero then
            put lineOffset("***END***", card field "TEMP
                FIELD" of card "title" of window "JEHT") into
                    THE_LINE
            put "TRUE" into LAST_UPDATE
        end if

        put line 1 of card field "TEMP FIELD" of card "title" of
            window "JEHT" into THE_CARD

        put line 3 to THE_LINE - 1 of card field "TEMP FIELD"
            of card "title" of window "JEHT" into background
                field "INFORMATION" of card THE_CARD of
                window "PERSONNEL"

        delete line 1 to THE_LINE of card field "TEMP FIELD"
            of card "title" of window "JEHT"

    end repeat

    set the lockScreen to false
    set the cursor to "hand"

end UPDATE
```

Once the insertion task is complete, we do a quick sanity check to make sure there are no blatant errors. In this case, the sanity check is to select the Update menu item. If the interface between the user interface and the background code was not maintained, the software will immediately issue an error message. When this was tried, no error message was displayed. Therefore, we are ready to move on to formal testing.

## TESTING

A reasonable amount of unit testing has already been accomplished. This testing was used to check the basic functionality and syntactical correctness of the software. We can now enter the two formal testing stages: requirements testing and error testing.

### Requirements Testing

The purpose of requirements testing is to assure that all of the user requirements are met by the software. The first thing to accomplish

in requirements testing is to establish a Testing document.  This
document is drawn directly from the requirements document.  For
the purpose of performing requirements testing on the JEHT
application, the following Testing document was derived:

2.0    **System Description**
    2.2    **Narrative of system operation**
        The Overview/Title screen will have a drawing of
the corporate hierarchy.  By clicking on any of the levels, the user will be presented with a picture of the person
who holds that position and some information on that
person and the position.  Some mechanism will be provided to hear the voice of the selected person.  The system
must be designed so that changes in corporate personnel
will not result in major changes to the software.  Drastic
changes in the corporate structure are not anticipated,
and therefore, need not be considered.

    2.5    **System inputs**
        From a user point of view, the system inputs will be a
series of mouse clicks which will be used to navigate
around the application.  From a maintainers point of
view, there will exist files that the system will draw upon
to obtain the most current personnel information.

    2.7    **Look and feel of the system**
        There will be no formal training on JEHT provided
to the users.  Therefore, the software should be intuitive
in nature with a great emphasis on an easy to use, graphical user interface.  Menu functions as necessary may
be utilized.

5.0    **System constraints**
    5.5    **Acceptable system response time**
        There should be a minimum of delay between an ac-
tion taken by the user and a response by the system.  The
customer understands that this is a vague requirement
and that this issue will be explored in further depth during the rapid prototyping phase.

    5.6    **Special reliability needs**
        The JEHT software should not fail because of any
software error.  The customer understands that failures
due to faults in the Macintosh operating system are unavoidable.

As you have noticed, the requirements document was followed exactly.  The sections on the overall purpose of the system, types of media utilized, available resources, and physical location of the sys-

tem were left out . All of these items are general information on the system and are not testable conditions. The sections on Flow Diagram, types of media utilized, system outputs, security needs, size limits, special power requirements, and others were also omitted. These items were left out because the Requirements document had no testable information concerning the item.

Of the sections that were left in, the narrative of system operation, look and feel of the system, and acceptable system response time will be tested by observation. The special reliability needs will be covered in the error-testing stage. Therefore, the only thing left to test in the requirements testing arena is system inputs.

If you remember, there was an update file that the Update menu item script used to obtain the latest personnel information.We must consider what will happen if, when performing an update, the wrong file is selected or the file does not contain any information. The file format that the script will be expecting is as follows:

```
***BEGIN***
Button you would click on to get to the changed card

this is the new information on the specified person
this is the new information on the specified person
this is the new information on the specified person
***NEXT***
Button you would click on to get to the changed card

this is the new information on the next person
this is the new information on the next person
this is the new information on the next person
this is the new information on the next person
***NEXT***
Button you would click on to get to the changed card

this is the new information on the next person
this is the new information on the next person
this is the new information on the next person
***END***
```

We must be sure that the menu item script adequately checks to be sure that the selected file is properly formatted. Currently, the section of the script that does this checking is as follows:

```
put lineOffset("***BEGIN***", card field "TEMP FIELD" of
    card "title" of window "JEHT") into THE_LINE
```

```
if THE_LINE is zero then
    exit UPDATE
end if
```

In this script, the lineOffset function will return a zero if it doesn't find the string "***BEGIN***" within the file and the script will be exited without updating the application. It would make sense here to double-check that the file is correct by looking for the "***END***" string. This is a very simple matter and is accomplished by adding the following script segment before the last one. The new script segment reads as follows:

```
put lineOffset("***END***", card field "TEMP FIELD" of
    card "title" of window "JEHT") into THE_LINE

if THE_LINE is zero then
    exit UPDATE
end if

put lineOffset("***BEGIN***", card field "TEMP FIELD" of
    card "title" of window "JEHT") into THE_LINE

if THE_LINE is zero then
    exit UPDATE
end if
```

Now we can be reasonably assured that the selected file is the correct one. There is one other possibility to consider. The selected file may be in the right format, but, not contain correct information. The information of prime concern is in the first line. This line contains the name of the card to be modified. If that name is misspelled, a script error will result. The script error will be brought to the attention of the user in the form of a dialog box. For this error, the dialog box is shown in Figure 6.5. Obviously, this dialog box may not be descriptive enough for your users to figure out what is going on. So, to be more descriptive, you can trap the error and issue your own error message.

A script segment that could be used to trap error messages would be located in the menu item script and may look like the following:

```
on scriptError The_Error

    if The_Error is 51 then
        answer "Recheck the Update file for errors" with "OK"
```

```
        else
            pass scriptError
        end if

    end scriptError
```

**Figure 6.5** This error message dialog box will pop up if there is an error in the Update file.

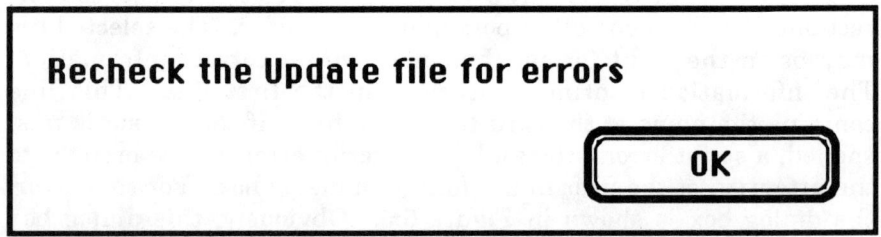

**Figure 6.6** The new error message dialog box indicates the source of the problem.

This script traps the error and puts the error number into the local variable The_Error.  Error number 51 is designated by SuperCard as the "Can't find card" error.  If the error is from some other source, then it will be passed through the normal channels.  But, if the "Can't find card" error is encountered , the dialog box in Figure

6.6 will be displayed.  This dialog box will give the user a concrete solution to the problem.  Instead of simply stating that the application can't find the card for no apparent reason, the user is told that the source of the problem is in the Update file.  This simple script will eliminate much confusion and allow your user to solve this problem without consulting you.

The requirements testing is now complete.  You can be reasonably assured that the users requirements are satisfied.  The next step is to accomplish error testing.

### Error Testing

For our purposes, there is only one code segment that must go through error testing.  That code segment belongs to the Update menu item script and reads as follows:

```
on itemSelect
    UPDATE
end itemSelect

on UPDATE

--   Get the location of the Update file from the user.

    put getFile("Select the Update File") into FILE_NAME
    if FILE_NAME is empty then
        exit UPDATE
    end if

--   Put the file contents into a local field.

    set the cursor to "watch"
    set the lockScreen to true

    open file FILE_NAME
    read from file FILE_NAME for 65000
    close file FILE_NAME

    put it into card field "TEMP FIELD" of card "title" of
        window "JEHT"

    put lineOffset("***BEGIN***", card field "TEMP FIELD"
        of card "title" of window "JEHT") into THE_LINE
```

```
            if THE_LINE is zero then
                exit UPDATE
            end if

            delete line THE_LINE of card field "TEMP FIELD" of card
                "title" of window "JEHT"

--      Repeat until all fields are updated
--          Put information into the correct fields
--      end Repeat

            put "FALSE" into LAST_UPDATE
            repeat while LAST_UPDATE = "FALSE"

                put lineOffset("***NEXT***", card field "TEMP
                    FIELD" of card "title" of window "JEHT") into
                    THE_LINE

                if THE_LINE is zero then
                    put lineOffset("***END***", card field "TEMP
                        FIELD" of card "title" of window "JEHT") into
                        THE_LINE
                    put "TRUE" into LAST_UPDATE
                end if

                put line 1 of card field "TEMP FIELD" of card "title" of
                    window "JEHT" into THE_CARD

                put line 3 to THE_LINE - 1 of card field "TEMP FIELD"
                    of card "title" of window "JEHT" into bg field
                    "INFORMATION" of card THE_CARD of
                    window "PERSONNEL"

                delete line 1 to THE_LINE of card field "TEMP FIELD"
                    of card "title" of window "JEHT"

            end repeat

            set the lockScreen to false
            set the cursor to "hand"

        end UPDATE
```

```
on scriptError The_Error

    if The_Error is 51 then
        answer "Recheck the Update file for errors" with "OK"
    else
        pass scriptError
    end if

end scriptError
```

To accomplish error testing on the above script, you must be sure that your test cases thoroughly evaluate the software. You should guarantee that all statements within the module are executed at least once, all logical decisions are evaluated on the true and false alternatives, all loops are executed at the boundaries and at nominal values, and all data structures are exercised to ensure their validity. Since we are intimately familiar with the code, we can use the application itself as a test driver to accomplish the previously mentioned tests.

For the one simple loop in the code, we will test by skipping the loop entirely, taking one pass through the loop, taking two passes through the loop, and taking many passes through the loop. Since the loop counter is established based on the Update file, the Update file will be varied to drive the test. And again, the application itself will be used as the test driver.

All of the testing has now been performed. No errors were uncovered in the testing, so we are essentially ready to field the software.


## MAINTENANCE

We have reached the final phase of the Parallel method. The purpose of the maintenance phase is to first field the product and then, when changes need to be made, determine the appropriate phase of the Parallel method to initiate that change. There are three distinct stages in the maintenance phase. Those stages are: fielding the product, performing routine maintenance, and performing system upgrades.


### Fielding the Product

Here, before fielding the software, we will first evaluate our software transition plan. This plan should address how you intend to field the software as well as how you plan to maintain it. In forming the plan, you can rely on the three keys to fielding a successful product: maintaining a close relationship with your customer throughout the development, providing a means of customer feedback, and responding to that feedback in a timely manner.

---

### Problem/Idea Report for JEHT

**Problem Hotline:   1-800-FIX-JEHT**


**Name:** _____         **Date:** _____


**Description of Problem or Idea:** _____
_____
_____
_____
_____
_____

**Resolution:** _____
_____
_____
_____
_____
_____
_____

---

**Figure 6.7** The format of the Problem/Idea Report.

We have maintained communication with the customer throughout the development of JEHT. In fact, you should have consulted several times with the customers to determine exactly how they wanted things to look and act. For the delivery, make sure that there is adequate time to train the appropriate personnel. And establish that, for a period of approximately six months, personnel will be available to maintain and upgrade the software. During that time, make sure that the person who will be taking over the maintenance of the software fully understands how the application works and how to maintain it.

The next item in our plan should be to establish a means of customer feedback. The JEHT application was developed for a specific customer, and for a period of time, the developer will be maintaining the software. So you should create some forum for the users of the software to provide feedback. This forum should also be adaptable so that the long term maintainer of the software will be able to use it as well. The forum selected is a Problem/Idea Report form. A sample format for this form is shown in Figure 6.7. As you can see from Figure 6.7, the Problem/Idea Report form provides spaces for the name of the originator, the date , a description of the problem or idea, and a resolution by the developer. Also included on the form is the hotline number that the customer can call to receive help or clarify a potential problem or idea. Now that the forum for change has been established, you should give your customer some indication that this is not just a paper exercise. Establish a schedule to pick up the Problem/Idea Reports on a regular basis. And, set a time period by which the reports will be returned to the initiator with some sort of a problem resolution written on the form. Any problems or ideas that come in on the hotline should be formalized on the same form and responded to in the same manner. When you set a time period for the response, be realistic. Remember, you only need to say how you will be dealing with the problem or idea, not actually solving the problem or incorporating the idea. For JEHT, it was decided that there would be a response to all Problem/Idea Reports on the initiators desk in one week.

When you receive the forms, you will need to classify them. There are three distinct classes for the problems and ideas: do nothing, routine maintenance action, or system upgrade action. Whichever class you decide to put the form in should be written in the resolution section of the form.

The do-nothing class indicates that either there was an operator error and no real problem or that the idea is not feasible given the current resources. If this is the case, then the resolution block on the form should contain instructions on how to avoid the problem in the future, or an explanation of why the idea is not feasible.

The routine-maintenance class is generally used to correct problems that affect the day to day working of the software. Any problem that causes the software to crash or issues an uninformative error message would fall into this class. The resolution block on the form should, in this case, contain an acknowledgement of the problem. A date for an actual fix to be released should also be included.

The system-upgrade class could be used for problems or ideas. If the problem is of the nature that a fix would require a major rework of the software functionality, it would fall into the system upgrade class. Ideas for new functionality of the software should also fall into this class. The resolution block on the form should indicate that the problem or idea is being considered for inclusion in the next major upgrade. A time frame for that upgrade should be specified.

Once you have classified the Problem/Idea Reports and returned them to the originator you should move on to the appropriate stage defined by the classification.

### Routine Maintenance

Errors that fall into this category are generally quick fix errors. The fix should not require a change in the overall functionality. Usually the problem is related to a software crash or an unexpected error message. Once a problem has been identified and classified as a routine maintenance action, you have to identify which phase of the Parallel method in which to accomplish the change. For routine maintenance, there is one of two places you will normally go: the implementation phase or the rapid prototyping phase.

If the change is a fix of a problem in the background software or a new algorithm for accomplishing the same thing in a more efficient manner, you will usually go to the implementation phase. Once you have made the change, you will go to the integration phase and thoroughly test the application once again before fielding the new version.

If the problem is related to navigation through the application or to the user interface in general, you would go to the rapid prototyping phase. There, you will make the changes to the user interface, obtain some sort of approval from the customer, and proceed to the modify user interface phase. There, you clean up the change and, again, move on to the integration phase for complete testing before fielding the new version. If the reason for the change is to fix an error, be sure to modify your test procedures to look for the new class of errors. Most of the changes that fall into the routine maintenance category will follow one of these two paths. If the change is to complex for this, it should be considered a candidate for the system upgrade stage.

### System Upgrades

The system upgrade stage requires some careful planning. The primary use of the system upgrade phase is incorporating enhancements that add new functionality to the software. These ideas should come from your customers in the form of the Problem/Idea Reports. Time frames are critical in this stage. You should establish a cutoff date after which no new ideas will be accepted for that cycle. Then, meet with a customer representative and analyze the reports for that cycle. The customer should make the decisions on which of the suggestions are incorporated into the application. You are only there to weed out ideas that are not feasible given the current resources.

Once a decision has been made on what changes are to be made, you must decide at what point it is appropriate to enter the Parallel method. If the new functionality is simple enough, you may be able to reenter an intermediate phase. But, most of the time a new software function should be treated as a new software requirement which you will take to the rapid prototyping phase. You would then proceed with the rest of the Parallel method as before culminating in a new release of the software upon reentering the maintenance phase.

## EXAMPLE 2 – Rolomap

In Chapter 5, the user interface and the background code of the Rolomap application were brought completely through the modify user interface and design and implementation phases. The application is now ready to come together and form one software unit.

## INTEGRATION

Since the key to the success of the integration phase is following the interface standards established in the preparation sub-phase, the standards for the two background code items we established for the Rolomap application will be repeated here.

## Add

1. **Launching user interface item**
   Menu:      File
   Item:      Add
2. **Description of required action**
   Put up a dialog box for the user to enter the new information. Extract the information from the dialog box and update the appropriate fields.
3. **Calling protocol**
   ADD_DATA
4. **Parameters**

A global variable called CARD_NAME containing the name of the card into which the information is to be placed must be initialized before going to the dialog box.

5. **Return values**
   None

## Delete

1. **Launching user interface item**
   Menu:     File
   Item:       Delete
2. **Description of required action**
   If an item is selected, delete the item and the information associated with it.
3. **Calling protocol**
   DELETE_DATA
4. **Parameters**
   None
5. **Return values**
   None

These interface standards defined the interface between the user interface and the background code. Since we rigidly adhered to the interface standard, we simply need to insert the background code into the calling objects script. In both cases, the calling object is a menu item. The complete script for the Add menu item is as follows:

```
on itemSelect
    ADD_DATA
end itemSelect

on ADD_DATA
    global CARD_NAME

    put the short name of this card into CARD_NAME
    open window "ADD ENTRY"

end ADD_DATA
```

The complete script for the Delete menu item is as follows:

```
on itemSelect
    DELETE_DATA
end itemSelect
```

```
on DELETE_DATA

    put the hilitedLines of bg field "NAME LIST" into
        LINE_NUM

    if LINE_NUM is not empty then
        answer "DELETE THIS ITEM?" with "YES" or "NO"
        if it is "NO" then
            exit itemSelect
        end if

        put line LINE_NUM of bg field "NAME LIST" into
            THE_NAME
        delete line LINE_NUM of bg field "NAME LIST"

        put lineOffset(THE_NAME, bg field "ADDRESS LIST")
            into NAME_LINE
        put lineOffset("*******", bg field "ADDRESS LIST",
            NAME_LINE) into END_LINE
        delete line NAME_LINE to NAME_LINE + END_LINE
            of bg field "ADDRESS LIST"
    end if

end DELETE_DATA
```

Once the insertion task is complete, we do a quick sanity check to make sure there are no blatant errors. In this case, the sanity check is to select the Add and Delete menu items. If the interface between the user interface and the background code was not maintained, the software will immediately issue an error message. When this was tried, no error message was displayed. Therefore, we are ready to move on to formal testing.

## TESTING

A reasonable amount of unit testing has already been accomplished. This testing was used to check the basic functionality and syntactical correctness of the software. We can now enter the two formal testing stages: requirements testing and error testing.

### Requirements Testing

The purpose of requirements testing is to assure that all of the user requirements are met by the software. The first thing to accomplish in requirements testing is to establish a Testing document. This document is drawn directly from the Requirements document. For the purpose of performing requirements testing on the Rolomap application, the following Testing document was derived:

### 2.0    System description
#### 2.2    Narrative of system operation
The Overview/Title screen will have a drawing of the United States. By clicking on any particular region, the user will be presented with a larger version of that region. Then, by clicking on a specific state, a list of points of contact for that state will appear. Some mechanism will be provided to add and subtract items from the list.

#### 2.5    System inputs
From a user point of view, the system inputs will be a series of mouse clicks which will be used to navigate around the application. There will also be user input in the form of additions to and removals from the database.

#### 2.7    Look and feel of the system
Initially, there will be no associated documentation. Rolomap is expected to be completely intuitive. Menu selections may be utilized as necessary.

### 5.0    System constraints
#### 5.5    Acceptable system response time
There should be a minimum of delay between an action taken by the user and a response by the system. I understand that this is a vague requirement and that this issue will be examined in greater detail during the Rapid Prototyping phase.

#### 5.6    Special reliability needs
The Rolomap software should not fail because of any software error. Macintosh Operating System errors are, of course, unavoidable.

As you have noticed, the requirements document was followed exactly. The sections on the overall purpose of the system, types of media utilized, available resources, and physical location of the system were left out. All of these items are general information on the system and are not testable conditions. The sections on Flow Diagram, types of media utilized, system outputs, security needs, size limits, special power requirements, and other were also omitted. These items were left out because the Requirements document had no testable information concerning the item.

Of the sections that were left in, the narrative of system operation, look and feel of the system, and acceptable system response time will be tested by observation. The special reliability needs will be covered in the error-testing stage. Therefore, the only thing left to test in the requirements testing arena is system inputs.

Upon examination of the Add and Delete menu item scripts, it was determined that there are no significant areas that are particularly succeptible to error. Therefore, the Requirements testing is complete and we are ready to move on to error testing.

**Error Testing**

For our purposes, there are only two code segments that must go through error testing. Those code segments belong to the Delete menu item script and the OK button script on the ADD ENTRY window. The Delete menu item script reads as follows:

```
on itemSelect
    DELETE_DATA
end itemSelect

on DELETE_DATA

    put the hilitedLines of bg field "NAME LIST" into
        LINE_NUM

    if LINE_NUM is not empty then
        answer "DELETE THIS ITEM?" with "YES" or "NO"
        if it is "NO" then
            exit itemSelect
        end if

        put line LINE_NUM of bg field "NAME LIST" into
            THE_NAME
        delete line LINE_NUM of bg field "NAME LIST"

        put lineOffset(THE_NAME, bg field "ADDRESS LIST")
            into NAME_LINE
        put lineOffset("*******", bg field "ADDRESS LIST",
            NAME_LINE) into END_LINE
        delete line NAME_LINE to NAME_LINE + END_LINE
            of bg field "ADDRESS LIST"
    end if

end DELETE_DATA
```

The OK button script reads as follows:

```
on mouseUp
    global CARD_NAME

        put card field "NAME" into THE_NAME
        if THE_NAME is empty then
            close window "ADD ENTRY"
            exit mouseUp
        end if

        put card field "ADDRESS" into THE_ADDRESS
        if THE_ADDRESS is empty then
            close window "ADD ENTRY"
            exit mouseUp
        end if

        put cr & THE_NAME after bg field "NAME LIST" of card
            CARD_NAME of window "STATES"

        put sortField(bg field "NAME LIST" of card CARD_NAME
            of window "STATES") into bg field "NAME LIST" of
            card CARD_NAME of window "STATES"

        put cr & THE_NAME & cr & THE_ADDRESS after bg field
            "ADDRESS LIST" of card CARD_NAME of window
            "STATES"

        put cr & "*****************" after bg field "ADDRESS
            LIST" of card CARD_NAME of window "STATES"

        close window "ADD ENTRY"
end mouseUp
```

To accomplish error testing on the above scripts, you must be sure that your test cases thoroughly evaluate the software. You should guarantee that all statements within the modules are executed at least once, all logical decisions are evaluated on the true and false alternatives, all loops are executed at the boundaries and at nominal values, and all data structures are exercised to ensure their validity. Since we are intimately familiar with the code, we can use the application itself as a test driver to accomplish the previously mentioned tests.

There are no loops in either of the code segments, so we do not need to be concerned with loop testing. All of the testing has now been performed. No errors were uncovered in the testing, so we are essentially ready to field the software.

## MAINTENANCE

We have reached the final phase of the Parallel method. The purpose of the maintenance phase is to first field the product and then, when changes need to be made, determine the appropriate phase of the Parallel method to initiate that change. There are three distinct stages in the maintenance phase: fielding the product, performing routine maintenance, and performing system upgrades.

### Fielding the Product

Here, before fielding the software, we will first evaluate our software transition plan. This plan should address how you intend to field the software as well as how you plan to maintain it. In forming the plan, you can rely on the three keys to fielding a successful product: maintaining a close relationship with your customer throughout the development, providing a means of customer feedback, and responding to that feedback in a timely manner.

In developing Rolomap, we, the developers, were the customer. Therefore, it is obvious that all of the above criteria will be met. Let us assume for a moment that plans are being made to market Rolomap. Formal training, in this case, cannot take place. But you must give your customers some avenue of learning about how to use the application. For an application the size of Rolomap, a simple users manual should be sufficient. An online help system could also be extremely helpful. Including both a users manual and an online help system is optimal. This will provide the users of your application with instant access to any information necessary to clear up questions that arise during use. Included with the manual should be some sort of a registration form. This will provide you with a list of the owners of your application. Then, when you are about to issue a new release of your software, you will know who to send it to.

The next item in our plan should be to establish a means of customer feedback. Again, we will assume that the application will be mass marketed. So, create some forum for the users of the software to provide feedback. In the mass marketing case, the only viable alternative is to provide a phone number and an address and ask for help. This information should, of course, be included in the users manual. But, it is generally accepted to provide an "About" menu item as shown in Figure 6.8.

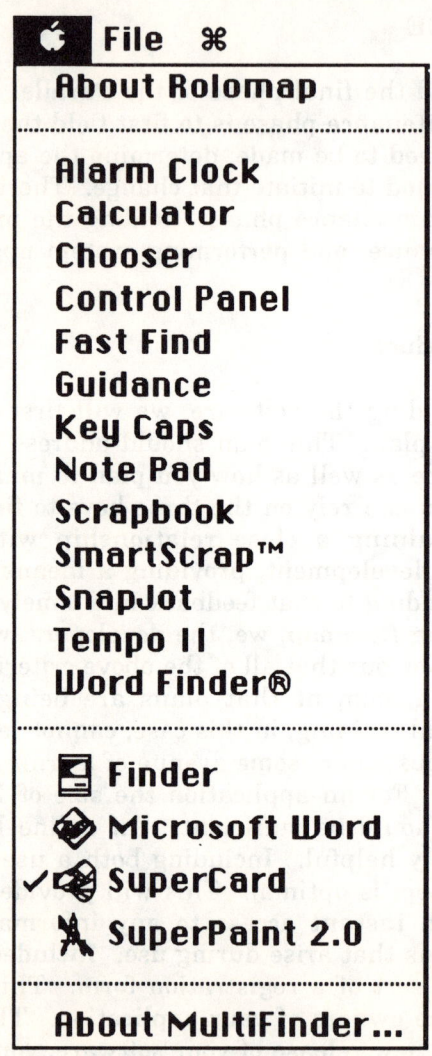

**Figure 6.8** The new Apple menu with the "About Rolomap" item.

When the user selects the About Rolomap menu item from the Apple menu, the dialog box in Figure 6.9 will be displayed. This dialog box gives the user a phone number to contact in search of help and an address to write to with suggestions or comments. If there is to be an online help system, it is commonly accessed through the same dialog box. You would simply put a help button on the dialog box that would launch the help portion of the application.

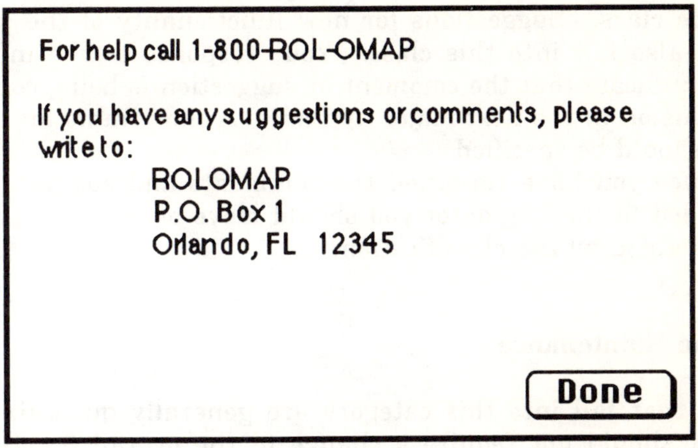

---

For help call 1-800-ROL-OMAP

If you have any suggestions or comments, please write to:

ROLOMAP
P.O. Box 1
Orlando, FL  12345

[ **Done** ]

---

**Figure 6.9** The "About Rolomap" dialog box.

Now that the forum for change has been established, you should give your customers some indication that you will do something about their concerns. If someone calls, of course, you should help them with their problem. But, if anyone calls or writes with a suggestion or a comment that may help improve your application, you should respond in writing. Tell the customer that you appreciate the comments and that they will be acted on appropriately with the next software release. If you are not planning on incorporating the comment, then explain why.

When you receive feedback, you will need to classify it. There are three distinct classes for the comments and suggestions:  do nothing, routine maintenance action, or system upgrade action.

The do-nothing class indicates that either there was an operator error and no real problem or that the idea is not feasible given the current resources or direction you want the application to head in. If this is the case, then indicate to the user how to avoid the problem in the future, or explain why the idea is not feasible.

The routine-maintenance class is generally used to correct problems that affect the day to day working of the software. Any problem that causes the software to crash or issues an uninformative error message would fall into this class. Hopefully, your own testing, or beta testers, will have uncovered all of these errors. Your response to the individual should contain an acknowledgement of the problem. A date for an actual fix to be released should also be included.

The system-upgrade class could be used for comments or suggestions. If the comment is of the nature that a fix would require a major rework of the software functionality, it would fall into the system upgrade class. Suggestions for new functionality of the software should also fall into this class. Your response to the individual should indicate that the comment or suggestion is being considered for inclusion in the next major upgrade. A time frame for that upgrade should be specified.

Once you have classified the comments and suggestions and responded to the originator you should move on to the appropriate stage defined by the classification.

## Routine Maintenance

Errors that fall into this category are generally quick-fix errors. The fix should not require a change in the overall functionality. Usually the problem is related to a software crash or an unexpected error message. Once a problem has been identified and classified as a routine maintenance action, you have to identify which phase of the Parallel method in which to accomplish the change. For routine maintenance, there is one of two places you will normally go: the implementation phase or the rapid prototyping phase.

If the change is a fix of a problem in the background software or a new algorithm for accomplishing the same thing in a more efficient manner, you will usually go to the implementation phase. Once you have made the change, you will go to the integration phase and thoroughly test the application once again before fielding the new version.

If the problem is related to navigation through the application or to the user interface in general, you would go to the rapid prototyping phase. There, you will make the changes to the user interface, obtain some sort of approval from the customer, and proceed to the modify user interface phase. There, you clean up the change and, again, move on to the integration phase for complete testing before fielding the new version. If the change involves fixing an error, be sure to modify your test procedures to look for the new class of errors. Most of the changes that fall into the routine maintenance category will follow one of these two paths. If the change is too complex for this, it should be considered a candidate for the system upgrade stage.

If, like in the case of Rolomap, the application is mass marketed, you should try to accumulate any errors of this type and incorporate them into the next system upgrade. However, if the application is only for your personal use or for the use of several known individuals, then make the required changes as part of the routine maintenance phase and distribute the new version of the software.

## System Upgrades

The system upgrade stage requires some careful planning. The primary use of the system upgrade phase is incorporating enhancements that add new functionality to the software. These ideas could come from your customers in the form of comments and suggestions or from ideas you have. Time frames are critical in this stage. You should establish a cutoff date after which no new ideas will be accepted for that cycle. Then, make the decisions on which of the suggestions are incorporated into the application.

Once a decision has been made on what changes are to be made, you must decide at what point it is appropriate to enter the Parallel method. If the new functionality is simple enough, you may be able to reenter an intermediate phase. But, most of the time a new software function should be treated as a new software requirement which you will take to the rapid prototyping phase. You would then proceed with the rest of the Parallel method as before culminating in a new release of the software upon reentering the maintenance phase.

# Software and Hardware Options

# Off-the-Shelf Software

In Section 2, we completely examined the Parallel method of software development. Along with the examination, we created two simple Hypermedia applications in order to apply and clarify the presented concepts. While the examples were developed using the SuperCard graphical scripting environment, the concepts covered in the discussion of the Parallel method were not specific to any software development environment or language. The reason for this is that there is no predefined Hypermedia programming language. In fact, Hypermedia applications can be developed using nearly any language. However, there are qualities of different types of programming environments that may help you (or hinder you) in the development of your application.

The purpose of this chapter is to provide you with the information necessary to make an informed decision concerning programming languages. It will cover three basic types of programming languages: traditional high-order languages, object-oriented languages, and graphical scripting environments. Specific languages will, of course, be used to illustrate the advantages and disadvantages of the different categories of development environments. However, the discussion will remain non-application specific at this time. The availability and quality of specific programming environments for different hardware platforms will be discussed in Chapters 8 and 9.

## SOFTWARE ENVIRONMENTS

There are a multitude of programming languages available for developing Hypermedia applications. In this chapter, the advantages and disadvantages of specific applications will not be covered. However, it will cover three different categories of software environments: traditional high-order languages, object-oriented languages, and graphical scripting environments.

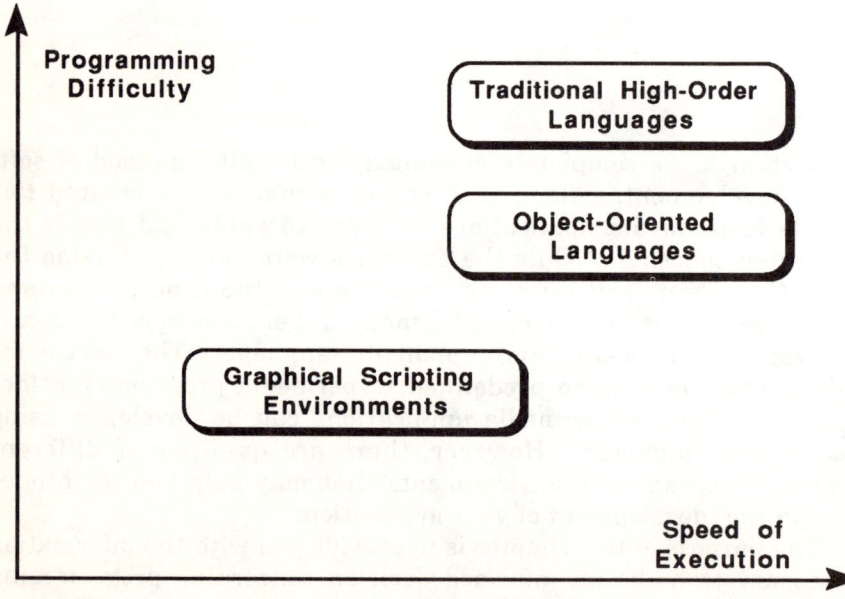

**Figure 7.1** The relationship of programming environments with respect to programming difficulty and speed of execution.

There are many things to consider when choosing an implementation language. Among these considerations are speed, programming difficulty, and maintainability. Figure 7.1 illustrates the general relationship of the three programming environment types with respect to programming difficulty and speed of execution.

As you can see, graphical scripting environments are the easiest to program. But, while they do well in ease of programming, they suffer in speed of execution. The reason for this is that graphical scripting environments are often interpreted languages. This means that each line of code is individually evaluated at execution time. In contrast, traditional high-order languages and object-oriented languages are generally compiled and linked into a single executable image. Compiled languages almost always execute faster than interpreted languages. Also, notice that while traditional high-order languages and object-oriented languages offer similar speed of execution, it is often easier to develop your application using an object-oriented language.

Maintainability is often something that is forgotten until it is too late. This is easy to do since, depending on the situation, someone besides the developer may be maintaining the software. Maintainability for the three classes of programming environments is roughly equal. Therefore, you should evaluate your particular situation and decide which environmental type is optimally maintainable. Some things to consider when making this decision are current computing environment, expertise within the maintenance organization, and willingness to change the two previous items if necessary. This highlights the main pitfall of maintainability. Don't consider change to be a bad thing. Change is always painful up front. But, staying the same can be more painful (and more expensive) in the long run.

## Traditional High-Order Languages

There are several high-order language environments available for personal computers. Among these are Ada, C, Pascal, Fortran, and Basic. The particular power of any of these languages generally does not come from the language itself, but from the libraries that are packaged with the environment. These libraries are machine-specific functions and routines (usually written in Assembly Language) that accomplish a multitude of low-level operations. Since the basic languages are not generally input/output oriented, the libraries are often centered around graphics functions that enable fancy screen output. All of the mentioned languages, except Basic, are compiled languages and, therefore, can be made to run very quickly. Basic, while easy to learn, is interpreted and is slow compared to compiled languages.

The main disadvantage of traditional high-order languages is the amount of code that it takes to implement basic Hypermedia objects such as windows, dialog boxes, buttons, and menus. This disadvantage will be fully illustrated in the examples at the end of this chapter.

### Object-Oriented Languages

Object-oriented languages are really an extension of traditional high-order languages. Any traditional high-order language can be programmed using object-oriented techniques. However, there are several languages (C++, Object Pascal, and Ada, for example) that are designed to be used with object-oriented programming techniques. These techniques allow the developer to define objects within the code and then perform actions on or with those objects to accomplish the desired task. As with traditional high-order languages, the power of the language comes with the libraries of functions that are packaged with the environment. Object-oriented languages are usually compiled and run as fast as traditional high-order languages.

While object-oriented languages can usually accomplish the same thing with fewer lines of code, it can still be extremely difficult to implement the basic Hypermedia objects. Again, this will be illustrated in the examples.

### Graphical Scripting Environments

Graphical scripting environments can be considered an extension of object-oriented languages. With object-oriented languages the objects are defined by code. But, in graphical scripting environments, the objects are actually objects on the screen. These environments usually come with a graphical editor for developing your user interface. All of the background programming ( event handling, error handling, etc.) is taken care of by the environment leaving you free to develop the meat of the application. What you must do is develop the code (scripts) that perform an action when some event happens (clicking on a button, selecting a menu item, etc.). The basic Hypermedia structures are all developed graphically with a few mouse clicks. These features will be illustrated in the examples at the end of the chapter in contrast to the traditional high-order languages and object-oriented languages.

The primary disadvantage of graphical scripting environments is speed. Often, these environments are interpreted and can run significantly slower than their compiled counterparts. With some environments, however, you can purchase a separate compiler if speed is a major concern.

## EXAMPLES

This examples section should provide you with an illustration of the amount of code it takes to implement some basic Hypermedia structures in the three different types of programming environments. These examples are meant to be representative of the three environment types and therefore do not fully describe all of the features of the particular programming language.

The programming examples for the traditional high-order language are written in C. C++ was used for the object-oriented examples. Both of these types are written for use with Windows on an IBM PC or compatible computer. Programming in Windows is remarkably similar to programming on a Macintosh. Therefore, the Macintosh was chosen to illustrate the graphical scripting environment with SuperCard. Note that there are often several files associated with a C or C++ program. All files will be included where applicable. The examples will cover a basic window, a dialog box with assorted buttons, and a menu.

### Basic Window Using a Traditional High-Order Language

A basic window in Windows or on a Macintosh is moveable, sizeable, has a "zoom" box for expanding or shrinking the window, and a close box for closing the window. What follows here is the C definition file for the program written using traditional programming techniques.

```
NAME          WIN_ONE
DESCRIPTION   'Fundamental Window'
EXETYPE       WINDOWS
CODE          PRELOAD MOVEABLE
DATA          PRELOAD MOVEABLE MULTIPLE
HEAPSIZE      1024
STACKSIZE     5120
EXPORTS       WndProc
```

What follows is the actual C program used to implement a basic window using traditional programming techniques.

```
#include <windows.h>
#include <stdlib.h>
#include <string.h>

long FAR PASCAL WndProc (HWND hWnd,
    WORD iMessage, WORD wParam, LONG lParam);
int PASCAL WinMain (HANDLE hInstance,
    HANDLE hPrevInstance, LPSTR lpszCmdParam,
        int nCmdShow)

{
HWND hWnd;
MSG Message;
WNDCLASS WndClass;

if (!hPrevInstance)
    {
    WndClass.cbClsExtra = 0;
    WndClass.cbWndExtra = 0;
    WndClass.hbrBackground =
                    GetStockObject(WHITE_BRUSH);
    WndClass.hCursor = LoadCursor(NULL, IDC_ARROW);
    WndClass.hIcon = LoadIcon (NULL, "END");
    WndClass.hInstance = hInstance;
    WndClass.lpfnWndProc = WndProc;
    WndClass.lpszClassName = "WIN_ONE";
    WndClass.lpszMenuName = NULL;
    WndClass.style = CS_HREDRAW | CS_VREDRAW;

    RegisterClass (&WndClass);
    }

hWnd = CreateWindow ("WIN_ONE",      /* class name */
        "Fundamental Window",    /* Caption */
        WS_OVERLAPPEDWINDOW,    /* Style */
        CW_USEDEFAULT,        /* x position */
        0,          /* y position */
        CW_USEDEFAULT,        /* cx - size */
        0,          /* cy - size */
        NULL,           /* Parent window */
        NULL,           /* Menu */
        hInstance,          /* Program Instance */
        NULL);          /* Parameters */

ShowWindow (hWnd, nCmdShow);
```

```
while (GetMessage (&Message, 0, 0, 0))
    {
    TranslateMessage(&Message);
    DispatchMessage(&Message);
    }
return Message.wParam;
}

/*************************************************/
/*          Window Procedure: WndProc           */
/*************************************************/

long FAR PASCAL WndProc (HWND hWnd,
    WORD iMessage, WORD wParam, LONG lParam)
{
switch (iMessage)
    {
    case WM_DESTROY:
        PostQuitMessage(0);
        return 0;
    default:
        return(DefWindowProc(hWnd, iMessage, wParam,
            lParam));
    }
}
```

## Basic Window Using an Object-Oriented Language

What follows here is the actual C++ file for the program written using object-oriented programming techniques.

```
#include  <owl.h>

class TBasicDemo : public TApplication
{
public:
    TBasicDemo(LPSTR AName) : TApplication(AName){}
    virtual void InitMainWindow();
};

void  TBasicDemo::InitMainWindow()
{
MainWindow = new TWindow(NULL, "Basic Window
Demonstration");
```

```
}

int PASCAL WinMain(HANDLE hInstance,
    HANDLE hPrevInstance, LPSTR lpCmdLine,
        int nCmdShow)
{
TBasicDemo  BasicDemo("Basic  Window");
BasicDemo.Run();
return(BasicDemo.Status);
}
```

### Basic Window Using a Graphical Scripting Environment

In a graphical scripting environment like SuperCard, you are usually presented with some sort of a project manager.  Figure 7.2 shows the project window for SuperCard.

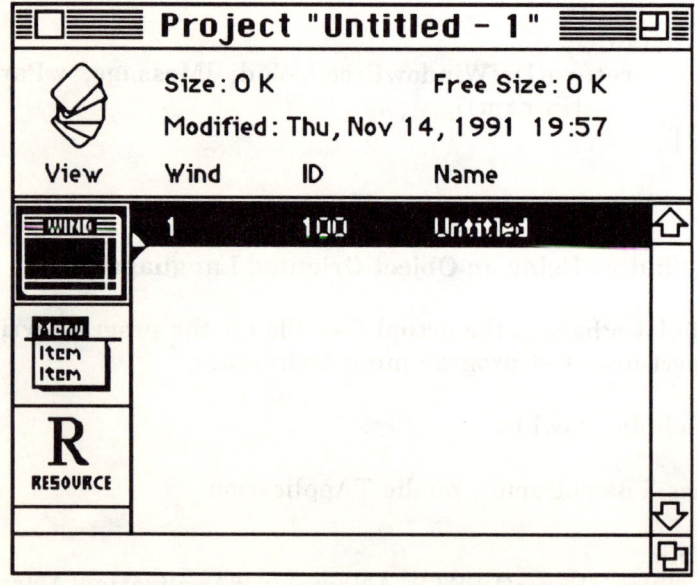

**Figure 7.2**  The Project window in SuperCard.

From this project window, you can create new windows in your project by double-clicking on the cards in the upper-left-hand corner, by choosing "New Window" from the edit menu, or by using a keyboard shortcut.  Of course, this new window will have some at-

tributes that need to be initialized.  This information can be modified from the "Window Info" window which is brought up by selecting "Window Info" from the edit menu or by using a keyboard
shortcut.  The "Window Info" window as shown in Figure 7.3 contains selections for all of the window attributes.  In this example we
need to create a window that is moveable, sizeable, has a "zoom" box
for expanding or shrinking the window, and a close box for closing
the window.

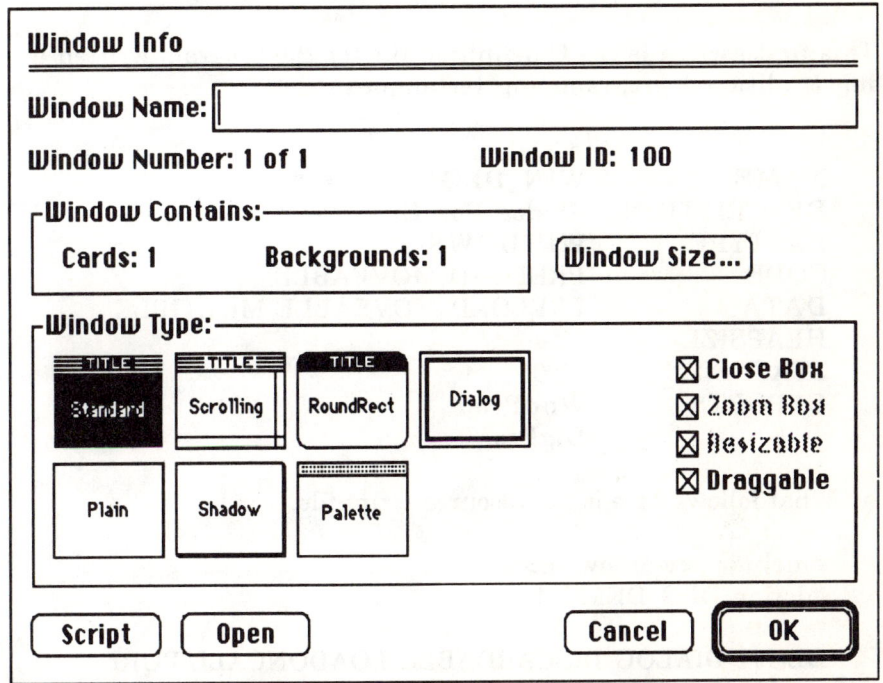

Figure 7.3  The Window Info window in SuperCard.

To implement this, click on the scrolling window type and click
in the boxes marked close box, zoom box, resizable, and draggable.
If you wish a specific default size for the window, you can click on
the "Window Size ..." button and be presented with window sizing
information.  When you are finished, you click on the "OK" button
and the window is created and initialized.

## Dialog Box

A dialog box is a window-like structure that is normally used to obtain information from or provide information to the user. Because of this nature, there are often buttons of various types associated with the dialog box. The following examples illustrate a dialog box with an assortment of buttons.

### Dialog Box Using a Traditional High-Order Language

This first section is the C definition file for the program written using traditional programming techniques.

```
NAME          WIN_DLG
DESCRIPTION   'Dialog Box Example'
EXETYPE       WINDOWS
CODE          PRELOAD MOVEABLE
DATA          PRELOAD MOVEABLE MULTIPLE
HEAPSIZE      1024
STACKSIZE     5120
EXPORTS       WndProc
              DlgProc
```

What follows here is the resource script file.

```
#include  <windows.h>
#define DLG_DEMO 1

DLG#1 DIALOG DISCARDABLE LOADONCALL PURE
     MOVEABLE 42, 38, 148, 108 STYLE WS_POPUP |
     WS_DLGFRAME | WS_SYSMENU
BEGIN
     CONTROL "Radio Button One" 101, "BUTTON",
        WS_CHILD| WS_VISIBLE | 0x4L, 38, 6, 74, 14
     CONTROL "Radio Button Two" 102, "BUTTON",
        WS_CHILD | WS_VISIBLE | 0x4L, 38, 25, 74, 14
     CONTROL "Checkbox One" 103, "BUTTON", WS_CHILD
        | WS_VISIBLE | WS_TABSTOP | 0x2L, 8, 45, 64, 12
     CONTROL "Checkbox Two" 104, "BUTTON", WS_CHILD
        | WS_VISIBLE | WS_TABSTOP | 0x2L, 8, 61, 64, 12
     CONTROL "Checkbox Three" 105, "BUTTON",
        WS_CHILD | WS_VISIBLE | WS_TABSTOP | 0x2L,
           75, 45, 72, 12
```

```
        CONTROL "Checkbox Four" 106, "BUTTON", WS_CHILD
           | WS_VISIBLE | WS_TABSTOP | 0x2L, 75, 61, 68, 12
        CONTROL "Cancel" 107, "BUTTON", WS_CHILD |
           WS_VISIBLE | WS_TABSTOP, 26, 87, 40, 12
        CONTROL "OK" 108, "BUTTON", WS_CHILD |
           WS_VISIBLE | WS_TABSTOP | 0x1L, 82, 87, 38, 12
END

DlgMenu MENU
{
POPUP "&Help"
    {
    MENUITEM "&Dialog Demo",  DLG_DEMO
    }
    }
```

What follows now is the actual C program used to implement a dialog box using traditional programming techniques.

```
#include <windows.h>
#include <stdlib.h>
#include <string.h>

long FAR PASCAL WndProc (HWND hWnd,
    WORD iMessage, WORD wParam, LONG lParam);

int PASCAL WinMain (HANDLE hInstance,
    HANDLE hPrevInstance, LPSTR lpszCmdParam,
        int nCmdShow)

#define DLG_DEMO 1

{
HWND hWnd;
MSG Message;
WNDCLASS WndClass;

if (!hPrevInstance)
    {
    WndClass.cbClsExtra = 0;
    WndClass.cbWndExtra = 0;
    WndClass.hbrBackground =
                    GetStockObject(WHITE_BRUSH);
    WndClass.hCursor = LoadCursor(NULL, IDC_ARROW);
    WndClass.hIcon = LoadIcon (NULL, "END");
```

```
         WndClass.hInstance = hInstance;
         WndClass.lpfnWndProc = WndProc;
         WndClass.lpszClassName = "WIN_DLG";
         WndClass.lpszMenuName = "DlgMenu";
         WndClass.style = CS_HREDRAW I CS_VREDRAW;
         RegisterClass (&WndClass);
         }

 hWnd = CreateWindow ("WIN_DLG",        /* class name */
     "Dialog Box Example",     /* Caption */
     WS_OVERLAPPEDWINDOW,      /* Style */
     CW_USEDEFAULT,        /* x position */
     0,        /* y position */
     CW_USEDEFAULT,        /* cx - size */
     0,           /* cy - size */
     NULL,            /* Parent window */
     NULL,            /* Menu */
     hInstance,       /* Program Instance */
     NULL);           /* Parameters */

 ShowWindow(hWnd,nCmdShow);
 UpdateWindow(hWnd);
 while (GetMessage (&Message, 0, 0, 0))
     {
     TranslateMessage(&Message);
     DispatchMessage(&Message);
     }
 return Message.wParam;
 }


 /*************************************************/
 /*        Dialog Procedure: DlgProc          */
 /*************************************************/

 BOOL FAR PASCAL DlgProc(HWND hDlg, WORD iMessage,
                    WORD wParam, LONG lParam)
 {
 WORD status;

 switch(iMessage)
     {
     case WM_INITDIALOG:

         CheckDlgButton(hDlg,101,1);
         return TRUE;
```

```
case WM_COMMAND:

    switch(wParam)
    {
    case 101:
        status = IsDlgButtonChecked(hDlg,101);
        if (status == 0)
            CheckDlgButton(hDlg,101,1);
        else
            CheckDlgButton(hDlg,101,0);
        return TRUE;

    case 102:
        status = IsDlgButtonChecked(hDlg,102);
        if (status == 0)
            CheckDlgButton(hDlg,102,1);
        else
            CheckDlgButton(hDlg,102,0);
        return TRUE;

    case 103:
        status = IsDlgButtonChecked(hDlg,103);
        if (status == 0)
            CheckDlgButton(hDlg,103,1);
        else
            CheckDlgButton(hDlg,103,0);
        return TRUE;

    case 104:
        status = IsDlgButtonChecked(hDlg,104);
        if (status == 0)
            CheckDlgButton(hDlg,104,1);
        else
            CheckDlgButton(hDlg,104,0);
        return TRUE;

    case 105:
        status = IsDlgButtonChecked(hDlg,105);
        if (status == 0)
            CheckDlgButton(hDlg,105,1);
        else
            CheckDlgButton(hDlg,105,0);
        return TRUE;
```

```
            case 106:
                status = IsDlgButtonChecked(hDlg,106);
                if (status == 0)
                    CheckDlgButton(hDlg,106,1);
                else
                    CheckDlgButton(hDlg,106,0);
                return TRUE;

            case 107:
                EndDialog(hDlg,FALSE);
                return TRUE;

            case 108:
                EndDialog(hDlg,TRUE);
                return TRUE;

            }
            break;
        }
    return FALSE;
    }


/**************************************************/
/*        Window Procedure: WndProc          */
/**************************************************/

long FAR PASCAL WndProc (HWND hWnd,
    WORD iMessage, WORD wParam, LONG lParam)
{
static FARPROC lpfnDlgProc;
static HANDLE hInstance;

switch (iMessage)
    {
    case WM_CREATE:
        hInstance = ((LPCREATESTRUCT)lParam)
            >hInstance;
        lpfnDlgProc = MakeProcInstance(DlgProc,hInstance);
    return 0;

    case WM_COMMAND:

    switch(wParam)
        {
        case DLG_DEMO:
```

```
            if(DialogBox(hInstance,"DLG#1",hWnd,
                lpfnDlgProc));
                InvalidateRect(hWnd,NULL,TRUE);
            return 0;
        }
        break;

    case WM_DESTROY:

        PostQuitMessage(0);
        return 0;

    }

    return(DefWindowProc(hWnd,iMessage,wParam,lParam));
}
```

### Dialog Box Using an Object-Oriented Language

This first section is the C++ resource script file for the program written using object-oriented techniques.

```
#include <windows.h>
#define DLG_DEMO 1

DLG#1 DIALOG DISCARDABLE LOADONCALL PURE
    MOVEABLE 42, 38, 148, 108 STYLE WS_POPUP |
        WS_DLGFRAME | WS_SYSMENU
BEGIN
    CONTROL "Radio Button One" 101, "BUTTON",
        WS_CHILD | WS_VISIBLE | 0x4L, 38, 6, 74, 14
    CONTROL "Radio Button Two" 102, "BUTTON",
        WS_CHILD | WS_VISIBLE | 0x4L, 38, 25, 74, 14
    CONTROL "Checkbox One" 103, "BUTTON", WS_CHILD
        | WS_VISIBLE | WS_TABSTOP | 0x2L, 8, 45, 64, 12
    CONTROL "Checkbox Two" 104, "BUTTON", WS_CHILD
        | WS_VISIBLE | WS_TABSTOP | 0x2L, 8, 61, 64, 12
    CONTROL "Checkbox Three" 105, "BUTTON",
        WS_CHILD | WS_VISIBLE | WS_TABSTOP | 0x2L,
            75, 45, 72, 12
    CONTROL "Checkbox Four" 106, "BUTTON", WS_CHILD
        | WS_VISIBLE | WS_TABSTOP | 0x2L, 75, 61, 68, 12
    CONTROL "Cancel" 107, "BUTTON", WS_CHILD |
        WS_VISIBLE | WS_TABSTOP, 26, 87, 40, 12
```

```
        CONTROL "OK" 108, "BUTTON", WS_CHILD |
            WS_VISIBLE | WS_TABSTOP | 0x1L, 82, 87, 38, 12
END

DlgMenu MENU
{
POPUP "&Help"
    {
    MENUITEM "Dialog Demo",  DLG_DEMO
    }
}
```

What follows now is the actual C++ program used to implement a dialog box using object-oriented programming techniques.

```cpp
#include <owl.h>
#include <dialog.h>

#define CM_DLG 1
#define ID_RADIOONE 101
#define ID_RADIOTWO 102
#define ID_CHECKONE 103
#define ID_CHECKTWO 104
#define ID_CHECKTHREE 105
#define ID_CHECKFOUR 106
#define ID_MYCANCEL 107
#define ID_MYOK 108

class TDlg : public TDialog
{
public:
    TDlg(PWindowsObject AParent, LPSTR AName)
        : TDialog(AParent, AName) {};
    virtual void RadioOne(TMessage& Msg) =
        [ID_FIRST + ID_RADIOONE];
    virtual void RadioTwo(TMessage& Msg) =
        [ID_FIRST + ID_RADIOTWO];
    virtual void CheckOne(TMessage& Msg) =
        [ID_FIRST + ID_CHECKONE];
    virtual void CheckTwo(TMessage& Msg) =
        [ID_FIRST + ID_CHECKTWO];
    virtual void CheckThree(TMessage& Msg) =
        [ID_FIRST + ID_CHECKTHREE];
    virtual void CheckFour(TMessage& Msg) =
        [ID_FIRST + ID_CHECKFOUR];
```

```
            virtual void MyCancel(TMessage& Msg) =
                [ID_FIRST + ID_MYCANCEL];
            virtual void MyOk(TMessage& Msg) =
                [ID_FIRST + ID_MYOK];
};
class TDlgWindow : public TWindow
{
public:
    TDlgWindow(PWindowsObject AParent, LPSTR ATitle);
    virtual void CMDlg(TMessage& Msg) =
            [CM_FIRST + CM_DLG];
};

class TDlgApp : public TApplication
{
public:
    TDlgApp(LPSTR AName): TApplication(AName) {};
    virtual void InitMainWindow();
};

void  TDlg::RadioOne(TMessage&)
{
WORD status;

status = IsDlgButtonChecked(HWindow,101);
if (status == 0)
    CheckDlgButton(HWindow,101,1);
else
    CheckDlgButton(HWindow,101,0);
}

void  TDlg::RadioTwo(TMessage&)
{
WORD status;

status = IsDlgButtonChecked(HWindow,102);
if (status == 0)
    CheckDlgButton(HWindow,102,1);
else
    CheckDlgButton(HWindow,102,0);
}

void  TDlg::CheckOne(TMessage&)
{
WORD status;
```

```
status = IsDlgButtonChecked(HWindow,103);
if (status == 0)
    CheckDlgButton(HWindow,103,1);
else
    CheckDlgButton(HWindow,103,0);
}
void  TDlg::CheckTwo(TMessage&)
{
WORD status;

status = IsDlgButtonChecked(HWindow,104);
if (status == 0)
    CheckDlgButton(HWindow,104,1);
else
    CheckDlgButton(HWindow,104,0);
}

void  TDlg::CheckThree(TMessage&)
{
WORD status;

status = IsDlgButtonChecked(HWindow,105);
if (status == 0)
    CheckDlgButton(HWindow,105,1);
else
    CheckDlgButton(HWindow,105,0);
}

void  TDlg::CheckFour(TMessage&)
{
WORD status;

status = IsDlgButtonChecked(HWindow,106);
if (status == 0)
    CheckDlgButton(HWindow,106,1);
else
    CheckDlgButton(HWindow,106,0);
}

void  TDlg::MyCancel(TMessage&)
{
EndDlg(0);
}

void  TDlg::MyOk(TMessage&)
```

```
{
EndDlg(0);
}

TDlgWindow::TDlgWindow(PWindowsObject AParent,
    LPSTR Title): TWindow(AParent, Title)
{
Attr.Menu = LoadMenu(Application->hInstance, "DlgMenu");
}

void TDlgWindow::CMDlg(TMessage&)
{
Application->ExecDialog(new TDlg(this, "DLG#1"));
}

void TDlgApp::InitMainWindow()
{
MainWindow = new TDlgWindow(NULL, "Dialogs");
}

int PASCAL WinMain(HANDLE hInstance,
    HANDLE hPrevInstance, LPSTR lpCmdLine,
        int nCmdShow)
{
    TDlgApp DlgApp("Dialogs");
    DlgApp.Run();
return (DlgApp.Status);
}
```

### Dialog Box Using a Graphical Scripting Environment

In our graphical scripting environment, we desire to create a dialog box with assorted buttons. To accomplish this, we once again go to the "Window Info" window as shown in Figure 7.4. From this window, you click on the dialog window type and establish the attributes of the window.

Once the dialog box is created, we desire to put some assorted buttons on it. To do this, we double click on the window from the project window of SuperCard. This will supply us a list of the cards that are in the window. You open one of these cards by again double clicking on it. When you do this, you will be presented with the actual card as shown in Figure 7.5. To the left of Figure 7.5 is a group of tools. There are four different tool palettes in SuperCard: the button palette, the field palette, the bitmap palette, and the drawing palette.

To create buttons, obviously, we choose the button palette. Then, by simply clicking on the graphic of the appropriate button on the palette and then selecting an area on the card, the button is created. As shown in Figure 7.5, several buttons of varying types have been created.

The next task would be to adjust the attributes of the individual buttons. This is accomplished by double-clicking on the button of interest. When you do this, you will be presented with something similar to Figure 7.6.

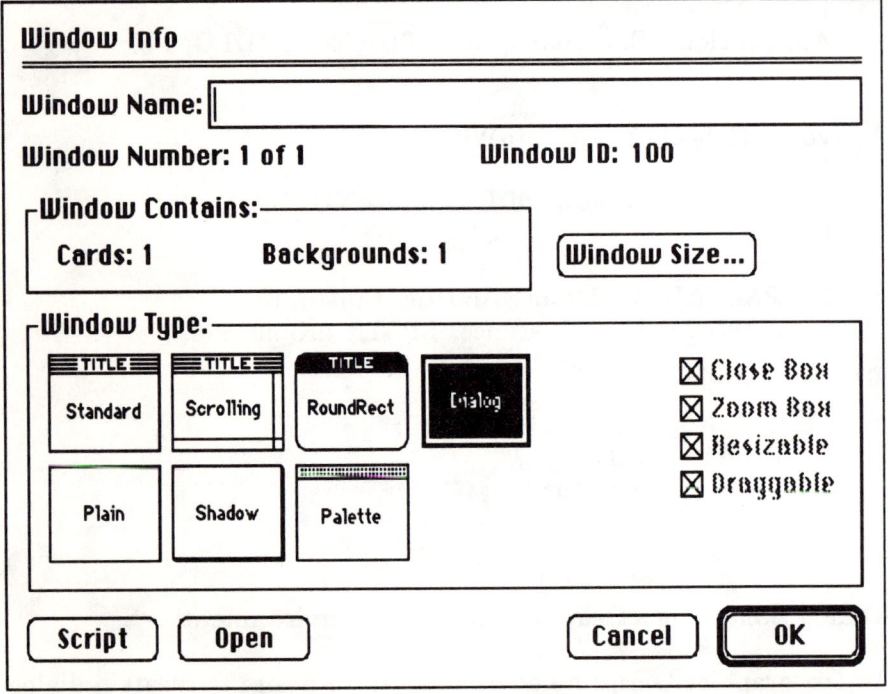

**Figure 7.4** Selecting a dialog box from the Window Info window in SuperCard.

This "Button Info" window allows you to name and set the attributes of your buttons. As you can see, the available button properties are show name, auto highlight, visible, disable button, default, and autowidth. The styles available for the button are round rectangle, rectangle, polygon, check box, and radio button.

A final point of concern is how to program the button to do something when a user clicks on it. If you were to click on the "Script" button on the "Button Info" window, you would go to a window that contains a text field that is specific to that particular button. In that text field, you write the script to accomplish whatever task is necessary. Sometimes these scripts are written in a high-order programming language like the ones we have been examining.

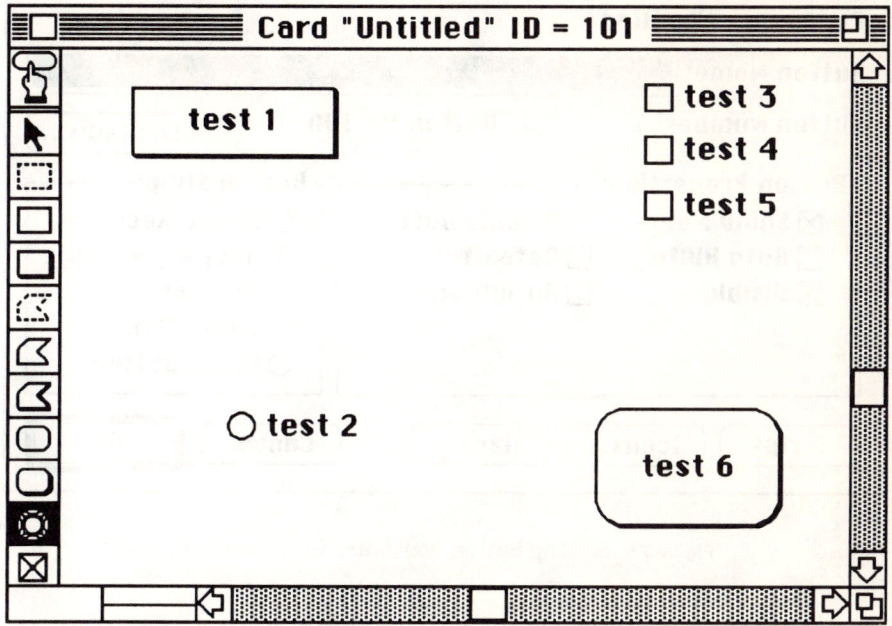

**Figure 7.5** Creating buttons on a card in SuperCard.

SuperCard, along with many other graphical scripting environments, has its own scripting language. The SuperCard scripting language, called SuperTalk, is quite English-like and can be learned by a competent programmer very quickly. The buttons in the previous examples had no actual functionality, so no actual script will be included.

## Menus

Menus are fairly self-explanatory. They are established to accomplish a number of different things ranging from basic editing features to Hypermedia navigation. One thing is certain, menus are an integral part of Hypermedia applications as well as most other types of applications.

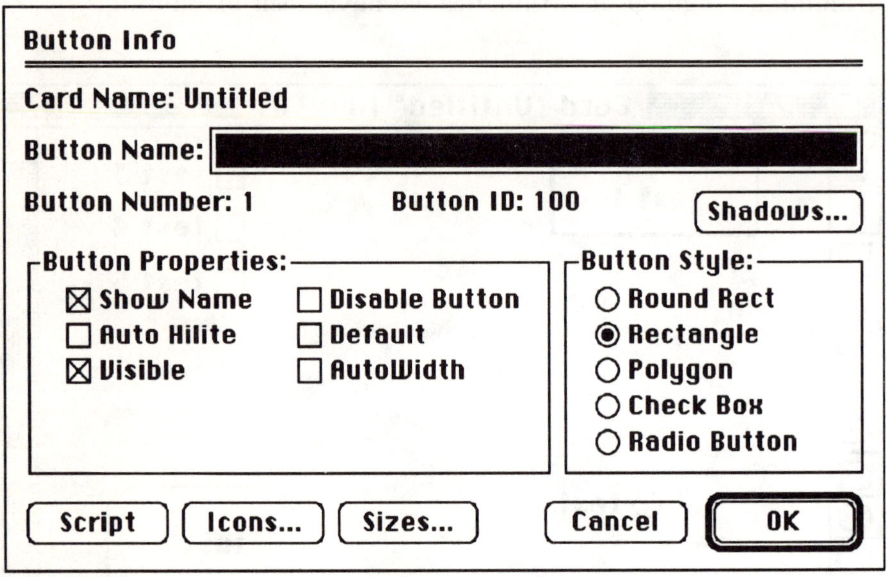

Figure 7.6  Setting button attributes in SuperCard.

## Menus Using a Traditional High-Order Language

This first section is the C definition file for the program written using traditional programming techniques.

```
NAME          WIN_MENU
DESCRIPTION   'Menu Example'
EXETYPE       WINDOWS
CODE          PRELOAD MOVEABLE
DATA          PRELOAD MOVEABLE MULTIPLE
HEAPSIZE      1024
STACKSIZE     5120
EXPORTS       WndProc
```

What follows here is the resource script file.

```
MENU  MENU LOADONCALL MOVEABLE PURE
   DISCARDABLE
BEGIN
   POPUP "Menu & One"
   BEGIN
      MenuItem "Item One", 2
      MenuItem "Item Two", 3
   END
   POPUP "Menu & Two"
   BEGIN
      MenuItem "Selection One", 5
   END
   POPUP "Menu & Three"
   BEGIN
      MenuItem "Checked Item #&1", 7, CHECKED
      MenuItem "Checked Item #&2", 8, CHECKED
   END
   POPUP "Menu & Four"
   BEGIN
      MenuItem "Menu Item One", 10
      MenuItem "Menu Item Two", 11
   END
END
```

What follows now is the actual C program used to implement a menu using traditional programming techniques.

```
#include <windows.h>
#include <stdlib.h>
#include <string.h>

BOOL CheckOne = MF_CHECKED;
BOOL CheckTwo = MF_CHECKED;

long FAR PASCAL WndProc (HWND hWnd,
   WORD iMessage, WORD wParam, LONG lParam);

int PASCAL WinMain (HANDLE hInstance,
   HANDLE hPrevInstance, LPSTR lpszCmdParam,
      int nCmdShow)

{
HWND hWnd;
MSG Message;
WNDCLASS WndClass;
```

```
if (!hPrevInstance)
    {
    WndClass.cbClsExtra = 0;
    WndClass.cbWndExtra = 0;
    WndClass.hbrBackground =
                         GetStockObject(WHITE_BRUSH);
    WndClass.hCursor = LoadCursor(NULL, IDC_ARROW);
    WndClass.hIcon = LoadIcon (NULL, "END");
    WndClass.hInstance = hInstance;
    WndClass.lpfnWndProc = WndProc;
    WndClass.lpszClassName = "WIN_MENU";
    WndClass.lpszMenuName = "MENU";
    WndClass.style = CS_HREDRAW | CS_VREDRAW;

    RegisterClass (&WndClass);
    }

hWnd = CreateWindow ("WIN_MENU",    /* class name */
    "Menu Example",     /* Caption */
    WS_OVERLAPPEDWINDOW,    /* Style */
    CW_USEDEFAULT,      /* x position */
    0,          /* y position */
    CW_USEDEFAULT,      /* cx - size */
    0,          /* cy - size */
    NULL,           /* Parent window */
    NULL,           /* Menu */
    hInstance,      /* Program Instance */
    NULL);          /* Parameters */

ShowWindow(hWnd,nCmdShow);
UpdateWindow(hWnd);
while (GetMessage (&Message, 0, 0, 0))
    {
    TranslateMessage(&Message);
    DispatchMessage(&Message);
    }
return Message.wParam;
}

/**************************************************/
/*         Window Procedure: WndProc          */
/**************************************************/

long FAR PASCAL WndProc (HWND hWnd,
    WORD iMessage, WORD wParam, LONG lParam)
```

```
{
HMENU hMenu;

switch (iMessage)
    {
    case WM_COMMAND:
        hMenu = GetMenu(hWnd);

    switch(wParam)
        {
        case 2:
            MessageBox(hWnd,"Item One","Menu Example",
                MB_ICONINFORMATION | MB_OK);
        return 0;

        case 3:
            MessageBox(hWnd,"Item Two","Menu Example",
                MB_ICONINFORMATION | MB_OK);
        return 0;

        case 5:
            MessageBox(hWnd,"Selection One",
                "Menu Example",
                    MB_ICONINFORMATION | MB_OK);
        return 0;

        case 7:
        if (CheckOne == MF_CHECKED)
            {
            CheckMenuItem(hMenu,7,MF_BYCOMMAND |
                MF_UNCHECKED);
            CheckOne = MF_UNCHECKED;
            }
        else
            {
            CheckMenuItem(hMenu,7,MF_BYCOMMAND |
                MF_CHECKED);
            CheckOne = MF_CHECKED;
            }
        return 0;

        case 8:
        if (CheckTwo == MF_CHECKED)
            {
            CheckMenuItem(hMenu,8,MF_BYCOMMAND |
```

```
                            MF_UNCHECKED);
                    CheckTwo = MF_UNCHECKED;
                    }
            else
                    {
                    CheckMenuItem(hMenu,8,MF_BYCOMMAND |
                        MF_CHECKED);
                    CheckTwo = MF_CHECKED;
                    }
            return 0;
            case 10:
                    MessageBox(hWnd,"Menu Item One",
                        "Menu Example",
                            MB_ICONINFORMATION | MB_OK);
            return 0;

            case 11:
                    MessageBox(hWnd,"Menu Item Two",
                        "Menu Example",
                            MB_ICONINFORMATION | MB_OK);
            return 0;
            }
        break;

    case WM_DESTROY:

            PostQuitMessage(0);
            return 0;

    default:

            return(DefWindowProc(hWnd, iMessage, wParam,
                lParam));
            }
        }
```

## Menus Using an Object-Oriented Language

This first section is the C++ resource script file for the program
written using object-oriented techniques.

```
MENU  MENU LOADONCALL MOVEABLE PURE
    DISCARDABLE
BEGIN
```

```
    POPUP "Player One"
    BEGIN
       MenuItem "Bob", 1, CHECKED
       MenuItem "Mary", 2, CHECKED
       MenuItem "John", 3, CHECKED
    END
    POPUP "Player Two"
    BEGIN
       MenuItem "Gary", 4, CHECKED
       MenuItem "Sue", 5, CHECKED
       MenuItem "Jane", 6, CHECKED
    END
    POPUP "Game"
    BEGIN
       MenuItem "Checkers", 7, CHECKED
       MenuItem "Chess", 8, CHECKED
    END
END
```

What follows now is the actual C++ program used to implement menus using object-oriented programming techniques.

```
#include <owl.h>

#define CM_BOB 1
#define CM_MARY 2
#define CM_JOHN 3
#define CM_GARY 4
#define CM_SUE 5
#define CM_JANE 6
#define CM_CHECKERS 7
#define CM_CHESS 8

class TMenuDemo : public TApplication
{
public:
    TMenuDemo(LPSTR AName) : TApplication(AName){}
    virtual void InitMainWindow();
    virtual void InitInstance();
};

class TMenuWindow : public TWindow
{
public:
    TMenuWindow(PWindowsObject AParent,
```

```
          LPSTR ATitle);
      virtual void CMBob(TMessage& Msg) =
          [CM_FIRST + CM_BOB];
      virtual void CMMary(TMessage& Msg) =
          [CM_FIRST + CM_MARY];
      virtual void CMJohn(TMessage& Msg) =
          [CM_FIRST + CM_JOHN];
      virtual void CMGary(TMessage& Msg) =
          [CM_FIRST + CM_GARY];
      virtual void CMSue(TMessage& Msg) =
          [CM_FIRST + CM_SUE];
      virtual void CMJane(TMessage& Msg) =
          [CM_FIRST + CM_JANE];
      virtual void CMCheckers(TMessage& Msg) =
          [CM_FIRST + CM_CHECKERS];
      virtual void CMChess(TMessage& Msg) =
          [CM_FIRST + CM_CHESS];
  };

TMenuWindow::TMenuWindow(PWindowsObject AParent,
    LPSTR ATitle) : TWindow(AParent, ATitle)
{
Attr.Menu = LoadMenu(Application->hInstance,"MENU");
CheckMenuItem(Attr.Menu, 1 ,MF_BYCOMMAND |
    MF_CHECKED);
CheckMenuItem(Attr.Menu, 2 ,MF_BYCOMMAND |
    MF_UNCHECKED);
CheckMenuItem(Attr.Menu, 3 ,MF_BYCOMMAND |
    MF_UNCHECKED);
CheckMenuItem(Attr.Menu, 4 ,MF_BYCOMMAND |
    MF_CHECKED);
CheckMenuItem(Attr.Menu, 5 ,MF_BYCOMMAND |
    MF_UNCHECKED);
CheckMenuItem(Attr.Menu, 6 ,MF_BYCOMMAND |
    MF_UNCHECKED);
CheckMenuItem(Attr.Menu, 7 ,MF_BYCOMMAND |
    MF_CHECKED);
CheckMenuItem(Attr.Menu, 8 ,MF_BYCOMMAND |
    MF_UNCHECKED);
};

void TMenuDemo::InitMainWindow()
{
MainWindow = new TMenuWindow(NULL,"Menus");
}
```

```
void TMenuDemo::InitInstance()
{
TApplication::InitInstance();
}


void TMenuWindow::CMBob(TMessage&)
{
CheckMenuItem(Attr.Menu, 1 ,MF_BYCOMMAND |
    MF_CHECKED);
CheckMenuItem(Attr.Menu, 2 ,MF_BYCOMMAND |
    MF_UNCHECKED);
CheckMenuItem(Attr.Menu, 3 ,MF_BYCOMMAND |
    MF_UNCHECKED);
MessageBox(HWindow, "Bob","Player One",MB_OK);
}
void TMenuWindow::CMMary(TMessage&)
{
CheckMenuItem(Attr.Menu, 1 ,MF_BYCOMMAND |
    MF_UNCHECKED);
CheckMenuItem(Attr.Menu, 2 ,MF_BYCOMMAND |
    MF_CHECKED);
CheckMenuItem(Attr.Menu, 3 ,MF_BYCOMMAND |
    MF_UNCHECKED);
MessageBox(HWindow, "Mary","Player One",MB_OK);
}


void TMenuWindow::CMJohn(TMessage&)
{
CheckMenuItem(Attr.Menu, 1 ,MF_BYCOMMAND |
    MF_UNCHECKED);
CheckMenuItem(Attr.Menu, 2 ,MF_BYCOMMAND |
    MF_UNCHECKED);
CheckMenuItem(Attr.Menu, 3 ,MF_BYCOMMAND |
    MF_CHECKED);
MessageBox(HWindow, "John","Player One",MB_OK);
}


void TMenuWindow::CMGary(TMessage&)
{
CheckMenuItem(Attr.Menu, 4 ,MF_BYCOMMAND |
    MF_CHECKED);
CheckMenuItem(Attr.Menu, 5 ,MF_BYCOMMAND |
    MF_UNCHECKED);
CheckMenuItem(Attr.Menu, 6 ,MF_BYCOMMAND |
    MF_UNCHECKED);
```

```
MessageBox(HWindow, "Gary","Player Two",MB_OK);
}

void TMenuWindow::CMSue(TMessage&)
{
CheckMenuItem(Attr.Menu, 4 ,MF_BYCOMMAND |
   MF_UNCHECKED);
CheckMenuItem(Attr.Menu, 5 ,MF_BYCOMMAND |
   MF_CHECKED);
CheckMenuItem(Attr.Menu, 6 ,MF_BYCOMMAND |
   MF_UNCHECKED);
MessageBox(HWindow, "Sue","Player Two",MB_OK);
}

void TMenuWindow::CMJane(TMessage&)
{
CheckMenuItem(Attr.Menu, 4 ,MF_BYCOMMAND |
   MF_UNCHECKED);
CheckMenuItem(Attr.Menu, 5 ,MF_BYCOMMAND |
   MF_UNCHECKED);
CheckMenuItem(Attr.Menu, 6 ,MF_BYCOMMAND |
   MF_CHECKED);
MessageBox(HWindow, "Jane","Player Two",MB_OK);
}

void TMenuWindow::CMCheckers(TMessage&)
{
CheckMenuItem(Attr.Menu, 7 ,MF_BYCOMMAND |
   MF_CHECKED);
CheckMenuItem(Attr.Menu, 8 ,MF_BYCOMMAND |
   MF_UNCHECKED);
MessageBox(HWindow, "Checkers","Game",MB_OK);
}

void TMenuWindow::CMChess(TMessage&)
{
CheckMenuItem(Attr.Menu, 7 ,MF_BYCOMMAND |
   MF_UNCHECKED);
CheckMenuItem(Attr.Menu, 8 ,MF_BYCOMMAND |
   MF_CHECKED);
MessageBox(HWindow, "Chess","Game",MB_OK);
}

int PASCAL WinMain(HANDLE hInstance,
   HANDLE hPrevInstance, LPSTR lpCmdLine,
```

```
        int nCmdShow)
{
TMenuDemo MenuDemo("Menu Window");
MenuDemo.Run();
return(MenuDemo.Status);
}
```

### Menus Using a Graphical Scripting Environment

To create menus in a graphical scripting environment you must return to the project window for SuperCard shown in Figure 7.7.

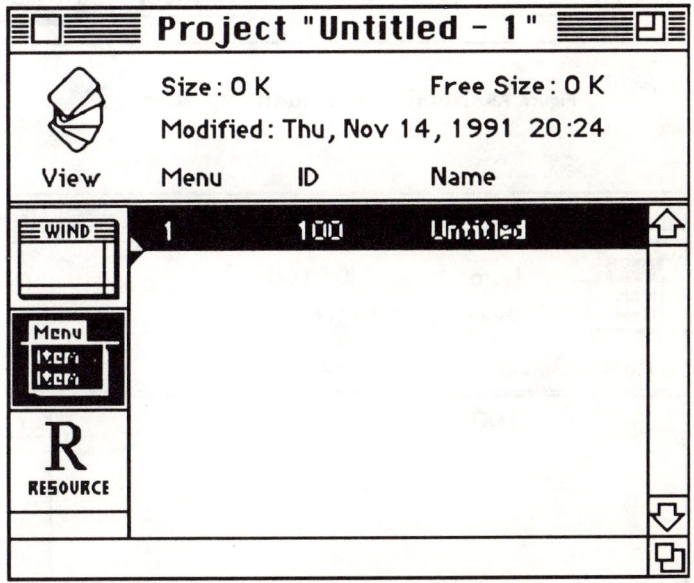

**Figure 7.7** Creating a menu in SuperCard.

By clicking on the middle icon on the left of the project window, you will enable the menu features of SuperCard. Each of the menus that will eventually appear at the top of the screen will be listed in the project window. To create new menus, simply double-click on the menu icon, select "New Menu" from the edit menu, or use the keyboard shortcut. The next thing to accomplish is naming the menu. By selecting "Menu Info" from the edit menu or by using a keyboard shortcut, the "Menu Info" window shown in Figure 7.8 will appear. With this window, you can name your menu, establish it as enabled or disabled upon initialization, and establish a script that will execute when the menu is activated.

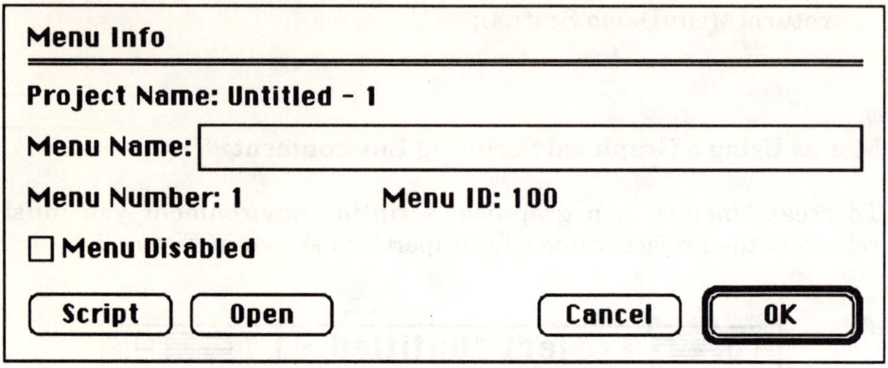

Menu Info

**Project Name: Untitled – 1**

**Menu Name:** [                                        ]

**Menu Number: 1**          **Menu ID: 100**

☐ **Menu Disabled**

( Script )    ( Open )              ( Cancel )    ( **OK** )

**Figure 7.8** Naming a menu in SuperCard.

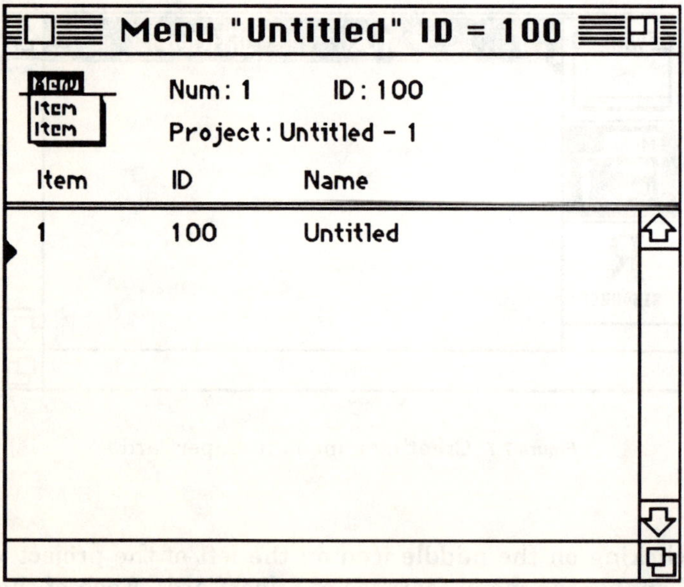

**Menu "Untitled" ID = 100**

Num: 1       ID: 100
Project: Untitled – 1

| Item | ID | Name |
|------|------|----------|
| 1 | 100 | Untitled |

**Figure 7.9** Creating menu items in SuperCard.

Once your menu has been enabled and initialized, you will probably want to create menu items that will pop up whenever the menu is clicked on. To create these menu items, you would double-click on the menu as it appears in the project window. When you do this, the window shown in Figure 7.9 will pop up. This window is specific to the menu you created. It will contain all of the menu items you wish to appear under the menu. From this window, you can create new menu items by double-clicking on the menu item icon in the upper-left-hand corner of the window, selecting "New Item" from the edit menu, or by using a keyboard shortcut. The new menu items will appear as a list within the window. Unfortunately, they will all be named "untitled" upon creation.

To name the menu items and to set the attributes of them, you will need to access the "Menu Item Info" window. To access this window, you can double-click on the menu item in the window shown in Figure 7.9, choose "Item Info" from the edit menu, or use the keyboard shortcut again. When you have accomplished this, the "Menu Item Info" window shown in Figure 7.10 will come into view.

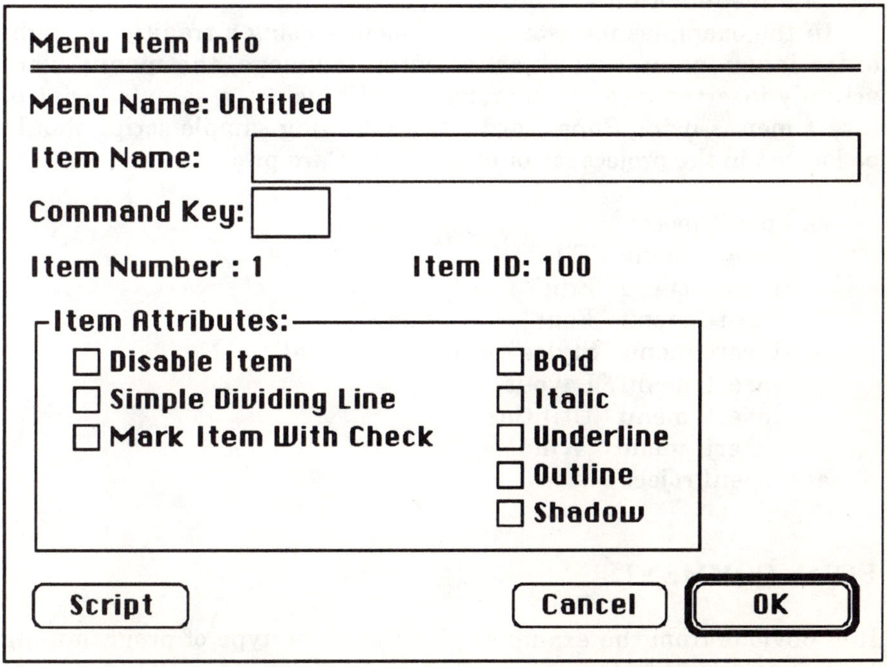

---

**Menu Item Info**

**Menu Name: Untitled**

**Item Name:** [                    ]

**Command Key:** [    ]

**Item Number : 1**            **Item ID: 100**

┌─ **Item Attributes:** ──────────────────┐
│  ☐ **Disable Item**        ☐ **Bold**
│  ☐ **Simple Dividing Line**   ☐ **Italic**
│  ☐ **Mark Item With Check**   ☐ **Underline**
│                           ☐ **Outline**
│                           ☐ **Shadow**
└───────────────────────────────────────┘

[ **Script** ]          [ **Cancel** ]   [ **OK** ]

---

**Figure 7.10** Assigning menu item attributes in SuperCard.

From the "Menu Item Info" window, you can establish the attributes of each individual menu item. The menu item should be named and you can specify a keyboard shortcut command sequence that will be displayed alongside the menu item. In addition, each item can be enabled or disabled at initialization or you can set the item up so that it displays a check mark by it when activated. The simple dividing-line option allows you to separate the menu items by a line if you wish. Along with these attributes, you can highlight your menu item by displaying it in **bold**, *italic*, <u>underline</u>, outline, shadow, or any combination of these selections. Also, from this window, you can click on the "Script" button in the lower-left-hand corner and write the script that will execute whenever the menu item is selected.

Now, all of your menus and menu items are created. This may have seemed like a lot of work, but keep in mind that you only have to create the menus one time. Once they are created and the project is launched, all you have to do is insert the menus into the menubar. Of course, if you want to have nested menus, you would simply insert a menu as a menu item in another menu. This will give the effect of a menu within a menu.

In the examples for establishing menus using a traditional high-order language and an object-oriented language, the menus were actually inserted into the menubar. I will include a sample script to insert menus using SuperCard. The following sample script should be located in the project script of the SuperCard project.

```
on openProject
    insert menu "File"
    insert menu "Edit"
    insert menu "Font"
    insert menu "Styles" into menu "Font"
    insert menu "Layout"
    insert menu "Utilities"
    insert menu "Window"
end openProject
```

## FINAL COMMENTS

It is obvious from the examples given that the type of programming language you choose is largely dependent on your personal preference. If you are a graphically oriented person, you may choose a graphical scripting environment. If not, you might select one of the high-order language options. For speed of development and ease of use, the graphical scripting environments win hands down. However, they tend to suffer where speed is concerned. If you must select a high-order language, using the object-oriented approach is highly recommended. You will find it to be a compromise between the graphical scripting environments and the traditional high-order language approach. With an object-oriented language, you can have the speed of a compiled language and end up writing less code. But because of the nature of object-oriented languages, you will probably end up with more understandable and maintainable code than with the traditional approach

# 8

# IBM PCs and Compatibles

Up to now, we have discussed Hypermedia and software development in general. We created our own hybrid software development method for use with Hypermedia applications. We have also built two Hypermedia applications using that software development method. And, finally, we discussed the advantages and disadvantages of three different types of off-the-shelf software development packages. We will now get a little more specific.

The purpose of this chapter is to provide you with the information necessary to make an informed decision concerning specific hardware platforms and software packages. This chapter will focus on IBM PCs and compatible computers. It will first describe some of the hardware options available and the pros and cons of those options with respect to Hypermedia. Then it will provide an overview of some programming environments that are currently available to develop your application. Naturally, this chapter can't cover every environment; however, it will cover a good sized sampling. It is not the intention to tell you which environment is best to use when developing Hypermedia applications. But it will make some general recommendations based on the information presented.

## HARDWARE

Selecting the appropriate hardware can sometimes be a difficult task. There are many things to consider. In developing a Hypermedia application, we must consider at least the relative speed and power of the system and the quality of the system input and output.

## MICROPROCESSORS

The microprocessor or Central Processing Unit (CPU) is the heart of any computer system. All of the computer's basic functions are either performed or monitored by the microprocessor. It is important, therefore, to understand the relative speed and power of the microprocessor in choosing the machine on which to develop your application.

All IBM PCs and compatibles utilize a microprocessor from the Intel 8086 family. This family has evolved over the years while still maintaining downward compatibility. In Figure 8.1, the Intel 8086 family and the major upgrade features for each microprocessor are illustrated.

### 8086/8088

The 8086/8088 microprocessor is Intel's first leap into a 16-bit machine. The 8086 and 8088 are virtually identical except that the 8086 has a 16-bit data bus while the 8088 maintains an 8-bit data bus. Each supports the ability to access only one megabyte of memory.

The Intel 8088 is the microprocessor used in the original IBM PC and in the PC XT. Both of these machines are vastly underpowered for all but the simplest of Hypermedia applications.

### 80286

The Intel 80286 was the IBM PC's first true 16-bit machine. Unlike the 8088, the 80286 has a full 16-bit data bus. One of the primary features added to the 80286 is multitasking capability. Multitasking is the property that makes the user of the computer feel as though two things are happening at once. An example of this would be editing a document while printing another one in the background. The 80286 accomplishes this by switching its processing between the separate tasks. The other upgrade feature is the incorporation of two different operating modes. In the protected mode, the 80286 sets aside a certain amount of memory for program execution. This memory is protected from use by any other program. Only in the protected mode can multitasking occur. The other operating mode is the real mode. The real mode forces the 80286 to act like the 8086, thus allowing complete downward compatibility.

The 80286 microprocessor is used in the IBM PC AT and assorted compatibles. This is the first IBM machine that would be considered marginally acceptable for Hypermedia applications.

| | Microprocessor | Upgrade Features |
|---|---|---|
| **Power and Speed** ↑ | 80486 | Enhanced 80386, 80387 math coprocessor, cache controller, on-chip cache memory, downward compatibility. |
| | 80386 | 32-bit microprocessor, 32-bit registers, memory management, downward compatibility. |
| | 80286 | 16-bit data bus, multitasking support, downward compatibility. |
| | 8086/8088 | 16-bit microprocessor, 16/8-bit data bus. |

**Figure 8.1** The relationship and upgrade features of microprocessors in the Intel 8086 family.

## 80386

The Intel 80386 is a full 32-bit high-speed microprocessor used in many IBM PCs and compatible computers. The 80386 supports both the real and protected modes of the 80286, thus providing multitasking capability and downward compatibility. In addition, the 80386 offers much more flexible memory management.

For the purpose of building Hypermedia applications, the IBM PC and compatible computers built around the 80386 are the first fully capable machines.

## 80486

As of this writing, the Intel 80486 is the newest member of the 8086 family. The primary upgrade features of the 80486 are speed, an integrated 80387 math co-processor, a cache controller, and an on chip cache memory. The 80486 accomplishes this while still maintaining the real and protected modes of its predecessors.

Obviously, computers based on the 80486 are faster and more powerful than 80386 based machines. Therefore, IBM PC and compatible computers designed around the Intel 80486 are completely usable for Hypermedia applications.

## INPUT/OUTPUT

One of the keys to good Hypermedia applications is the quality of the computer system's input and output (I/O). For the purpose of discussion, the I/O category has been broken down into keyboard, mice, and others for the system input and displays and sound for the system output.

### Keyboards, Mice, and Others

The computer keyboard has been and will continue to be one of the primary sources of input for all types of applications. The real up-and-coming challenge to the keyboard is voice response computing. There are several input devices designed around voice recognition concepts. For the most part, though, these are severely limited. Cost-effective voice-response computing is still many years in the future.

The mouse and trackball (which is essentially an upside down mouse) have made great gains in the last several years as the input devices of choice. For Hypermedia applications, these devices are vital. It would be extremely awkward to navigate using only the keyboard cursor keys. And, while IBM PCs are traditionally text based machines, they have in the past few years, particularly with the advent of Windows, become nearly as dependent on a pointing device as the Macintosh personal computer. In fact nearly all IBM PC clone resellers include a copy of Windows and a mouse with every CPU purchase. Therefore, you can safely assume that there will be some sort of a pointing device available for the user to provide input to your application.

There are several other input schemes that have garnered some level of popularity recently. Voice recognition software has already been discussed. The digitizer tablet is a hybrid of the mouse which allows precise coordinate input. Two conceptually closely related devices are touch screens and light pens. Both devices allow the user to interact directly with the screen. Of these two, the light pen would seem to show more promise. With touch screens, it is sometimes difficult to discern the precise point the user is trying to activate with something as large as a finger. An alternative is to provide the user a pointing device. But, if the user has to pick up a pointing device anyway, the device might as well be a light pen.

### Displays

A quality display system is critical to the acceptance level of your application. While appearance isn't everything, it does play a great part in the initial reaction of the user to an application. And, we all know how lasting that first impression can be. For IBM PC and compatible computers, there are many video options. Of all those options, though, there are three that have established themselves as virtual standards: Color Graphics Adapter (CGA), Enhanced Graphics Adapter (EGA), and Video Graphics Array (VGA). All three of these video options maintain two general modes of operation: text mode and graphics mode. Each of these modes within each video option may support several predefined colors and screen resolutions. Figure 8.2 shows the mode, screen resolution, and colors supported by each option.

### CGA

The Color Graphics Adapter (CGA) is the oldest of the video systems. CGA came standard with the original IBM PC and is still common in many home systems. It supported both text and graphics modes and had five sub-modes. Four of those sub-modes support a 320 x 200 pixel screen resolution with four colors. The fifth sub-mode, CGA-HI, supports a 640 x 200 screen resolution, but only two colors.

For Hypermedia applications, the CGA is of too low a resolution to support decent graphics and is therefore unacceptable. The cost difference between CGA and the now-recognized standard, VGA, is minimal. In fact, you will find that virtually all of the new IBM PC and compatible computer systems purchased will come equipped with VGA adapters and monitors. Therefore, you should not concern yourself with the CGA problem.

| Option | Mode | Screen Resolution | Colors Supported |
|--------|------|-------------------|------------------|
| CGA | CGAC0 | 320 x 200 | 4 |
|  | CGAC1 | 320 x 200 | 4 |
|  | CGAC2 | 320 x 200 | 4 |
|  | CGAC3 | 320 x 200 | 4 |
|  | CGAHI | 640 x 200 | 2 |
| EGA | EGALO | 320 x 200 | 16 |
|  | EGAHI | 640 x 350 | 16 |
|  | EGA64LO | 320 x 200 | 16 |
|  | EGA64HI | 640 x 350 | 4 |
|  | EGAMONOHI | 640 x 350 | 2 |
| VGA | VGALO | 640 x 200 | 16 |
|  | VGAMED | 640 x 350 | 16 |
|  | VGAHI | 640 x 480 | 16 |

**Figure 8.2** The three video standards and their relative modes of operation, screen resolution, and supported colors.

## EGA

The Enhanced Graphics Adapter (EGA) is the next step up from CGA. And, it supports all the text and graphics modes of the CGA standard. In addition, EGA has five sub-modes. Two of those sub-modes, EGALO and EGA64LO, have a 320 x 200 pixel screen resolution and support 16 colors. The other three, EGAHI, EGA64HI, and EGAMONOHI, have a 640 x 350 pixel screen resolution and support 16, four and two colors respectively.

EGA is moderately acceptable for Hypermedia applications. But, as in the CGA discussion, the cost difference between EGA and VGA is nearly insignificant and most IBM and compatible computer systems are now shipping with a VGA adapter and monitor.

## VGA

The Video Graphics Array (VGA) is currently the standard for displays in the IBM PC and compatible domain. VGA supports all CGA and EGA modes as well as three of its own. VGALO has a 640 x 200 pixel screen resolution. VGAMED has a 640 x 350 screen resolution. And, VGAHI has a 640 x 480 screen resolution. All modes support 16 colors.

VGA should be the current choice for Hypermedia applications. The higher screen resolutions and more color choices give the developer better flexibility in developing the application.

### Sound

For IBM PC and compatible computers, sounds are foreign. The audio system in a PC compatible is designed for little more than beeps and boings and the is no standard option for sound input. However, there are options available. There are third-party expansion boards available that can process sounds. The cost of these boards ranges from approximately $200 - $500. With the addition of an external speaker, you are now prepared to incorporate sounds into your application. Unfortunately, if you are developing your application with the intention of mass marketing, all buyers of the software will have to have those items to run your application. You may be forced to reevaluate the need for sound in your application or your choice in hardware platform.

### Video

The video situation for IBM PC and compatible computers is similar to that of the audio. You will have to buy an expansion board to process and display video. The difference is that video is a little more expensive. The first purchase will probably be a laserdisk to store the video images for around $1000. Then, you must purchase a board to overlay the video images on the computer screen. The cost of these boards ranges from approximately $700 - $2500. Of course, all systems that will run your application must have these items as well.

## SOFTWARE

There are two major items to consider under the software umbrella. The first is which operating system will be the basis for the application. This concern comes particularly into play if you plan on using a traditional high-order or object-oriented language to develop your application. Then, depending on which type of Hypermedia authoring tool you have chosen, you must select a specific environment.

## OPERATING SYSTEMS

For Hypermedia application development on an IBM PC or compatible computer, the operating systems you need to be concerned with are MS-DOS and Windows.

## MS-DOS

The Microsoft Disk Operating System (MS-DOS) is the most popular operating system on IBM PC and compatible computers. MS-DOS is the recognized standard and is shipped with virtually all PC purchases. MS-DOS is a command line, text-based operating system. Of course, this does not mean that your application must be the same. It does mean, however, that you may have to do a little more programming work to set up windows and buttons within your application.

### Windows

Microsoft Windows (or Windows, for short) is actually on operating system on top of an operating system. Windows is dependent on and will not run without MS-DOS. There are several advantages to Windows, however. The first is that for 80386 and higher-based machines, Windows breaks the 640 K RAM limit imposed by MS-DOS. Also, Windows offers a graphical user interface remarkably similar to the recognized leader in graphical user interfaces: the Apple Macintosh. In addition, Windows offers IBM PC and compatible users multitasking capabilities.

Programming in Windows is also very similar to programming a Macintosh. This is more difficult in some respects as this type of programming is usually event driven, not sequential. However, once that obstacle is overcome, Windows programming can actu-

ally be easier.  The operating system is already graphically oriented and understands windows, dialog boxes, buttons and menus.
All you must do is learn to manipulate these objects from within
your application.

If it is your intention to use a traditional high-order language or
an object-oriented language, use Windows as your foundation.  If
you intend to use a graphical scripting environment, then it doesn't
matter.  You will only use Windows if the application uses it.


## AUTHORING PACKAGES

It is assumed, at this point, that after reading Chapter 7, you have
decided on what type of programming environment in which you
will develop your application.  Therefore, you will probably only be
interested in one of the following sections.  An overview will be
given of the available traditional and object-oriented environments
and then cover graphical scripting environments that are designed
for authoring Hypermedia applications.


## TRADITIONAL AND OBJECT-ORIENTED ENVIRONMENTS

There are numerous compilers and environments available for the
IBM PC and compatible computers.  However, Hypermedia applications are primarily authored in some form of C or Pascal.  The primary reason for this is that, generally, the compilers for these two
languages come bundled with libraries containing a  great number
of graphics functions.  These graphics functions enable the programmer to develop graphical user interfaces with relative ease.
While others are available, Borland and Microsoft are the prime
vendors of quality large and small scale C and Pascal packages.

For traditional and object-oriented programmers, there are, from
both companies, several options on C, C++, Pascal, and Object Pascal.  Also, both companies provide versions for Windows that offer a
full Windows development environment.  The advantages and
disadvantages of each option will not be listed.  The decision
whether to choose traditional or object-oriented techniques has already been covered in Chapter 7.  And choosing C or Pascal is a personal decision based upon preference since the development environments are similar in features and functions provided.

## HYPER SPECIFIC ENVIRONMENTS

If you have selected a graphical scripting environment to build your application, there are many options available to you. Eight Hypermedia authoring environments have been chosen for review. By no means are these eight the only ones available. But, they represent a wide range of cost and capability. Your choice should be based upon which authoring package best meets your needs and your personal preference. The eight packages chosen are, in low- to high-cost order, TransText, xText, Hyper–Word, Hyperties, HyperWriter, Guide, SmarText, and Folio VIEWS Professional.

### TransText

The first and least expensive of the Hypermedia authoring applications reviewed is TransText. Some of the key features of TransText are shown in Figure 8.3.

| TransText<br>Support for: | YES | NO |
|---|---|---|
| Mouse | | √ |
| Text | √ | |
| Drawings | √ | |
| Pictures | √ | |
| Animation | | √ |
| Sound | | √ |
| Video | | √ |
| Other Applications | | √ |
| Scripting Language | | √ |

Figure 8.3 A summary of key Hypermedia features supported by TransText.

TransText is primarily a word processing program that allows you to insert links to other documents. As you can see from Figure

8.3, TransText does not support a mouse, animation, sound, video, other programs or a scripting language. It does provide some limited support for linking to pictures and drawings. You can build a decent text-based application using TransText. However, the application has several disadvantages. First, the application does not support a mouse. This makes for very klutzy navigation. The navigation that is provided by TransText is quite primitive. And, you can't add to that capability because TransText does not have a scripting language. Probably the prime disadvantage of TransText is that it is actually part of a series of applications that are used to build, edit, and run your Hypermedia application. This tends to make the TransText authoring tool very confusing and difficult to use.

| xText Support for: | YES | NO |
|---|---|---|
| Mouse | √ | |
| Text | √ | |
| Drawings | | √ |
| Pictures | | √ |
| Animation | | √ |
| Sound | | √ |
| Video | | √ |
| Other Applications | | √ |
| Scripting Language | | √ |

Figure 8.4 A summary of key Hypermedia features supported by xText.

## xText

The next Hypermedia authoring application is xText. Some of the key features of xText are shown in Figure 8.4. xText was initially created to develop memory resident help systems that are text-based. As you can see from Figure 8.4, xText is rather weak in the features department. There is no support for any media form aside from text. However, xText does have a couple of advantages over Trans-Text. It has a much simpler program layout. There are only two parts of the program: the compiler and the reader. All of the authoring of the application is done in your own word processor. xText currently includes special support for Microsoft Word 5.0 and WordPerfect 5.0. If you do not use one of these word processors, you will have to deal with straight ASCII text. When creating your document, you imbed the xText commands into the text of the application. After entering the text, the application is compiled. Then, the reader can be used to perform simple navigation on the application. There is no scripting language, so navigation enhancements are not possible. While there is no multimedia support whatsoever, at least xText does support the use of a mouse.

| Hyper-Word<br>Support for: | YES | NO |
|---|---|---|
| Mouse | √ | |
| Text | √ | |
| Drawings | | √ |
| Pictures | | √ |
| Animation | | √ |
| Sound | | √ |
| Video | | √ |
| Other Applications | | √ |
| Scripting Language | √ | |

**Figure 8.5** A summary of key Hypermedia features supported by Hyper-Word.

## Hyper-Word

The next Hypermedia authoring application is Hyper-Word. Some of the key features of Hyper-Word are shown in Figure 8.5. Hyper-Word is slightly more sophisticated than TransText or xText.

While all three of the programs are text based, Hyper-Word is the first authoring program to offer a scripting language. This gives the author the freedom to customize the application somewhat. As you can see from Figure 8.5, there is no support for any media form aside from text. In fact, Hyper-Word is actually a decent word processor with the ability to place Hypertext links. Hyper-Word does support several other word processors as well as ASCII. The Hyper-Word reader utilizes the mouse, but, requires keyboard interaction at the same time to navigate.

| Hyperties Support for: | YES | NO |
|---|---|---|
| Mouse | √ | |
| Text | √ | |
| Drawings | √ | |
| Pictures | √ | |
| Animation | | √ |
| Sound | | √ |
| Video | √ | |
| Other Applications | √ | |
| Scripting Language | | √ |

**Figure 8.6** A summary of key Hypermedia features supported by Hyperties.

## Hyperties

The first three authoring packages reviewed were text based. But, all of them were priced under $150, offering an inexpensive entry point into the world of Hypermedia for IBM PC and compatible computers. Hyperties, as you can see from Figure 8.6, is a more full-featured authoring environment. Of course this comes at a price; Hyperties costs approximately $350.

Again refering to Figure 8.6, Hyperties is the first application to offer support for drawings and pictures in addition to text. In addition, Hyperties can control video and can launch other applications. Some of the disadvantages of Hyperties are the lack of support for animation and sound and the lack of a scripting language. This does not allow the developer to fully customize the application.

Hyperties uses the encyclopedia metaphor. That is, you must have a cover, preface, table of contents, a series of articles with illustrations, and an index. Navigation within Hyperties begins with the table of contents. There, you select an item of interest and that particular article is displayed. While this skeletal layout can be very efficient, it is unfortunate that there are no facilities for user identified links.

| HyperWriter Support for: | YES | NO |
|---|---|---|
| Mouse | √ | |
| Text | √ | |
| Drawings | √ | |
| Pictures | √ | |
| Animation | | √ |
| Sound | √ | |
| Video | √ | |
| Other Applications | √ | |
| Scripting Language | √ | |

**Figure 8.7** A summary of key Hypermedia features supported by HyperWriter.

## HyperWriter

HyperWriter, as you can see from Figure 8.7 is the most versatile of the applications we have examined. It has full support for all media types except animation. It can access other applications. It supports text, drawings, pictures, sound, and can control a video disk. And, HyperWriter has its own scripting language allowing the developer to customize the application under development. HyperWriter has a full-featured word processor, but, can also accept ASCII text from another source if necessary. It also includes a graphics capture program and a variety of linking metaphors.

One of the key features of HyperWriter is the link map. The link map is a graphic display of all the links in the system. The link map resembles a flow chart giving an overview of the major links in the application. If the readers so choose, they can even navigate using the link map instead of the information itself. HyperWriter also supports some other valuable features. Among these are full use of menus, scroll bars, and dialog boxes, macros, group authoring, and password protection.

| Guide<br>Support for: | YES | NO |
|---|---|---|
| Mouse | √ | |
| Text | √ | |
| Drawings | √ | |
| Pictures | √ | |
| Animation | | √ |
| Sound | | √ |
| Video | √ | |
| Other Applications | √ | |
| Scripting Language | √ | |

Figure 8.8 A summary of key Hypermedia features supported by Guide.

## Guide

Guide is the first Windows application that we have examined. Because of its ties to windows, Guide gives the developer the ability to create a quality graphical user interface that is consistent with that of other Windows programs. As you can see from Figure 8.8, Guide provides support for text, drawings, pictures, and other applications. It can control a video disk and comes with an outstanding scripting language. The scripting language is much like Pascal and allows complete customization of the application. There are no link maps, bookmarks, or reading histories, but, you could develop these items using the scripting language. Unfortunately, Guide does not support animation or sound.

Guide, like most of the other application builders, has its own word processor. It can, though, accept ASCII text exported from some other source. One of Guide's key features is its graphics handling. Guide accepts multiple graphics formats and allows total control over the images including placement, sizing, cropping, and combining with other images. Guide also supports links to and from graphics images. With all of these abilities and Windows support, Guide has the capability to provide the highest quality presentation of any of the previously examined packages.

| SmarText Support for: | YES | NO |
|---|---|---|
| Mouse | √ | |
| Text | √ | |
| Drawings | √ | |
| Pictures | √ | |
| Animation | | √ |
| Sound | | √ |
| Video | | √ |
| Other Applications | √ | |
| Scripting Language | | √ |

**Figure 8.9** A summary of key Hypermedia features supported by SmarText.

## SmarText

SmarText is a Windows program like the very versatile Guide that we just examined. Unfortunately, the similarities to Guide stop there. As shown in Figure 8.9, SmarText only offers support for text, drawings, pictures, and other applications. There is no support for animation, sound, or video. And SmarText does not have a scripting language. One of the key disadvantages of SmarText is that it does not have a built-in word processor. The developer must create the document in another word processor and then import the document. Since there is no ability whatsoever to format documents, the look of the application suffers greatly. Another disadvantage is that the reader module must be purchased separately for an additional $100.

To its advantage, SmarText makes extensive use of icons and menus for everything from linking to opening and closing documents. An important feature of SmarText not seen before is automated linking. Whenever a document is imported, links are automatically placed based on a user set degree of linking. SmarText performs an analysis of the document looking for single occurrences of words and linking them the places where the word occurs more frequently. There are two disadvantages to this automated linking. First, the user must manually place all links to graphics, other applications, and places where there is applicable information but not the identical wording. Also, there is the possibility of overlinking the document and providing links to areas that you don't want linked. Living with these disadvantages, may or may not be better than entering all of the links manually. Overall, SmarText provides an outstanding user interface and an important step towards automated linking. But, it is woefully lacking in customizability with a scripting language, and in basic editing and formatting features.

## Folio VIEWS Professional

Folio VIEWS Professional is exactly what its name and price imply: a professional tool. As with many tools of this nature, Folio VIEWS Professional imposes a particular organizational method upon the information entered into it. In this case, the Folio VIEWS Professional document is called an infobase. The infobase containing all of the necessary text, sound, graphics, and animation is organized into blocks of information called folios. These folios are roughly equivalent to concepts or ideas. Once the information is sorted into the appropriate format, the reader is supplied with some

powerful tools to navigate the folios. The developer has two options
in creating the application. Folio VIEWS Professional has its own
editor for infobase building, or the files can be imported. Folio
VIEWS Professional understands 41 different file formats, so you
can use virtually any word processor. When importing a file, Folio
VIEWS Professional assigns a conversion method to that file. The
most common conversion method puts every paragraph of the file
into its own folio. Once all the files are imported, the developer can
edit, create, or delete the folios at will to suit the particular needs of
the application.

| Folio VIEWS Professional<br>Support for: | YES | NO |
|---|---|---|
| Mouse | √ | |
| Text | √ | |
| Drawings | √ | |
| Pictures | √ | |
| Animation | √ | |
| Sound | √ | |
| Video | | √ |
| Other Applications | √ | |
| Scripting Language | √ | |

Figure 8.10 A summary of key Hypermedia features supported
by Folio VIEWS Professional.

As you can see from Figure 8.10, Folio VIEWS Professional provides support for all media types except, surprisingly, video. It can
access other applications and has its own scripting language allowing the developer to customize the application.

There are only two apparent disadvantages to Folio VIEWS Professional. The first is the forced folio concept which does not allow
developers the freedom to organize information as they please. The
second is Folio VIEWS Professional's limited graphics editing capability. Text and graphics can't be combined. The position and

size of an image can't be altered once it is entered. And, you can't link from an image to more that one location in the infobase.

## FINAL RECOMMENDATIONS

The final recommendations, as you might expect, are wishy-washy. You should choose the hardware and software that is right for the application, not force the application onto inadequate platforms. The purpose of this chapter was to provide you with the information necessary to make informed decisions on hardware and software platforms based upon your particular application. Therefore, any recommendation made would be contradictory to this concept. However, an exception can be made to any established rule. In order to develop an effective Hypermedia application using an IBM PC or compatible computer, there is a minimum hardware configuration. Since Hypermedia applications tend to be graphics-intensive, speed and quality of display can be severely hampered by an underpowered computer. Therefore, as a minimum configuration, a 80386 based machine with a VGA board and monitor is recommended.

# 9

# The Macintosh

As we all know, many years ago, two inventive geniuses, finding themselves fed up with the current computing platforms, formulated Apple Corporation. As the years passed, one of these geniuses, Steven Jobs, was sparked with the desire to create a new standard in the computing world. The machine he would have a hand in creating would have a graphical user interface that was intuitive and easy to learn. The machine would be easily expandable with built in support for networking. All the software run on it would behave in a similar manner making training for applications virtually obsolete.

In 1984, Apple Corporation announced the release of the Macintosh Plus. While there were earlier versions of the Macintosh, the Macintosh Plus is considered by many to be the first real Macintosh. The reason for this is that the Macintosh Plus was the first expandable platform. The buyer could select from 1 to 4 megabytes of RAM. But, more importantly, the Macintosh Plus had a built-in Small Computer System Interface (SCSI) port. This SCSI port enabled the buyer to daisy-chain up to seven external peripheral devices to the computer. Also, at about the same time, third-party software developers began producing a great quantity of applications targeted to the Macintosh operating system. Many of these applications were, and still are, integrated, allowing easy sharing of data between applications.

Over the years, the Apple Macintosh family has grown. Apple has developed new and much more powerful computers while still maintaining the standards set years before. In fact, the Macintosh operating system is widely recognized as the standard for graphical user interfaces. The proliferation of entries into the Macintosh family, though, could lead to some confusion over which particular computer would be best suited for a given task.

No, this chapter will not be a long advertisement for the Macintosh. The purpose of this chapter is to provide you with the information necessary to make an informed decision concerning specific hardware platforms and software packages. Unlike Chapter 8, this chapter will focus on the Apple Macintosh computer. It will first describe some of the hardware options available and the pros and cons of those options with respect to Hypermedia. Then it will provide an overview of some programming environments that are currently available to develop your application. Naturally, this chapter can't cover every environment; however, it will cover a good sized sampling. It is not the intention to tell you which environment is best to use when developing Hypermedia applications. But this chapter will make some general recommendations based on the information presented.

## HARDWARE

Selecting the appropriate hardware can sometimes be a difficult task. There are many things to consider. For our purpose, developing a Hypermedia application, we must consider at least the relative speed and power of the system and the quality of the system input and output. Since there are currently no Macintosh clones, we will examine all of the desktop versions (portables are excluded) of the Macintosh that Apple supports as of this writing.

## THE MACINTOSH FAMILY

As of this writing, there is a total of 15 versions of the Macintosh that are being supported by Apple. Four of those are laptop versions and will not be considered here. The other 11 in increasing order of cost and performance are the Macintosh Classic, Macintosh LC, Macintosh LC II, Macintosh Classic II, Macintosh SE/30, Macintosh IIsi, Macintosh IIci, Macintosh IIfx, Macintosh Quadra 700, Macintosh Quadra 900, and Macintosh Quadra 950. It is important to understand the relative speed and capabilities of each system before choosing the machine on which to develop your application.

All the members of the Macintosh family run the Macintosh.graphical user interface. Since a mouse or other pointing device is mandatory to run the interface, all Macintosh computers ship with a mouse. And, consequently, all Macintosh applications are mouse-driven. Also, all Macintosh computers are equipped with some version of a SCSI interface to link external peripherals. The complete commonality of the individual systems ends there. Each of the Macintosh versions will now be discussed with respect to its applicability to Hypermedia applications.

### Macintosh Classic

The Macintosh Classic is Apple's entry level Macintosh. The Classic is actually the replacement for the aging Macintosh Plus that was discussed in the introduction to this chapter. Figure 9.1 shows some pertinent information on the Macintosh Classic.

**Macintosh  Classic**

| | |
|---|---|
| **Processor/Speed** | 68000/8Mhz |
| **Math  Coprocessor** | no |
| **RAM** | 1MB-4MB |
| **Expansion  Slots** | 0 |
| **Sound  Input/Output** | no/mono |
| **Built-in  Video/Resolution** | b&w/512 by 342 |

**Figure 9.1** Some of the key features of the Macintosh Classic.

The Macintosh Classic is built in a similar fashion to the original Macintosh. That is, it is not a modular system. The entire system, including the built-in monitor is enclosed in a single case. Unlike the original Macintosh, the Classic is somewhat expandable. Additional RAM can be added, and there is room in the case for an internal hard drive.  Of course, there is a built-in SCSI port and an internal 1.4 megabyte floppy drive.  The monitor is a black and white nine-inch screen with a resolution of 512 x 342 pixels.

For Hypermedia purposes, the Macintosh Classic is adequate for small applications.  However, for large graphics-intensive applications, the 68000 processor will seem a little slow.  The video resolution is sufficient, but, black and white on a nine inch screen might be a little limiting.  The sound output is of good quality, but, unfortunately, Apple chose not to offer built-in sound input.  Inexpensive, quality sound-input devices can be purchased from third-party vendors to make up for this oversight.

## Macintosh LC

The Macintosh LC is considerably different from the Classic.  The features of the Macintosh LC are summarized in Figure 9.2.

### Macintosh LC

| | |
|---|---|
| Processor/Speed | 68020/16Mhz |
| Math Coprocessor | no |
| RAM | 2MB-10MB |
| Expansion Slots | 1 |
| Sound Input/Output | yes/mono |
| Built-in Video/Resolution | color/640 by 480 |

Figure 9.2 Some of the key features of the Macintosh LC.

Probably the first noticeable difference is the case.  The LC is modular in nature, giving the purchaser the option of choosing a monitor.  That is not to say that you must buy a card though.  If you select a 13- or 14-inch color monitor, no separate card purchase is necessary.  This alludes to the second noticeable difference.  The Macintosh LC is a color-capable machine.  The LC is an extremely capable machine for its price.  It supports 2 to 10 megabytes of memory and has one internal expansion slot.  The one possible disadvantage of the Macintosh LC is that it is powered by a 68020 microprocessor with a 16-bit data path and no coprocessor.  For extreme color graphics-intensive applications, the Macintosh LC may be a little slow.  On the plus side, though, it does have quality sound output and a sound input jack.  Overall, for the cost the Macintosh LC is an outstanding Hypermedia platform.

**Macintosh LC II**

The Macintosh LC II, as its name suggests, is an upgrade to the original Macintosh LC.  The features of the Macintosh LC II are summarized in Figure 9.3.

### Macintosh LC II

| | |
|---|---|
| Processor/Speed | 68030/16Mhz |
| Math Coprocessor | no |
| RAM | 4MB-10MB |
| Expansion Slots | 1 |
| Sound Input/Output | yes/mono |
| Built-in Video/Resolution | color/640 by 480 |

**Figure 9.3** Some of the key features of the Macintosh LC II.

The Macintosh LC is Apple Corporation's response to the primary complaint about the Macintosh LC: the 68020 microprocessor.  The main advantage of the Macintosh LC II is the addition of a 68030 microprocessor which allows the machine to support virtual memory.  Virtual memory is a feature which allows the CPU to treat part of the hard drive as Random Access Memory (RAM).  Unfortunately, the new microprocessor is essentially the only difference in the two machines.  The Macintosh LC II has the same clock speed (16 megahertz) and data path width (16-bits) as the original Macintosh LC.  Therefore, the machines are virtually identical in performance.

Another oddity on the Macintosh LC II is its memory scheme. To keep the cost down, Apple used the same memory controller in both machines. This memory controller is only capable of accessing 10 megabytes of RAM. However, with four megabytes of RAM built-in, you must install a total of 12 megabytes of RAM in order to utilize the 10 megabyte maximum. Without some third-party support, the extra two megabytes of RAM is wasted. In spite of its faults, the Macintosh LC II is still a sound purchase since it is a slight improvement over the Macintosh LC and it is the same price.

**Macintosh Classic II**

The Macintosh Classic II actually came out about a year after the original Classic. The Classic II is Apple's answer to the need for a low cost, entry-level 68030-based machine. Some of the features of the Classic II are shown in Figure 9.4.

### Macintosh Classic II

| | |
|---|---|
| Processor/Speed | 68030/16Mhz |
| Math Coprocessor | optional |
| RAM | 1MB-10MB |
| Expansion Slots | 0 |
| Sound Input/Output | yes/mono |
| Built-in Video/Resolution | b&w/512 by 342 |

**Figure 9.4** Some of the key features of the Macintosh Classic II.

As you can see, the Classic II is much more powerful than the original Classic. The addition of the 68030 microprocessor, an optional math coprocessor, and the capability to upgrade to 10 megabytes of RAM result in a tremendous power increase. The two share a near identical case so there is room for an internal hard drive. Of course, there is a built-in SCSI port and an internal 1.4 megabyte floppy drive. The monitor is the same black and white nine-inch screen with a resolution of 512 x 342 pixels.

For Hypermedia purposes, the Macintosh Classic II is far better equipped than the Classic. However, it does suffer from the small-screen syndrome. The sound output is of good quality, and, there is a built-in microphone jack for sound input. The Macintosh Classic, while quite inexpensive, is the first full-featured Hypermedia platform in the traditional Macintosh case.

### Macintosh SE/30

The Macintosh SE/30 is a step forward and a step back at the same time. Some of the features of the Macintosh SE/30 are shown in Figure 9.5.

**Macintosh  SE/30**

| | |
|---|---|
| Processor/Speed | 68030/16Mhz |
| Math  Coprocessor | yes |
| RAM | 1MB-32MB |
| Expansion  Slots | 1 |
| Sound  Input/Output | no/stereo |
| Built-in  Video/Resolution | b&w/512 by 342 |

**Figure 9.5** Some of the key features of the Macintosh SE/30.

In moving forward, the Macintosh SE/30 contains a 16-megahertz 68030, a math coprocessor, and a full 32-bit data path. The Macintosh SE/30, like the Macintosh LC, has one internal expansion slot, but, it is capable of housing 32 megabytes of RAM. Unfortunately, the Macintosh SE/30 takes a step back by returning to the original nonmodular Macintosh case and small black and white screen. In another unusual move, Apple included high-fidelity stereo output but did not put in a sound-input jack. The Macintosh SE/30 is quite a powerful machine. And the inclusion of stereo output is a great leap.  But without the support for sound input and a larger color monitor, the platform is found to be somewhat lacking when compared to the next Macintosh, the IIsi, which is only slightly more expensive.

## Macintosh IIsi

The Macintosh IIsi is the first in a series of three workstation class 68030-based Macs called the Macintosh II series.  The Macintosh II series computers are all powered by a 68030 microprocessor with a full 32-bit data path.  The pertinent features of the Macintosh IIsi are shown in Figure 9.6.

### Macintosh  IIsi

| | |
|---|---|
| Processor/Speed | 68030/20 Mhz |
| Math  Coprocessor | optional |
| RAM | 2MB-17MB |
| Expansion  Slots | 1 |
| Sound  Input/Output | yes/stereo |
| Built-in  Video/Resolution | color/640  by  480 |

**Figure 9.6** Some of the key features of the Macintosh IIsi.

The only noticeable fault of the Macintosh IIsi is that you must pay extra for the math coprocessor.  A 20-megahertz 68030 is at the heart of the machine which can contain up to 17 megabytes of RAM.  The Macintosh IIsi contains one expansion slot and the standard 1.4 megabyte internal floppy drive all in a small modular case.  There is built-in support for 13- or 14-inch color or gray-scale monitors.  The resolutions supported are 640 x 480 pixels with 256 colors or gray shades, 640 x 780 pixels with 16 gray shades, and 512 x 382 pixels with 256 colors.  Also, Apple finally got the sound situation right.  The Macintosh IIsi has not only high-fidelity stereo sound output, but also a sound-input port.

Overall, for the cost (around $2500), the Macintosh IIsi is probably the most capable Macintosh for Hypermedia applications. There is support for large-screen color monitors, internal expansion, and stereo sound. With the addition of a $250 math coprocessor, the Macintosh IIsi becomes the platform of choice.

## Macintosh IIci

With the Macintosh IIci, Apple again manages to move forward and take a small step backward at the same time. Some of the features of the Macintosh IIci are shown in Figure 9.7.

### Macintosh IIci

| | |
|---|---|
| Processor/Speed | 68030/25Mhz |
| Math Coprocessor | yes |
| RAM | 1MB-32MB |
| Expansion Slots | 3 |
| Sound Input/Output | no/stereo |
| Built-in Video/Resolution | color/multiple |

Figure 9.7 Some of the key features of the Macintosh IIci.

The Macintosh IIci is more capable, at a cost of nearly $1000 more, than the Macintosh IIsi in almost every area. It is powered by a 68030 running at 25 megahertz and comes standard with a math coprocessor. The Macintosh IIci can contain up to 32 megabytes of RAM and has three internal expansion slots in a slightly larger modular case. While stereo sound output was included, sound input was omitted on the Macintosh IIci. The built-in video options are identical to the Macintosh IIsi. There is support for 13- or 14-inch color or gray-scale monitors. The resolutions supported are 640 x 480 pixels with 256 colors or gray shades, 640 x 780 pixels with 16 gray shades, and 512 x 382 pixels with 256 colors.

The Macintosh IIci is obviously the most powerful machine we have yet examined.  However, there is some question as to whether that power increase is completely offset by the lack of a built-in sound input port and additional expense.

## Macintosh IIfx

The Macintosh IIfx is the last and most powerful of the Macintosh II series.  Some of the features of the Macintosh IIfx are shown in Figure 9.8.

### Macintosh  IIfx

| | |
|---|---|
| Processor/Speed | 68030/40Mhz |
| Math  Coprocessor | yes |
| RAM | 1MB-32MB |
| Expansion  Slots | 6 |
| Sound  Input/Output | no/stereo |
| Built-in  Video/Resolution | none |

Figure 9.8  Some of the key features of the Macintosh IIfx.

Once again, with the Macintosh IIfx, Apple managed to provide a more powerful machine while still leaving some holes.  The 68030 microprocessor running at 40 megahertz is an incredible leap.  A math coprocessor comes standard as does a memory-management unit.  Two other items shipped with the system for the first time are a static RAM cache and dedicated I/O processors.  The Macintosh IIfx can contain up to 32 megabytes of RAM and has six internal expansion slots.  Of course, the price of those six slots is paid in the size of the case.  Once again stereo-sound output was provided while sound input was omitted altogether.  Noticeably missing from the Macintosh IIfx, and a first for any Macintosh, is any built-in support for video.  One of the six expansion slots must be used to house a video card.

The Macintosh IIfx is by far the most powerful Macintosh we have yet examined.  However, for the purpose of building Hypermedia applications, the platform is somewhat lacking especially when you consider the approximately $5000 price tag.

### Macintosh Quadra 700

The most recent addition to the Macintosh family is the 68040-based Quadra series.  The first in that series is the Macintosh Quadra 700. Some of the features of this machine are shown in Figure 9.9.

**Macintosh  Quadra  700**

| | |
|---|---|
| Processor/Speed | 68040/25Mhz |
| Math  Coprocessor | built  in |
| RAM | 4MB-64MB |
| Expansion  Slots | 2 |
| Sound  Input/Output | yes/stereo |
| Built-in  Video/Resolution | color/multiple |

**Figure 9.9** Some of the key features of the Macintosh Quadra 700.

The Macintosh Quadra 700 was obviously built with Hypermedia in mind.  It comes with a 68040 microprocessor which has a built-in math coprocessor and static RAM cache.  It can contain up to 64 megabytes of RAM and has two internal expansion slots.  Apple finally reverted to supporting stereo sound output as well as a sound input port on the Macintosh Quadra 700.  And, the video options are greatly expanded.  The Macintosh Quadra 700 comes with 500 kilobytes of video RAM that is separate from the main memory to speed up screen response.  Also, the Macintosh Quadra 700 supports not only the standard Macintosh monitors, but also, the IBM compatible Video Graphics Array (VGA) standard.  Another first for the Macintosh Quadra 700 is built-in Ethernet support.

Overall, the Macintosh Quadra 700, while a bit pricey at approximately $5500, is a terrific platform for Hypermedia application authoring and reading.

### Macintosh Quadra 900

The next version of the Macintosh family is the Macintosh Quadra 900. Some of the features of the Macintosh Quadra 900 are shown in Figure 9.10.

### Macintosh Quadra 900

| | |
|---|---|
| Processor/Speed | 68040/25Mhz |
| Math Coprocessor | built in |
| RAM | 4MB-256MB |
| Expansion Slots | 5 |
| Sound Input/Output | yes/stereo |
| Built-in Video/Resolution | color/multiple |

Figure 9.10 Some of the key features of the Macintosh Quadra 900.

With the Macintosh Quadra 900, Apple concentrated on making the system better than its predecessor in nearly every respect. While both the Macintosh Quadra 700 and the Macintosh Quadra 900 are driven by the same 25 megahertz 68040 microprocessor, the Macintosh Quadra 900 can contain up to 256 megabytes of RAM and has five internal expansion slots. The sound input is the same except for the capability in the Macintosh Quadra 900 of bringing music directly off an internal CD-ROM drive. The sound output is also slightly different. The Macintosh Quadra 900 has a considerably larger speaker and its own amplifier.

The only noticeable disadvantages of the Macintosh Quadra 900 are size and price. The unit is not made to be desktop-bound unless that is all you want on you desk. The expected price of a Macintosh Quadra 900 is in the neighborhood of $7500.

## Macintosh Quadra 950

The final addition and top-of-the-line of the Macintosh family is the Macintosh Quadra 950. Some of the features of the Macintosh Quadra 950 are shown in Figure 9.11.

**Macintosh  Quadra  950**

| | |
|---|---|
| Processor/Speed | 68040/33Mhz |
| Math  Coprocessor | built  in |
| RAM | 8MB-256MB |
| Expansion  Slots | 5 |
| Sound  Input/Output | yes/stereo |
| Built-in  Video/Resolution | color/multiple |

**Figure 9.11** Some of the key features of the Macintosh Quadra 950.

With the Macintosh Quadra 950, Apple sought to make improvements on the previous high-end Macintosh, the Macintosh Quadra 900. Both systems are driven by a 68040 microprocessor. However, the Macintosh Quadra 950 operates at 33 megahertz. Another primary difference is in the built-in video. The Macintosh Quadra 950 has built-in support for 19-inch color monitors. The other new features of the Macintosh Quadra 950 involve general fine-tuning of the system. The Macintosh Quadra 950 is expected to be the same price as that of a Macintosh Quadra 900. This fact makes the Macintosh Quadra 950 the obvious choice for the high-end user.

## SOFTWARE

There are two major items to consider under the software umbrella. The first is which operating system will be the basis for the application. This concern comes particularly into play if you plan on using a traditional high-order or object-oriented language to develop your application. Then, depending on which type of Hypermedia authoring tool you have chosen, you must select a specific environment.

## OPERATING SYSTEMS

For Hypermedia application development on a Macintosh computer, there is only one operating system you need to be concerned with. Unfortunately, there are two versions of the Macintosh operating system and they are not necessarily compatible.

### System 6 or System 7

System 6 (Version 6.0.7 was the last System 6 release) is the traditional Macintosh operating system. It has evolved over years of upgrades into the standard by which all graphical user interfaces are judged. The highest compliment you can pay to an IBM PC or workstation software developer is to state that the user interface of their application is Mac-like. As more powerful Macintosh platforms were developed, some of the weaknesses of System 6 were encountered. Not the least of these weaknesses was the fact that System 6 utilized only 24 of the 32 bits available for addressing memory. This limited the RAM access of any platform using System 6 to eight megabytes.

With the arrival of the Macintosh II and Quadra series, it became obvious that the eight megabyte barrier must be broken. Macintosh platforms are now able to house up to 256 megabytes of RAM. Being restricted to eight is intolerable. System 7 is Apple's solution to the problem. System 7 is 32-bit clean, meaning that it can access up to 2048 megabytes of RAM. This should be sufficient for the near future.

Several other changes also went into System 7. Among these changes is one that is expected to revolutionize Hypermedia. This new feature is called QuickTime. Up until now, it has been said that interactive Hypervideo is far too expensive for the average developer. With QuickTime, it is virtually free. There are three main features of QuickTime. The movie toolbox allows developers to create, edit, and play video, animation, or sound. Then these movies can be added into any application. The component manager allows the consistent adding of new features such as new compression and decompression techniques and digitizing software. Finally, the image compression manager controls the application of various compression schemes. There is a separate photo compressor, video compressor, and animation compressor. The only apparent disadvantage of QuickTime is that it does not run on older Macintosh computers.

So, if System 7 is a large enhancement over System 6, why is there a decision to make? Well, in a year or so, there will be no decision. The only holdback is that some software developed by third-party vendors is not System 7 compatible. This is not Apple Corporation's fault. Apple warned developers for years to make their applications 32-bit clean, but, only a few listened. All Macintosh computers are now shipped with System 7. And, most third-party software developers have revisions in the works that will make their applications System 7 compatible. Therefore, my recommendation is to develop your application under the more capable System 7.

## AUTHORING PACKAGES

It is assumed, at this point, that after reading Chapter 7, you have decided on which type of programming environment to develop your application. Therefore, you will probably only be interested in one of the following sections. An overview of the available traditional and object-oriented environments will be given and then graphical scripting environments that are designed for authoring Hypermedia applications will be covered.

## TRADITIONAL AND OBJECT ORIENTED ENVIRONMENTS

There are numerous compilers and environments available for the Macintosh computer. However, Hypermedia applications are primarily authored in some form of C or Pascal. The primary reason for this is that, generally, the compilers for these two languages come bundled with libraries containing a great number of graphics functions. These graphics functions enable the programmer to develop graphical user interfaces with relative ease.

For traditional and object-oriented programmers, there are several options on C, C++, Pascal, and Object Oriented Pascal. The advantages and disadvantages of each option will not be listed. The decision whether to choose a traditional or object-oriented techniques has already been covered in Chapter 7. Choosing C or Pascal is a personal decision based upon preference since the development environments are similar in features and functions provided.

There are some programming environments available, MacApp for one, that offer extremely easy incorporation of the graphic elements in a typical Macintosh application. What these packages essentially are is a library of commands and functions that can be called from a native high-order language to manipulate those graphical images. If you plan to implement your application in a traditional or object-oriented high-level language, it is strongly recommended that you look into these types of packages. They can save you a tremendous amount of programming time and help you to make your application look very professional.

## HYPER SPECIFIC ENVIRONMENTS

If you have selected a graphical scripting environment to build your application, there are many options available to you. Seven Hypermedia authoring environmentshave been chosen for review. By no means are these seven the only ones available. But they represent a wide range of cost and capability. Your choice should be based upon which authoring package best meets your needs and your personal preference. The seven packages chosen for review are, in low- to high-cost order, HyperCard, SuperCard, Spinnaker Plus, MacroMind Director, Course Builder, Authorware Professional, and Linx Industrial.

### HyperCard

The first and least expensive of the Hypermedia authoring applications for review is HyperCard. HyperCard is actually the grand-father of the Hypermedia authoring tools. The original Macintosh computers came bundled with HyperCard, giving it instant notoriety. What truly sparked the popularity of HyperCard, though, was that it allowed novice programmers to enter the world of programming on a Macintosh. The only other alternative was to learn the extremely complex Macintosh operating system. With HyperCard, Macintosh owners without this knowledge could develop applications (be they Hypermedia or not) that would enhance their productivity on a day-to-day basis. HyperCard gave these new developers the capability to bring up multiple windows, customize menus, create or incorporate pictures, and incorporate sounds into their applications with great ease and at a bargain price. Up until 1990, HyperCard was free. Then Apple licensed it to Claris Corporation. The current list price is approximately $200. Another HyperCard first was the creation of the card stack metaphor. Each card of a stack of cards was considered a node. These nodes could contain any of the media forms we have previously discussed and could be linked to other nodes through HyperTalk, the HyperCard scripting language. Many other popular authoring environments on the Macintosh and on the IBM PC have adopted this metaphor.

| HyperCard<br>Support for: | YES | NO |
|---|---|---|
| Animation | | √ |
| Graphics | √ | |
| Video | | √ |
| Sound | √ | |
| Menus | √ | |
| XCMD and XFCN | √ | |
| Debugging | √ | |
| Multiple Windows | √ | |
| Scripting Language | √ | |
| Standalone Applications | | √ |
| IBM PC Version | | √ |

Figure 9.12 A summary of key Hypermedia features supported by HyperCard.

As you can see from Figure 9.12, HyperCard is a very capable authoring program. But, it lack some of the sophistication of more expensive tools. HyperCard claims support for animation, but, it is quite weak. The animation support comes from the ability to flip cards very quickly. With a slightly different view on succeeding cards, simple animation can occur much in the same manner as the flip books children use to simulate moving pictures. Also, Hyper-Card has no built-in support for controlling a video disk and does not support video output on the screen. These problems can be overcome through the use of external commands (XCMDs) and external functions (XFCNs). XCMDs and XFCNs are actually programs written in a high-order language that can be imported and called from within the application to accomplish tasks that are beyond the capabilities of HyperCard. The one key disadvantage of HyperCard is that it does not have the capability of making a standalone application. All users of your program must own a copy of HyperCard in order to run the application.  For the price, though, HyperCard is a viable alternative to traditional programming.

| SuperCard Support for: | YES | NO |
|---|---|---|
| Animation | √ | |
| Graphics | √ | |
| Video | | √ |
| Sound | √ | |
| Menus | √ | |
| XCMD and XFCN | √ | |
| Debugging | √ | |
| Multiple Windows | √ | |
| Scripting Language | √ | |
| Standalone Applications | √ | |
| IBM PC Version | | √ |

Figure 9.13  A summary of key Hypermedia features supported by SuperCard.

## SuperCard

The next most expensive Hypermedia authoring application is Aldus SuperCard.  Some of the key features of SuperCard are shown in Figure 9.13.  SuperCard was initially created by a small company called Silicon Beach Software to compete with HyperCard.  While it is slightly more expensive than HyperCard (list price for SuperCard is approximately $300), SuperCard fills in many of the gaps and even maintains some compatibility with HyperCard.  In fact, one of the keys to the popularity of SuperCard is that you can directly import existing HyperCard stacks.  The scripting languages of HyperCard and SuperCard are remarkably similar, so there is an instant familiarity.  The fact that there are several features added by Super-

Card while maintaining compatibility leads you to believe that SuperCard is a superset of HyperCard; this is true. Nearly all of the features of HyperCard are duplicated in SuperCard. Some of the additional features are built in drawing tools, ink effects, and integrated color support. In addition, SuperCard supports true animation, not just the simple card flipping used in HyperCard. SuperCard actually has its own animation format and commands in the scripting language to control the action. Probably one of the most important added features of SuperCard is the ability to create standalone applications. With this capability, you can create your application and freely distribute it without worrying about whether the recipients of the application have the correct software to run it. Of course, this capability comes at a cost. The final product, after becoming a standalone application, is in the neighborhood of 300K larger than a non-standalone application. Unfortunately, like HyperCard, SuperCard has no built in support for controlling a video disk and does not support video output on the screen. These problems can be overcome through the use of external commands and external functions, though just like in HyperCard. All in all, SuperCard is more capable than HyperCard. The animation support and standalone creation capabilities alone make it worth the extra hundred dollars.

## Plus

The next most expensive Hypermedia authoring application (coming in at approximately $500) is Spinnaker Plus by Spinnaker Software. Some of the key features of Spinnaker Plus are shown in Figure 9.14. As you can see from this figure, Spinnaker Plus actually supports fewer features than either of the previously examined applications. There is no support for animation outside of the card flipping utilized by HyperCard. Also left out are a debugging facility, customizable menus, multiple window support, and the ability to create standalone applications. A runtime version of Plus that allows Hypermedia reading, but not authoring, must accompany anything that is distributed. Like HyperCard and SuperCard, Spinnaker Plus has no built-in support for controlling a video disk and does not support video output on the screen. But, also like HyperCard and SuperCard, the scripting language included with Spinnaker Plus can make up for that deficit.

Spinnaker Plus does have an interesting feature that, for some, may make it worth the extra money. That feature is that there is an IBM PC version of Spinnaker Plus. If cross platform capability is important to you, then Spinnaker Plus could be a viable alternative.

If not, then you would be better off with one of the less expensive, but more capable authoring tools.

| Plus Support for: | YES | NO |
|---|:---:|:---:|
| Animation | | √ |
| Graphics | √ | |
| Video | | √ |
| Sound | √ | |
| Menus | | √ |
| XCMD and XFCN | √ | |
| Debugging | | √ |
| Multiple Windows | | √ |
| Scripting Language | √ | |
| Standalone Applications | | √ |
| IBM PC Version | √ | |

Figure 9.14 A summary of key Hypermedia features supported by Plus.

## MacroMind Director

The next authoring tool to examine is MacroMind Director. This application takes a rather large leap in cost (list price is approximately $1000) over the next-lowest-priced competitor. Some of the key features of MacroMind Director are shown in Figure 9.15.

As you can plainly see, MacroMind Director is an extremely capable application that is actually geared for Hypervideo. MacroMind Director has built in support to put video in a window on the Macintosh screen. Any feature that MacroMind Director does not have, and there are not many, can be added through the use of it's scripting language and use of external commands and external functions. There is even an IBM PC version of the program avail-

able so you can develop your application across the two vastly different platforms. MacroMind Director also has full support for animation and can create a standalone application. There are only two
apparent disadvantages to MacroMind Director outside of cost. The
first is that there are minimal drawing tools to create your own
graphics. Anything slightly sophisticated must be created in another application and imported. And, strangely, MacroMind Director cannot directly control a video disk. If you can afford it, though,
MacroMind Director is the authoring tool of choice.

| MacroMind Director Support for: | YES | NO |
|---|---|---|
| Animation | √ | |
| Graphics | √ | |
| Video | √ | |
| Sound | √ | |
| Menus | √ | |
| XCMD and XFCN | √ | |
| Debugging | √ | |
| Multiple Windows | √ | |
| Scripting Language | √ | |
| Standalone Applications | √ | |
| IBM PC Version | √ | |

**Figure 9.15** A summary of key Hypermedia features supported
by MacroMind Director.

## Course Builder

Course Builder is the next application to be examined. Some of the
important features are shown in Figure 9.16. For its cost

(approximately $1500), Course Builder actually supports less of these key features than did MacroMind Director. In fact, Course Builder is remarkably less capable than MacroMind Director except for a couple of areas. Course Builder does have a complete set of drawing tools. And, Course Builder has a built-in video disk controller. Unfortunately, it is not capable on its own of video output. Some of the other features Course Builder lacks are a scripting language, a debugging facility, customizable menus, and support for multiple windows. To its credit, Course Builder does have built-in animation support and can create a standalone application.

| Course Builder Support for: | YES | NO |
|---|---|---|
| Animation | √ | |
| Graphics | √ | |
| Video | | √ |
| Sound | √ | |
| Menus | | √ |
| XCMD and XFCN | √ | |
| Debugging | | √ |
| Multiple Windows | | √ |
| Scripting Language | | √ |
| Standalone Applications | √ | |
| IBM PC Version | | √ |

Figure 9.16 A summary of key Hypermedia features supported by Course Builder.

## Authorware Professional

Some of the key features of Authorware Professional are shown in Figure 9.17. For the most part Authorware Professional is a very capable program. It had better be at a cost of nearly $8000.

Essentially, Authorware Professional is a complete development environment with support for animation, sound modification, controlling a video disk, and creating standalone applications. It does have some rather surprising drawbacks. There are virtually no painting or drawing tools, no scripting language, and does not support multiple windows. Even at the educational price of approximately $1000, Authorware Professional pales compared to the competition.

| Authorware Professional Support for: | YES | NO |
|---|---|---|
| Animation | √ | |
| Graphics | √ | |
| Video | | √ |
| Sound | √ | |
| Menus | √ | |
| XCMD and XFCN | √ | |
| Debugging | √ | |
| Multiple Windows | | √ |
| Scripting Language | | √ |
| Standalone Applications | √ | |
| IBM PC Version | √ | |

Figure 9.17 A summary of key Hypermedia features supported by Authorware Professional.

## Linx Industrial

Linx Industrial is the last of the authoring programs for review. Some key features of Linx Industrial are shown in Figure 9.18. Linx Industrial was chosen for review to illustrate the extreme cost that is often times associated with video presentations. The price of Linx Industrial is approximately $9000. The program does offer some sophisticated features that are not shown in Figure 9.18. Linx Industrial can control up to six monitors simultaneously and split each of the monitor screens up into nine different zones. Each of the monitors or zones can be displaying a different image. And, Linx Industrial is the only one of the applications we examined to contain both a video disk controller and video output capability. Unfortunately, Linx Industrial lacks a few of the basics. There is no support for internal drawing or painting tools, built in animation, external commands or external functions, debugging, or customizable menus. As of this writing, the makers of Linx Industrial, Warren-Forthought, have introduced a scaled down version of Linx Industrial called Linx Lite. Linx Lite will sell for around $250. But, it will not support multiple monitors or built in video, and will have a limited scripting language.

| Linx Industrial Support for: | YES | NO |
|---|---|---|
| Animation | | √ |
| Graphics | √ | |
| Video | √ | |
| Sound | √ | |
| Menus | | √ |
| XCMD and XFCN | | √ |
| Debugging | | √ |
| Multiple Windows | √ | |
| Scripting Language | √ | |
| Standalone Applications | | √ |
| IBM PC Version | | √ |

Figure 9.18 A summary of key Hypermedia features supported by Linx Industrial.

## FINAL RECOMMENDATIONS

The final recommendations, as you might expect, are wishy-washy. You should choose the hardware and software that is right for the application, not force the application onto inadequate platforms. The purpose of this chapter was to provide you the information necessary to make informed decisions on hardware and software platforms based upon your particular application. Therefore, any recommendation made would be contradictory to this concept.

Some rough guidelines for an authoring platform and environment will be offered. All of the Macintosh models considered are more than adequate for Hypermedia applications. Therefore, your decision comes down to how much you are willing to spend. If your budget is unlimited, then buy the best. If you are on a limited budget, then purchase the Macintosh IIsi. It is relatively inexpensive for the power it offers. The same holds true for authoring environments. If money is not a concern, then MacroMind Director would offer the most capabilities. If money is tight, then Aldus SuperCard would be an excellent choice.

# References

Barrett, Edward, eds (1989). *The Society of Text: Hypertext, Hypermedia and the Social Construction of Information* MIT Press Cambridge, MA

Boehm, Barry W. (1990). "A Spiral Model of Software Development and Enhancement" *Software Engineering Project Management* IEEE Computer Society Press Los Alamitos, CA

Berk, Emily and Joseph Devlin, eds (1991). *The Hypertext/Hypermedia Handbook* McGraw-Hill New York, NY

Carlson, David A. and Sudha Ram (1990). "HyperIntelligence: the Next Frontier" *Communications of the ACM* July, v33, n3, pp 311-322.

Fersko-Weiss, Henry (1991). "3-D Reading with the Hypertext Edge" *PC Magazine* May, pp 241-282.

Halasz, Frank G. (1988). "Reflections on NoteCards: seven issues for the next generation of hypermedia systems" *Communications of the ACM* July, v31, n7, pp 836-853.

Heid, Jim (1992). "More For Less: An Updated LC and Laserwriter Duo" *MacWorld* May, pp 137-141.

King, David (1988). *Creating Effective Software* Prentice Hall Engelwood Cliffs, NJ

McCord, James W. (1992). *Developing Windows Applications with Borland C++3* SAMS Carmel, IN.

Meyrowitz, N. (1990). "The Link to Tomorrow" *UNIX Review*, vol 8, no 2, pp 58-67.

Nielsen, Jakob (1990). "The Art of Navigating in Hypertext" *Communications of the ACM* July, v33, n3, pp 296-310.

Poole, Lon (1990). "The Macintosh Family Evolves" *MacWorld* December, pp 169-175.

Poole, Lon (1991). "Macintosh Classic II" *MacWorld* December, pp 148-151.

Poole, Lon (1992). "The Quadra 950" *MacWorld* July, pp 148-153.

Pressman, Roger S. (1988). *Software Engineering - A Beginner's Guide* McGraw-Hill New York, NY.

Schach, Stephen R. (1990). *Software Engineering* Asken Associates Boston, MA.

Schneiderman, Ben and Greg Kearsley (1989). *Hypertext Hands-On!* Addison-Wesley Reading, MA.

Van Dam, Andries (1988). Hypertext '87 keynote address (transcript) *Communications of the ACM* July, v31, n7, pp 887-896.

Webster, Bruce F. (1991). "Macintosh Quadras" *MacWorld* December, pp 140-147.

West, Nick (1991). "Multimedia Design Tools" *MacWorld* November, pp 195-201.

# Index

## ABOUT THE AUTHOR

Gary Thomas Howell is a staff engineer at Sverdrup Corporation. He was formerly a project engineer with the United States Air Force working on a number of projects involving the design and implementation of Hypermedia systems.